'We live in a complex world where causes, meanings and contexts interweave. Useful research relies on sophisticated and creative methodologies that respond to this complexity. This book offers excellent exemplars of such research and decisively advances the case for mixed methods designs. More than ever in health and wellbeing research, we need to free ourselves from traditional methodological constraints to successfully grapple with the urgent problems of our time. This book is an important, creative and timely contribution to that project.'

Professor Andrew Cooper, Professor of Social Work, The Tavistock and Portman Foundation Trust

'This important and original book has pulled together a broad collection of fascinating studies that illuminate and explore different mixed methods approaches. It is thoroughly recommended for anyone learning how to do health and wellbeing research or grappling with how to do it better.'

Dr Simon Fraser, Associate Professor of Public Health, Faculty of Medicine, University of Southampton, UK

'This is essential reading for all who are planning mixed methods and multimodal research, not only in the arenas of wellbeing and health. Through practical, diverse and policy orientated examples, it clearly illuminates the why, how, impact, successes and challenges of such approaches. A much-needed addition to the research literature.'

Professor Judith Lathlean, Visiting Professor, Faculty of Environmental and Life Sciences, School of Health Sciences, University of Southampton, UK

'This book provides a welcome and timely collection of chapters that encourage a fresh view of mixed methods research in health and wellbeing, together with a critical overview that invites discussion and reflection. It promises to help move forward the field of health and wellbeing research, opening possibilities for new research questions, new voices and with new implications for policy and practice.'

Professor Jane Payler, Faculty of Wellbeing, Education and Languages Studies, The Open University, UK

MIXED-METHODS RESEARCH IN WELLBEING AND HEALTH

Mixed-Methods Research in Wellbeing and Health brings together nine examples of high-quality research into wellbeing and health using a range of mixed methods. Research that employs mixed methods can yield robust data that is both more reliable and valid than that arising from a single-method approach.

Mixed-methods research is a vital component in responding to recent changes to the more complex needs of an increasingly diverse society and its health sector. This book covers how mixed-methods research can be designed creatively and applied sensitively in the context of wellbeing and health research. The editors have included a set of bespoke questions for reflection at the end of each chapter. The expert editorial commentary highlights the benefits and methodological challenges of mixed-methods research as well as 'thinking points' for researchers as they plan and carry out mixed-methods research on wellbeing and health topics. Within a holistic view of wellbeing and health, the mixed-methods research designs are applied appropriately in both practice and community settings. The research can be shaped by pragmatism and the actual needs of a study rather than purely theoretical considerations.

This practical book makes high-quality, mixed-methods research design and execution guidance readily accessible to health-care practitioners and researchers working in the fields of health, social care and wellbeing services and to undergraduate and postgraduate students in courses in research and health-care studies, as well as health management.

Rachel Locke is Senior Lecturer in International Development and Global Health in the Faculty of Health and Wellbeing at the University of Winchester, UK.

Amanda Lees is Senior Researcher in the Health and Wellbeing Research Group at the University of Winchester, UK.

MIXED-METHODS RESEARCH IN WELLBEING AND HEALTH

Edited by Rachel Locke and Amanda Lees

LONDON AND NEW YORK

First published 2022
by Routledge
2 Park Square, Milton Park, Abingdon, Oxon OX14 4RN

and by Routledge
605 Third Avenue, New York, NY 10158

Routledge is an imprint of the Taylor & Francis Group, an informa business

© 2022 selection and editorial matter, Rachel Locke and Amanda Lees; individual chapters, the contributors

The right of Rachel Locke and Amanda Lees to be identified as the authors of the editorial material, and of the authors for their individual chapters, has been asserted in accordance with sections 77 and 78 of the Copyright, Designs and Patents Act 1988.

All rights reserved. No part of this book may be reprinted or reproduced or utilised in any form or by any electronic, mechanical, or other means, now known or hereafter invented, including photocopying and recording, or in any information storage or retrieval system, without permission in writing from the publishers.

Trademark notice: Product or corporate names may be trademarks or registered trademarks, and are used only for identification and explanation without intent to infringe.

British Library Cataloguing-in-Publication Data
A catalogue record for this book is available from the British Library

Library of Congress Cataloging-in-Publication Data
A catalog record has been requested for this book

ISBN: 978-0-367-20776-2 (hbk)
ISBN: 978-0-367-20778-6 (pbk)
ISBN: 978-0-429-26348-4 (ebk)

DOI: 10.4324/9780429263484

Typeset in Bembo
by SPi Technologies India Pvt Ltd (Straive)

We dedicate this book to our families and our colleagues from the Health and Wellbeing Research Group, who were our work family for four great years.

CONTENTS

List of figures	*xi*
List of tables	*xii*
List of boxes	*xiii*
List of contributors	*xiv*
Foreword by Andrée le May	*xviii*
Foreword by Simon Jobson	*xx*
Acknowledgements	*xxiii*

Introduction   1

1   Methodological issues in researching everyday music
therapy practice   9
Claire Flower

2   Using a mix of qualitative methods to investigate vulnerability
in the medical profession   32
Rachel Locke, Jane Bell and Samantha Scallan

3   Qualitative methods to optimise design and conduct
of randomised controlled trials with clinical populations   54
Andrew Mitchelmore

4   Mixed methods and wellbeing: Issues emerging from
multiple studies into mentoring for doctors   79
Alison Steven and Gemma Wilson

x Contents

5 Mixing methods and data: Exploring health and wellbeing
on a social scale 110
David Harrison, Asta Medisauskaite and Eliot L. Rees

6 Community-participatory investigation of the
health-environment-wellbeing nexus of WaSH in rural Eswatini 133
Michelle R. Brear

7 Using mixed and multi-modal methods in psychological
research with young people 156
Debra Gray, Rachel Manning and Shokraneh Oftadeh-Moghadam

8 A multimethods approach for defining a strategy to engage
vulnerable families in research 174
Amanda Lees and Kit Tapson

9 Mixed methods in community-based health and wellbeing
practices 197
Geoffrey Meads

Conclusion: Developing mixed-methods research practice
in wellbeing and health 216

Index 224

FIGURES

1.1	Example from graphic score	25
3.1	Kolb's reflective cycle	57
3.2	Gibbs' reflective cycle	58
3.3	How does it feel to have a stroke and then be a participant in research?	68
4.1	Study 2 design	88
4.2	BMA study design	93
4.3	Conceptual diagram of context, mechanism outcome relationships	94
5.1	Health and wellbeing at the individual, environmental, and system levels	116
6.1	Community map with images of selected water sources	145
7.1	Young peoples' collaborative spatial maps of their local areas	159
8.1	Example of LSOA maps	189
8.2	Example mapping exercise	191

TABLES

1.1	Integrated themes	19
1.2	Segmented timings with descriptors	22
2.1	Types of educational interventions to help manage harmful stress in doctors	38
3.1	What do recent students and stroke research participants think are the most important traits in a researcher?	70
4.1	Overview of studies	85
4.2	Composite vignette	95
5.1	Types of primary data	112
5.2	Advantages and disadvantages of primary and secondary data	114
6.1	WaSH infrastructure and related practices	134
6.2	Data sources from which the WaSH dataset was constructed	138
6.3A	Standardised and corresponding unique water survey variables developed for the participatory health capability study	140
6.3B	Standardised and corresponding unique sanitation survey variables developed for the participatory health capability study	142
6.3C	Standardised and corresponding unique hygiene survey variables developed for the participatory health capability study	144
8.1	Findings from PPI groups	187
8.2	The seven domains of the IMD	188
8.3	The ethnic breakdown for three LSOAs	190
9.1	Relational wellbeing networks for older people: leadership exemplars	206
9.2	Exemplar senior/older people's networks: characteristics and cultures	207
9.3	Relational variables: examples of integration	210

BOXES

2.1	Focus group participants' views of harmful stress	39
5.1	Case study 1: Description of the UKMACS	117
5.2	Case study 2: Description of study on UCCiP	119
5.3	UKMACS: Why mix data?	121
5.4	UCCiP: Why mix data?	122
5.5	UKMACS: Developing integrated research instruments	124
5.6	UKMACS: Ethics and consent	126
5.7	UCCiP: Sampling	127
5.8	UKMACS: Widening coverage	127
5.9	UCCiP: Challenges with using big datasets	128

CONTRIBUTORS

Dr Jane Bell is Senior Lecturer in Medical Education at the University of Winchester. She has a clinical background in general practice and has worked for many years in medical education within both the general practice and secondary care postgraduate education arenas. She has been involved with the MA medical education programme at the University of Winchester since its inception. Her research interests are primarily around the professional development of medical educators.

Dr Michelle R. Brear is Senior Research Associate in Anthropology and Development Studies at the University of Johannesburg. She is a health social scientist with a special interest in methodological innovation and systems thinking. She focuses on using participatory and complex mixed-methods approaches through which indigenous and scientific knowledge can be combined to better understand how physical and social environments influence health and wellbeing in postcolonial contexts. Her public health research draws on methods and theories from a range of social science disciplines, including anthropology, gender and cultural studies and human geography.

Dr Claire Flower works at Chelsea and Westminster Hospital, London, where she jointly leads the music therapy team within Child Development Services. Claire also runs a supervision practice and is involved in training music therapists. She recently completed her doctoral studies on aspects of music therapy practice with children and parents and has a particular interest in the fit of research methods and everyday practice.

Dr Debra Gray is Reader in Social Psychology at the University of Winchester. She is a critical social psychologist whose research focuses on the relationship between participation, social/discursive identities and intergroup relations. She currently leads the Volunteering Research Hub, which examines how social and community identities shape participation in volunteering and provide people with important health and wellbeing resources, such as collective resilience.

Dr David Harrison is Research Fellow at University College London, Research Department of Medical Education on the UK Medical Applicant Cohort Study project. A philosopher turned education researcher, he enjoys exploring different methods of acquiring knowledge and has a passion for widening participation in higher education.

Professor Simon Jobson is Dean of the Faculty of Health and Wellbeing at the University of Winchester. Simon is a sport and exercise physiologist known for his work in the field of cycling science. Simon has published research findings in many areas related to cycling performance, including efficiency, allometric scaling and the ecological validity of laboratory testing. Simon is Associate Editor for the *Journal of Sports Sciences*, Section Editor for the *Journal of Sports Science and Medicine* and sits on the editorial boards of *Sports* and the *Journal of Science and Cycling*. As a British Association of Sport and Exercise Science (BASES)-accredited sport and exercise scientist, Simon applies the findings of his research when providing sport science support to many top athletes.

Dr Amanda Lees is Visiting Researcher in the University of Winchester's Health and Wellbeing Research Group. She obtained her undergraduate degree from the University of Reading in 1994 and her PhD from the University of Southampton in 2013. She has over 20 years of experience in health and social care–focused research, having worked in the private, local authority and academic sectors. Previous to working at the University of Winchester, she held research roles at the University of Oxford and the University of Southampton. In her role within the Health and Wellbeing Research Group, Amanda works in partnership with a range of collaborators from the National Health Service, local authorities, community and faith-based organisations and other universities to develop and conduct research and evaluation. As part of her collaborative work, she is also Research Lead for the Wessex-wide Healthier Together network. Amanda's research interests relate to the *experience* of care delivery from the perspectives of both those in receipt of services and those delivering them. She is particularly interested in psycho-socially informed research methods, (which consider psychological and emotional aspects, alongside social and systemic factors) and ethnographic approaches to understanding the experience of delivering and receiving care. She is also interested in the use of creative and responsive research methods for groups that may be 'hard to reach' in terms of research and engagement with services.

Professor Andrée le May is a nurse, teacher and researcher. Her work concentrates on how people working in and using health- and social care services use knowledge in practice, and whenever possible she combines this with her clinical specialism

xvi Contributors

of elderly care. Her interest in mixed-methods research and wellbeing started with her PhD studies in the 1980s when she explored qualitatively and quantitively how nurses' use of touch impacted older people's wellbeing. More recently, she has spent time developing and evaluating implementation techniques, especially communities of practice, co-producing evidence-based practice/policy change and researching quality improvement skills. She is Professor Emerita at the University of Southampton, Co-editor in Chief of the *Journal of Research in Nursing* and Joint Implementation Lead at the East of England Applied Research Collaboration.

Dr Rachel Locke is Senior Lecturer in International Development in the University of Winchester's Faculty of Health and Wellbeing. She is Convenor of the Centre for Global Health at the university. Rachel is Senior Journal Editor of *The Clinical Teacher*. As a researcher, she leads collaborative research concerning health professional education, development and practice underpinned by substantial funding. Rachel's work employs distinctive qualitative research methods that explore the experiences of professionals and broker their narratives to wider audiences. Her commitment is to collaborative insider research with practitioners and academic researchers to uncover what may otherwise be taken for granted about professional practice. Rachel's educational research expertise enables her to identify and (re) frame issues and explore solutions to the challenges associated with contemporary work, including professional learning with particular focus on what works well and professional practice, including the vulnerabilities of health professionals and their support and wellbeing.

Dr Rachel Manning is Senior Lecturer in Psychology at the University of Buckingham. She is a social psychologist with research interests that cover a range of spatial and collective phenomena, informed by social identity, place identity and discursive psychological approaches.

Professor Geoffrey Meads is Emeritus Professor of Wellbeing Research at the University of Winchester. He is an organisational sociologist with international experience of policy and practice in primary and community care. His publications in these subject areas have focused on innovations in general practice and inter-professional developments across health and social care.

Dr Asta Medisauskaite is Senior Research Fellow at University College London, Research Department of Medical Education. Asta is an organisational psychologist who is passionate about research on the mental health and wellbeing of medical doctors.

Dr Andrew Mitchelmore is Lecturer in Exercise and Health Physiology at Oxford Brookes University. He completed his PhD at the University of Winchester in 2019. This PhD investigated different ways of measuring arterial health in older populations and immediately after stroke. His main research interests are cardiovascular disease, healthy ageing and the interactions between lifestyle choices and mental health.

Shokraneh Oftadeh-Moghadam is a PhD student, and hourly paid Lecturer, at the University of Winchester. The focus of her PhD is the development and evaluation of a digital sleep intervention for adolescents using the Person-Based Approach to intervention development. She has previously worked on interventions for weight management, survivorship support in primary care for cancer patients and reducing and preventing cognitive impairment in older adults.

Dr Eliot L. Rees is National Institute for Health Research Academic Clinical Fellow in General Practice at University College London and Lecturer in Medical Education at Keele University. His research interests are in selection, widening access and faculty development. He has a particular passion for developing novice researchers.

Dr Samantha Scallan leads the master's in medical education at Winchester University and is Wessex Primary Care Education Research Lead for the General Practice Education Unit, University Hospitals Southampton. She has been a researcher and educator in the field of medical education for many years, with a particular interest in general practice education. She has extensive experience in designing research into training for general practice, typically with an emphasis on qualitative methods. Samantha is Deputy Editor of Education for Primary Care and a regular reviewer for a range of medical education journals.

Professor Alison Steven is Professor of Research in Nursing and Health Professions Education at Northumbria University. She has been involved in health services and health professions research for over 20 years, has published widely and undertakes research focused on education and practice development for the enhancement of knowledge translation, staff wellbeing, safety and quality in professional practice.

Dr Kit Tapson is Senior Research Associate in the Faculty of Creative and Cultural Industries at the University of Portsmouth where she studies moral injury. Kit pursued her interest in health and wellbeing at the University of Surrey researching the effect of mindfulness on front-line health-care professionals. Her knowledge was enhanced at the University of Winchester through studies of how the arts can improve the welfare and happiness of community groups.

Dr Gemma Wilson is Senior Research Fellow in Applied Health at Northumbria University, and a chartered psychologist/registered health psychologist. She has widely published on issues surrounding psychosocial wellbeing, ageing, preventative health and staff wellbeing.

FOREWORD BY ANDRÉE LE MAY

In the same year as Rachel Locke and Amanda Lees began to formulate their proposal for this book, I wrote an editorial for a 'mixing methods' focus issue of the *Journal of Research in Nursing* (le May, 2017). A coincidence, of course, but one that reflected the sustained interest in, and appreciation of, the value of this versatile approach to research. In my editorial, I urged readers to continue to embrace Ann Oakley's (1999) enthusiasm for mixing methods to gain better insights into the situations that social scientists research. This book provides a response to that request by showing readers not only the methodological possibilities that mixed-methods designs offer but also how mixed methods can bring alive some of the challenging and 'under-voiced' issues of our time – those that centre on wellbeing and health.

In their introduction to the book, Amanda and Rachel say that their 'core aim is to make a difference in the way in which research in wellbeing and health is conducted…(and) intend that the book showcases mixed-methods research designs as a means to give voice to those who are still seldom heard and to yield robust and useful findings in the domain of policy and practice'. They have certainly achieved that through the thoughtful and thought-provoking chapters that lie ahead.

I have read this book on many different levels. I was able to focus on methods and techniques; to learn more about different therapies, interventions, and professional groups; and learn about reinvigorating data. But above all, I was stimulated to consider how I might use mixed-methods designs to unlock greater understandings of some of the everyday problems I see in my work as a health-care professional, educator and researcher and in my ordinary life, now, during a pandemic. I considered how I could use mixed-methods more proficiently to answer certain pressing questions, for instance: What does wellbeing feel like to my colleagues whose jobs have been manifestly altered during the last year? What effect does being away from school have on children and their parents in terms of mental and physical wellbeing? How do people living in less resource-rich countries than I do reduce the

Foreword by Andrée le May **xix**

spread of infection? Why and how have the excess deaths this pandemic has brought been 'normalised' so that we scarcely 'see' the people behind the numbers? Mixed-methods designs would allow me to answer these questions and many more.

In addition to giving voice and adding richness to our understandings of simple *and* complex concerns, mixed-methods designs bring people together. Their very nature requires research teams to work together to overcome philosophical and practical differences that might otherwise have kept them apart. Sharing skills and expertise, as well as learning from others, is a critical facet of all research and the implementation of research findings, as well as academic study, but it is not always easy to achieve. Neither is it easy for researchers and non-researchers to work together – mixing methods can enable greater co-production of research accompanied by the swifter implementation of improvements in, for example, services, environments and care. Helping readers to question, learn and appreciate the skills and expertise required for successful mixed-methods research is central to this book and facilitated by the questions Rachel and Amanda keep posing to prompt readers to think further.

Twenty years ago, Oakley (2000) and others catalysed a quiet but steady revolution; they inspired researchers to be more flexible and to be less intimidated by paradigmatic loyalties. Rachel Locke and Amanda Lees have brought together many authors in this 'reader' to show the ongoing success of mixed-methods research and this revolution. Their book will continue to inspire and inform generations of students, researchers, and practitioners for years to come.

Enjoy the read and keeping mixed-methods designs at the forefront of health and wellbeing research.

Andrée le May, Cambridge, UK, February 2021

References

le May, A. (2017) Editorial. *Journal of Research in Nursing*, 22 (4), 259–260.

Oakley, A. (1999) Paradigm wars: some thoughts on a personal and public trajectory. *International Journal of Social Research Methodology*, 2 (3), 247–254.

Oakley, A. (2000) *Experiments in Knowing: gender and method in social science*. Cambridge: Polity Press.

FOREWORD BY SIMON JOBSON

The worldwide shift away from planned economies towards laissez-faire capitalism in the late 20th century stimulated an unprecedented boost to the wealth of many nations and their citizens. Success was, for many, defined by material accumulation and display. In contrast, the early decades of the 21st century have witnessed a growing awareness of the interconnectedness of all life. The individualism of the freewheeling 1980s and 1990s has been replaced by an understanding that success is a complex, multifactorial phenomenon. A high gross domestic product is no longer sufficient to demonstrate a healthy and successful nation, just as a high salary is no longer sufficient to define a healthy and successful citizen.

Where basic markers of external success – the type of car he drives and the postcode of her home – once dominated, it is becoming increasingly common to take a holistic view, a view that considers an individual's 'wellbeing'.

Building from the results of a UK Office for National Statistics consultation that asked people across the nation 'what matters most to them', the What Works Centre for Wellbeing suggested that 'Wellbeing, put simply, is about "how we are doing" as individuals, communities and as a nation and how sustainable this is for the future' (https://whatworkswellbeing.org/about-wellbeing/what-is-wellbeing/). Here wellbeing is recognised as having ten broad dimensions: (1) the natural environment, (2) personal wellbeing, (3) our relationships, (4) health, (5) what we do, (6) where we live, (7) personal finance, (8) the economy, (9) education and skills, and (10) governance (https://www.ons.gov.uk/peoplepopulationandcommunity/wellbeing/articles/measuresofnationalwellbeingdashboard/2018-04-25).

Similar definitions of wellbeing are provided by philosophers of wellbeing, though a narrower view is taken in order to focus on prudential value (e.g. 'how well my life goes *for me*'; emphasis added; Fletcher, 2016, p. 3). Such clarity allows the formation of precise theories of wellbeing, the dominant examples being hedonism, desire-fulfilment theory (subjectivism) and objective list theory.

Hedonism is the view that pleasure – any and all – is the only thing with prudential value; wellbeing is determined solely by the balance of pleasure and pain (Fletcher, 2016). Desire-fulfilment theory introduces an important nuance by suggesting that something is good for you if and only if it fulfils a desire of yours. Both might be grouped into a subjectivist view that 'nothing can be good for us unless we desire, prefer, or endorse this good' (Alexandrova, 2017). Objectivists disagree, suggesting, for example, that a loving relationship is good for us whether or not we want it. The challenge for objectivist theorists is in justifying any given list of 'goods', whether they be pleasures, desires or otherwise.

The technical details of these philosophical approaches to wellbeing are important because they have implications for how wellbeing is evaluated and how 'interventions' are applied in attempts to improve wellbeing. Are we seeking to evaluate individual or community wellbeing? Will an intervention improve an individual's wellbeing if hedonism is 'true' and objective list theory 'false', or vice versa?

As researchers, how then do we investigate 'wellbeing'? Alexandrova (2017) described the systematic and empirical study of wellbeing – the 'science of wellbeing' – as incorporating the fields of happiness studies, positive psychology and studies of life satisfaction, flourishing and welfare. In such fields, research projects are *explicitly* about wellbeing, but Alexandrova (2017) also highlighted that projects in many other fields should also be included under the 'science of wellbeing' umbrella. patient-reported outcome measures (PROMs) are frequently collected by health researchers to assess the quality of care from the patient perspective. Though PROMs may be just one of many dependent variables in any given investigation of a health intervention or similar, such investigations are nevertheless *implicitly* about wellbeing.

The science of wellbeing is thus a complex and multifaceted endeavour. Echoing the earlier question, how then do we carry out such science? 'If you treasure it, measure it', said Gus O'Donnell, British cabinet secretary, when addressing the All-Party Parliamentary Group on Wellbeing Economics in 2011. Here O'Donnell implied that wellbeing is an eminently 'measurable' phenomenon, but we should heed those who have questioned such a conclusion. McClimans and Browne (2012) challenged the use of PROMs because they treat wellbeing as an outcome rather than as a process, whilst Hausman (2015) suggested that wellbeing cannot be reliably measured because it is too 'person-relative'. Whilst these concerns are valid – *general wellbeing* may be unmeasurable! – enough of the factors that contribute to general wellbeing are common and measurable that we can still make significant progress in our investigations of wellbeing. These factors can and must require a plethora of investigatory methods, ranging from formal questionnaires and experience sampling to ethnographies, open interviews and many more besides.

The relentless march of increased specialisation means that many researchers are becoming highly skilled in the use of only a small number of research methods. But, as we have seen, wellbeing is a construct composed of many and diverse elements, each of which may demand its own investigatory technique. Thus, to truly understand wellbeing, we must investigate it from many angles; we must use

xxii Foreword by Simon Jobson

a mixed-methods approach. For this very reason, in this book, Rachel Locke and Amanda Lees have come to the rescue of arch specialists and mixed-methods neo-phytes alike to provide an invaluable *mixed-methods research in wellbeing and health.*

Professor Simon Jobson is Dean of the Faculty of Health and Wellbeing at the University of Winchester

References

Alexandrova, A. (2017). *A philosophy for the science of well-being.* New York: Oxford University Press.

Fletcher, G. (2016). *The philosophy of well-being: an introduction.* New York: Routledge.

Hausman, D. M. (2015). *Valuing health: well-being, freedom, and suffering.* New York: Oxford University Press.

McClimans, L. and Browne, J. P. (2012). Quality of life is a process not an outcome. *Theoretical Medicine and Bioethics, 33,* 279–292.

ACKNOWLEDGEMENTS

We are grateful to all our academic colleagues who commented on draft chapters. We would like to thank Hannah Shakespeare at Routledge for her consistent encouragement, which certainly helped us to keep up momentum for the project. Penelope Bates at the University of Winchester was instrumental in supporting the book in its early stages, and Professor Geoffrey Meads provided guidance and valuable input. We would especially like to thank Dr Lucy Wallis at the University of Winchester for her significant work on the production of the book.

INTRODUCTION

We were invited to produce a proposal for this book following an abstract we submitted for the British Educational Research Association conference in 2017. The study we presented at the conference (referred to in Chapter 2, Locke, Bell and Scallan) investigated ways to prevent harmful stress amongst doctors and combined a systematic literature review and focus groups. The commissioning editor explained that she was interested in producing books on mixed methods and asked if we felt there was a gap in teaching and research concerning these areas. This intrigued us. Whilst, as academic researchers of long-standing experience, we had both worked on many mixed-methods research studies, we felt it was certainly the case that more focus is given (in teaching and the research literature) on single-methods approaches and the aims, methods and underpinning philosophical positions of these. It seemed perhaps that mixing methods is something that researchers do in practice once we have learned about single methods in theory. In producing this book, we have been afforded the privilege of focusing on mixed methods as a research approach in its own right. We have done this in partnership with the book's contributing authors. To kick start the book, we hosted an event at the University of Winchester to which all contributors, as well as other interested parties, were invited. This served to encourage the cross-fertilisation of ideas and to make links between individual contributions as authors presented their ideas for the chapters, and feedback and discussion were encouraged. We have continued to develop our understanding of mixed methods as an editorial team and through engagement with the wider scholarship. Questions that have guided us throughout the process have included the following:

- How can we define mixed-methods research in the context of wellbeing and health research?
- What happens to 'philosophical position' when we mix approaches from two different paradigms?

DOI: 10.4324/9780429263484-1

2 Introduction

- Why employ mixed methods in wellbeing and health research?
- What are the challenges and benefits of mixed-methods research designs?

The chapter contributions in this book are made from researchers who are working in the area of health and wellbeing. Although mention of wellbeing is everywhere now, it was relatively new at the time, although interest in the concept was growing. This was reflected in an increasing number of related courses in higher education but also changes in structural organisation in this sector, with an increasing number of schools and faculties incorporating 'wellbeing' into their scope/remit and titles. Indeed, our own university (the University of Winchester) established a Faculty of Health and Wellbeing, which followed a health and wellbeing research group to which we as editors belonged. The What Works Centre for Wellbeing (2018) suggests,

> Wellbeing, put simply, is about 'how we are doing' as individuals, communities and as a nation and how sustainable this is for the future.

Drawing on past research, we have used a recognised framework for wellbeing which identifies its ten broad dimensions: (1) the natural environment, (2) personal wellbeing, (3) our relationships, (4) health, (5) what we do, (6) where we live, (7) personal finance, (8) the economy, (9) education, and (10) skills and governance (see What Works Centre for Wellbeing, 2020). In this reader, we adopt an understanding of health as one component of wellbeing, which is closely linked with the other dimensions. Health is viewed broadly and includes positive mental and physical health. We highlight the sensitivities of researching wellbeing in the 21st century and provide examples from research in practice around how these may be addressed to stimulate thought and enable students to see creative ways of researching in action.

The authors range from early career academics who have recently completed doctoral work to academics who are more established in their fields. These authors all provide good reasons for mixing methods in wellbeing and health research based on the academic literature and their own experiences. For example, Harrison, Medisauskaite and Rees (Chapter 5, p. x) refer to Bryman's (2011) review into the most frequently cited reasons for conducting mixed-methods research, these were as follows:

> Enhancement – using a second research method (quantitative or qualitative) to build on the findings of the first.
>
> Sampling – using one research method to identify cases to sample for the second (e.g. using responses to a questionnaire to facilitate purposive sampling for interviews).
>
> Completeness – to generate more comprehensive findings by using both approaches.
>
> Triangulation – defined by Denzin (1978) as 'the combination of methodologies in the study of the same phenomenon', triangulation describes the uses of multiple different sources, researchers, theories or methods to

approach a topic from different angles to fully illuminate a topic. It is also considered to demonstrate greater validity if similar findings are generated from different approaches.

Diversity of views – combining the perspectives of participants (through qualitative) and researchers (through their interpretation of quantitative deductions) and combining an understanding of the relationship between quantitative variables with their qualitative meanings.

This is a useful list, and we see examples of these reasons throughout the chapters. In addition, there is a strong sense that the research described here has enabled a 'giving voice' to research participants who have often been marginalised. This has been achieved through a commitment to employing a range of techniques (that may often fall outside of the 'traditional researcher toolbox') to ensure the most complete picture and understanding possible. The findings from the included research also have a strong policy and practice orientation. This is particularly relevant in such times as those of a pandemic or tsunami, when effective national strategies may be restricted by their reliance on statistical indicators largely derived from the medical sciences, economics and trials-based data capture.

The authors also deal with the question of what type of research designs may be encompassed by the term 'mixed methods'. A 'traditional' starting point for this might be viewed as the collection, analysis and integration of both qualitative and quantitative data in a single study (Morse, 2016). This, for example, is called for in Andrew Mitchelmore's chapter (Chapter 3). A broader definition of mixed methods is adopted in the contributions to this book, so, as well as those applying a mix of quantitative and qualitative approaches, we include chapters that apply a mix of methods within the qualitatively designed research. This adheres closely to Morse's (2016) definition of 'mixed-method' designs in which the research is qualitative and the main method fits this approach, and any additional strategies may be qualitative or quantitative. There is a sense, however, that in seeking to respond to the more complex needs of an increasingly diverse society and its health sectors, our contributors have further developed the definition and rationale for the use of mixed-methods approaches. As Michelle Brear writes in her chapter (Chapter 6, p. x):

> Mixed methods approaches plausibly generate more robust understandings of phenomenon and provide more policy- and change-relevant insights. However, mixed-methods research remains an emerging field, still dominated by the assumption that it involves adding a small qualitative enquiry to 'supplement' the 'real' quantitative data (Morse and Cheek, 2015). Although the importance of qualitatively driven approaches to mixed-methods research is receiving increasing attention, practical examples of how to de-centre quantitative methods are limited.

We hope that this reader provides you with a number of practical examples of just this. These chapters contain details of creative research designs that have employed a

4 Introduction

range of methods from across the quantitative/qualitative divide to yield robust data that is both more reliable and valid than that arising from a single-method approach alone. Gray, Manning and Oftadeh-Moghadam (Chapter 7, p. x) call for researchers to move beyond mixed to 'multi-modal' methods:

> Researchers working in this tradition point out that human experience is vastly multi-modal – including also the visual, the spatial, the temporal and 'the body' (Reavey, 2012). Therefore, we require methods that enable us to work with participants in different ways, in different places, at different times to understand their perspectives and practices.
>
> (Chamberlain, Cain, Sheridan and Dupuis, 2011)

Indeed, these chapters include examples of several innovative, multi-modal techniques, allowing access to understandings of space and place. For example, in two chapters, we see the use of Google Maps as a base on which to map/identify local facilities (Chapter 6, Brear, and Chapter 8, Lees and Tapson) and in another we see participants being asked to draw their own maps to illustrate their interpretations of their local neighbourhood (Chapter 7, Gray, Manning and Oftadeh-Moghadam). We also see the use of photography and the creative combining of insights from secondary and primary data, including the linking of data (Chapter 5, Harrison, Medisauskaite and Rees; and Chapter 9, Meads). For each research team involved, it seems that undertaking these studies has been rewarding yet challenging and requiring the development of existing skill sets. Such a willingness to adapt to the needs of context within new circumstances is likely to be all the more pressing in the current context of a global pandemic – where we see increased reliance on technology and digital approaches to research that for the moment must be conducted at a distance. At such a time, opportunism becomes a virtue in both identifying and accessing data sources and flexibility in methodological application absolutely essential.

This unprecedented time also raises questions about whether mixed-methods designs must be driven by one particular paradigm (that is, the positivist/realist paradigm most associated with quantitative approaches versus constructivist/interpretivist most associated with qualitative ones) or whether they belong to a 'third' paradigm shaped by pragmatism and practical needs of the study rather than theoretical considerations. We see some authors take qualitatively driven approaches (e.g. Chapter 1, Flower; Chapter 2, Locke, Bell and Scallan; Chapter 6, Brear; and Chapter 7, Gray, Manning and Oftadeh-Moghadam); Mitchelmore's chapter (Chapter 3) describes a quantitatively driven approach, whilst Harrison, Medisauskaite and Rees (Chapter 5); Lees and Tapson (Chapter 8); and Meads (Chapter 9) situate their stance as having taken a pragmatic approach driven by the questions to be answered rather than one dominant paradigm.

We intend that the book be primarily of interest to students, researchers and practitioners working in the fields of health, social care and wellbeing services. The purpose of the reader is to help them to appreciate the value of the use of mixed methods in this and similar fields. To this end, authors share the benefits and challenges that they found with such an approach in their chapters. These are also drawn together in our discussion in the conclusion, along with answers to the other guiding questions listed at the start of this introduction. We would also encourage readers to adopt a critical stance not only to our positioning on mixed methods but also the reports and reflections in each of the chapters. With this in mind, the editors have included a set of bespoke questions for discussion to aid further reflection at the end of each chapter. These questions will assist teaching and learning, as educators can use these as discussion points to help students reflect on the content of each of the chapters. In addition to this student-friendly feature, these questions give readers of this book more generally, whether readers of research, researchers and/or practitioners, the opportunity to help develop their insights on the material further.

Within our holistic view of wellbeing and health, we have contributions from authors who have dealt with these topics within traditional practice settings, as well as those whose research has been conducted within the broader community. It has become apparent as we have read these that, in how the research approaches described are shaped by the context within which the research is situated and within our chapters, we have a mix of community and health-care-service focused studies with designs ranging from a clinical trial within a UK hospital setting to health promotion work with a remote community in South Africa. In ordering the chapters in the book, we have broadly divided them, for ease of access, into studies that are based within practice settings and those that are community based. The first four chapters are based within health settings, and their design and conduct reflect this fact. The final four chapters have designs that are more 'community facing', and these also have a number of similarities that may become apparent as you work your way through. One chapter in the middle reports two studies, one of which is based in practice and the other in the community.

Chapter synopsis and ordering

P1 Claire Flower's chapter reports her doctoral research into the musical-social processes that occur in the context of music therapy practice for children within one National Health Service Child Development Service. Hers is a qualitatively driven, mixed-methods study using observational data derived in a clinical setting as the basis for two qualitative methods of video elicitation interview and video microanalysis. Flower's chapter highlights the complexity of choosing a research design capable of investigating creative and emergent practice whilst also meeting the demands of the clinical institutions within which research and practice take place. The author deals reflectively with the challenges of practitioner research and how to give voice to children who cannot participate in research in a 'traditional' way.

P2 Rachel Locke, Jane Bell and Samantha Scallan reflect on a cluster of three mixed-methods studies concerned with supporting doctors in their practice. These studies are all somewhat sensitive because they dealt with issues that challenged the stereotype of doctors as 'high-flyers' and even invincible, not usually in need of support.

6 Introduction

They relate to vulnerability in terms of harmful stress, learning difficulties and clinical practice performance issues. The authors describe how they use a mix of methods, 'informants' and recruitment strategies to examine these issues in a holistic way and to remove as many barriers as possible to participation. From their reframing of their work the authors highlight some key principles (i.e. inclusivity, methodological and analytical rigour and experience and voice) in their approach to mixed methods. They draw out some of the wider lessons for researchers contemplating the use of mixed methods to carry out research with other groups, particularly those involving wellbeing and health.

P3 Andrew Mitchelmore speaks of his experience of the 'human side' of recruiting to a clinical trial for stroke survivors. The chapter lays out some of the challenges for trialists with regards to recruitment and retention of participants and signals the potential of mixed-methods designs incorporating qualitative elements before, during or post-trial to enhance the design and conduct of randomised control trials.

P4 Alison Steven and Gemma Wilson describe four studies that took place between 2002 and 2017 on the subject of mentoring for doctors' wellbeing. Their chapter introduces the context of mentoring in medicine research and discusses a range of methodological, practical and ethical issues stemming from carrying out mixed-methods research in this field. The authors also illustrate the ways in which the research context, and the mix of employed methods and designs, facilitated the emergence of unanticipated findings related to wellbeing.

P/C 5 David Harrison, Asta Medisauskaite and Eliot L. Rees's chapter describes and reflects on two projects that have used mixed methods: the UK Medical Applicant Cohort Study, which investigated the factors that affect potential medical students' applications to medical school, and the Understanding Career Choices in Psychiatry study, which considers the factors leading to trainee's attrition from psychiatry training. Both studies used a mix of quantitative and qualitative methods. The studies also accessed a mix of data 'types', and the authors provide an interesting discussion about the benefits and challenges of mixing primary (defined as 'data that are collected for the specific research problem at hand, using procedures that fit the research problem best') and secondary data ('data originally collected for a different purpose and reused for another research question'). This has led the authors to adopt a pragmatic and broad definition of mixed methods, with a focus on 'practical real-world research and making effective use of available data'.

C6 Michelle Brear's chapter describes a participatory, qualitatively driven, mixed-methods study of water, sanitation and hygiene (WaSH) and wellbeing in rural Eswatini, southern Africa. She describes how the use of qualitatively derived techniques, including observations, mapping, photography, focus groups and interviews supplemented and enhanced data available from large-scale household surveys, including national censuses, demographic and health surveys and living standards measurement surveys. This enabled insights to be drawn about the profound barriers to WaSH access associated with poverty, the additional importance of WaSH in settings with a high burden of infectious disease and areas in which standardised surveys might provide invalid or unreliable data. The chapter draws attention to the ability of mixed-methods designs to 'plausibly generate more robust understandings of phenomenon and provide more policy- and change-relevant insights'.

C7 Debra Gray, Rachel Manning and Shokraneh Oftadeh-Moghadam discuss the use of mixed and multi-modal methods in psychological research with young people. The first qualitatively driven study engaged young people in an exploration of their experiences of public outdoor spaces in their local communities. The second is a PhD study which developed, refined and tested the feasibility of a digital sleep intervention for adolescents using a person-based approach. The authors explain their use of mixed but also multi-modal methods – i.e. techniques to engage with participants in different (and often innovative) ways – allowing access to different elements of participants' experiences. The chapter discusses the strengths of these approaches in representing complexity, disrupting 'reality', engaging and giving voice to young people. The authors also highlight the challenges of managing large amounts of data, seeking authority on how to ensure research quality and the need to develop skillsets amongst researchers.

C8 Amanda Lees and Kit Tapson describe a formative piece of research that they undertook to help them design a subsequent main study to recruit and engage vulnerable parents in the process of developing a community-based health literacy intervention to empower them to manage their young children's health and appropriately navigate health services. The authors use the term 'multi-methods' to describe the mix of quantitative and qualitative approaches they took to help them design a study that would be sensitive to the needs of its vulnerable participants. Methods employed involved a literature review, an analysis of secondary data and mapping exercise, along with focus groups.

C9 Geoffrey Meads' chapter describes a mix of methods for working with secondary data within the context of policy-oriented research. The chapter signals the usefulness of secondary data for acquiring transferable learning for developing contexts where there is not yet an extant body of primary studies. This chapter is not about reviewing published research studies in the form of literature reviews but rather making creative and opportunistic use of resources that may have been collected for or are geared to other purposes, such as observational and interview data or the use of published statistics. The chapter shows how existing data sources can be used in the prospective applications of trend or network analyses, agency models, case exemplars or future scenarios. These are particularly useful for policy and decision-making within new and emerging contexts of health and wellbeing, such as the contemporary emergence of social enterprise and faith agencies as providers in mixed economies of wellbeing.

We have drawn our own conclusions to our 'guiding questions' (p.217) as we have progressed with editing the book. However, the point of this book is not to be a textbook or a 'how-to guide' that espouses a single viewpoint. Instead, it is an opportunity for health and wellbeing researchers to share examples of their work in practice, to describe and reflect on the questions they have sought to answer, the research designs that they have undertaken and the associated benefits and challenges. In reading these chapters, we hope that you will see that there can be several

8 Introduction

answers to the previous questions and that these depend on the context and purpose of the individual study.

In putting together this book, we purposefully sought out researchers who we felt had thoughtfully and sensitively applied their research designs to meet the unique demands of the study's context. Whilst deliberately not involving those who espouse a single 'realist' approach for evaluation or evidence synthesis, we do share with them a conviction that understanding the impact of changing contexts is increasingly important. New technologies, governance and complex systems, not least across increasingly novel wellbeing services, mean a new journey of personal and intellectual exploration is underway for researchers. Accordingly, at the end of the conclusion, we have highlighted a series of 'thinking points' that we would strongly urge you to consider in developing your own practice in mixed-methods research. They are designed to encourage careful consideration about methods as 'ways of finding out' in designing and carrying out research. Ultimately, our core aim is to make a difference in the way in which research in wellbeing and health is conducted. We intend that the book showcases mixed-methods research designs as a means to give voice to those who are still seldom heard and to yield robust and useful findings in the domain of policy and practice.

References

Bryman, A. (2011). Why do researchers integrate/combine/mesh/blend/mix/merge/fuse quantitative and qualitative research?. In M. Bergman (ed.), *Advances in mixed methods research*, London: SAGE Publications, 86–100.

Chamberlain, K., Cain, T., Sheridan, J. and Dupuis, A. (2011). Pluralisms in qualitative research: from multiple methods to integrated methods. *Qualitative Research in Psychology*, 8 (2), 151–169.

Denzin, N. (1978). *The research act: A theoretical introduction to sociological methods.* Thousand Oaks: SAGE Publications.

Morse, J. M. (2016). *Essentials of qualitatively-driven mixed-method designs.* New York: Routledge.

Morse, J. M. and Cheek, J. (2015). Introducing qualitatively-driven mixed-method designs. *Qualitative Health Research*, 25, 731–733.

Reavey, P. (2012). The return to experience: psychology and the visual. In P. Reavey (ed.), *Visual methods in psychology*. Routledge, pp. 40–52.

What Works Centre for Wellbeing. (2018). *What is wellbeing?* What Works Centre for Wellbeing. Available at: https://whatworkswellbeing.org/about-wellbeing/what-is-well-being/. (Accessed November 2020).

What Works Centre for Wellbeing. (2020). *About wellbeing.* What Works Centre for Wellbeing. Available at: https://whatworkswellbeing.org/about-wellbeing/. (Accessed November 2020).

1

METHODOLOGICAL ISSUES IN RESEARCHING EVERYDAY MUSIC THERAPY PRACTICE

Claire Flower

Background and introduction

In the music therapy room of the National Health Service (NHS) Child Development Service (CDS), a three-year-old boy sits on the floor by a large floor drum. His mother sits to his left, a music therapist to the right. In his left hand, he holds a beater, gripping it briefly before his hand loosens, and it drops to the floor. His mother picks it up, and hands it to him saying to the therapist as she does so, 'You don't mind if I help him, do you?', to which the therapist quickly replies, 'Oh, of course, of course'. The therapist leans forward toward the mother as she speaks and then out again, as though giving space to parent and child as they negotiate the new opportunities that having a beater affords. As the child beats the drum, she hands the parent another beater and then, reaching sideways, picks up a guitar. The child watches her while still beating the drum. As she begins to strum in time with his drumming, he pauses and then drops the beater to reach towards the guitar. 'Oh dear, have I distracted you?' the therapist sings as the child looks towards her. Parent and therapist both laugh as the parent, with a beater still in her hand, beats once more on the drum.

This is an account of a brief moment in time between a child, parent and music therapist written as part of a microanalysis of video material from a single session. Written in simple descriptive terms, the narrative hints at the complex actions and interactions that are continually negotiated and enacted in music therapy practice with children and their parents. It is this complexity that has been the focus of a qualitative research study into the enactment of music therapy between child, parent and therapist. Based within a specific NHS children's service, the health and wellbeing of the child lie at the heart of music therapy practice in this setting. Developing robust and methodologically credible ways to research practice that is characterised by its emergent, improvisatory nature is a challenge for the music therapy profession.

DOI: 10.4324/9780429263484-2

10 Claire Flower

Mixed methods, such as those employed in this study, afford flexible frameworks that can be tailored to the demands and opportunities of both practice and research.

This chapter gives a brief introduction to music therapy practice within this specific health-care setting and the perspective such practice brings to bear on questions of health and wellbeing. It charts my own journey from practitioner to researcher, by way of a growing curiosity about particular aspects of practice within the institutional frame of the NHS. While the focus of the chapter is not on the study per se, my intention is to explore the uses made of clinical video material as a methodological thread, considering two distinct ways in which it was utilised. Examples illustrate the ways in which video material enriched the mixed methods used within the study, as well as offering a way of making research methods and everyday practice congruent. The chapter includes discussion of the ethical sensitivities of researching everyday practice, particularly when, as was the case here, the research setting is also the practitioner's place of work. I argue in this chapter for the benefits of video as a flexible tool both within this study and in future research across disciplines.

A context for practice and research

The CDS within which both the practice and research explored in this chapter are situated is a community paediatric service within a large London NHS Trust. It describes itself as providing 'specialist assessment and healthcare therapy for children with significant developmental needs, including those who are likely to have difficulty learning' (Chelsea and Westminster Hospital NHS Foundation Trust, 2017a). Music therapy has been part of therapeutic provision within the CDS for more than two decades. As part of the multidisciplinary team, music therapists work closely with, amongst others, paediatricians, physiotherapists, occupational and speech and language therapists, offering individual or group sessions with children.

Music therapy is one of a group of professions in the UK collectively described as allied health professions and regulated by the Health Care and Professions Council. A broad definition of music therapy, and further information, can be found by visiting the British Association for Music Therapy website. A more site-specific description of music therapy can be found on the Trust's website, where music therapy is described as follows:

> Music therapy uses shared music-making to help children cope more effectively with their lives and difficulties, and allows them to show their potential. It is based on the understanding that all human beings are able to respond to music irrespective of ability or disability…. In our sessions the therapist and the child make music together – it is shared and spontaneous – through this the two establish a musical relationship.
> (Chelsea and Westminster Hospital NHS Foundation Trust, 2017b)

In keeping with the majority of music therapy practice within the UK, music therapy in this setting has at its core an improvisatory, participatory music making. This, by its nature, can be characterised as emergent and co-created.

A central tenet of music therapy, as outlined earlier, is an understanding of people as essentially musical, regardless of ability. Whatever difficulties a child may be considered to have, they can be understood as being able to respond to, and generate, musical sounds and structures (Pavlicevic, 1999). Whether in the smallest frames of rhythmic breathing and tiny vocal sounds or in expansive and sophisticated drumming and complex song, the underlying principle is one of acknowledging and amplifying the child's innate musical resources. For families of children who may have multiple and complex developmental difficulties, the child's potential for agency and active participation in music therapy may hold significant value (Flower, 2008).

The World Health Organization definition of health, written in the 1940s, stresses that health is not only an absence of illness but also the presence of a 'state of complete physical, mental, and social well-being' (World Health Organization, 1948, as cited in MacDonald, Kreutz, and Mitchell, 2012). Arguing that such an ideal state is unattainable, Misselbrook proposes a model of health as 'unimpaired flourishing' (Misselbrook, 2014, 582). This he describes as a 'functional model', driven not by biomedical definitions of disease or illness but rather by what individuals define as important to themselves in living well. As such, it aligns with the understanding of 'wellbeing' that I adopt as being concerned with 'feeling good and functioning well' (Aked et al., 2008).

This description resonates well with the way music therapy itself 'works': functioning well becomes inextricably linked with experiences of personal and social flourishing (Stige et al., 2010; Ansdell, 2014). Nor is this only perceived as occurring within the music therapy session itself, but rather through the uses individuals, families and social groups make of their own musical resources in everyday life to enable wellbeing (Trondalen and Bonde, 2012; Rolvsjord, 2015; Flower, 2019).

Music therapy, in the particular setting described here, can be seen to contribute both to the wellbeing of the child, and of those closest to them. It has a focus on developmental, functional goals for the child, which is appropriate given the nature of the health-care setting. In parallel, however, it privileges the experience of the child, for whom a sense of themselves as a musically active contributor is central. That sense, of what Ansdell calls 'musical flourishing' (Ansdell, 2014, 305) of both child and family lies at the heart of an understanding of wellbeing within this context.

Such a perspective however has to find its place within the practice and discourse of the CDS, which could be understood as operating under an overarching medical model. As such, the individual – in this context, the child – may be understood in terms of deficit, presenting with particular difficulties which require assessment, diagnosis and, if possible, treatment (Aigen, 2014). This prevailing medical model has distinct value in many ways. The complex medical and neurodevelopmental conditions which children attending the CDS may have clearly require skilled diagnosis

12 Claire Flower

and effective treatment. The difficulty perhaps lies in an underlying tension between a medical frame that can too easily be understood to focus on deficit and disability and the musically tailored approach of music therapy in which the resources, skills and potential of the child and wider family are privileged. In the ongoing everyday practice of the multidisciplinary team, this tension is widely acknowledged and creatively addressed. Music therapy finds a distinctive role, positioning itself as an improvisatory, co-created approach through which families and other professionals witness the child being themselves as fully as possible.

There is a further tension to be seen, however, between the public statement about music therapy – 'in our sessions therapist and child make music together' (Chelsea and Westminster Hospital NHS Foundation Trust, 2017b) – and everyday practice. In reality, co-creation in music therapy does not only happen between therapist and child. Within the CDS, children attending music therapy are generally of preschool age, predominantly between 18 months and 4 years. Given their age and the possible complexity of their needs, parents or carers usually attend sessions with their children. Their attendance and active involvement are crucial, particularly in terms of optimising a child's communications or participation in sessions (Wood, Sandford and Bailey, 2016). Child, parent and therapist then form what I have termed, as shorthand, the music therapy trio.

My research interest grew from pragmatic dilemmas about working within a trio rather than the more conventional therapist-child duo. Over time, I became aware that my role and activity as a music therapist shifted as parents became more involved, an awareness shared by colleagues. This showed itself in musical ways: when a child handed a parent a beater to play the drum together, I musically 'stepped back', accompanying the pair as they played; or when a parent's enjoyment of playing the piano drew their child in to play alongside them, I might find myself sitting silently, not needing to offer anything overtly musical. At times, these dynamics created uncomfortable practice dilemmas. How, for instance, was a therapist to respond when a parent began to drum at what seemed, to the therapist, like an inopportune moment? Given that the main focus of therapy, within the CDS context, was on meeting the specific developmental needs of the child, how were parent, child and therapist to negotiate the shifting interactive musical ground between themselves to keep that focus in mind? These were the practice dilemmas that led to the study at the heart of this chapter.

Researching music therapy practice

Across the profession internationally, there has been a significant increase in recent years in the literature reporting on practice involving parents and families (Oldfield and Flower, 2008; Edwards, 2011; Jacobsen and Thompson, 2017). Research has tended to focus on the outcomes of parental involvement in a child's music therapy. Studies investigating practice in a range of settings can be broadly shown to offer positive outcomes in three discrete areas: (1) for the children themselves, in terms of developmental gains (Allgood, 2005; Chiang, 2008; Walworth, 2009); (2) for parents,

Methodological issues in researching everyday music therapy practice **13**

particularly in terms of improved mental health (Williams et al., 2012); and (3) for parent–child relationships (Thompson, 2012; Thompson and McFerran, 2013; Jacobsen, McKinney, and Holck, 2014).

The focus of this study was not on outcomes, although these did emerge as a side product of the investigation. Rather, research interest concentrated on the processes and events through which such outcomes might be reached. My concern, arising from the context-specific dilemmas in everyday practice with children and parents, was to uncover the activities and experiences of people as they do music therapy together. This gave the study a clear ontological (what do I understand music therapy with a child and parent to be) and epistemological (how can it be known) position. My intention was to consider music therapy practice with a child and parent as what might be termed a phenomenon, something that warranted investigative attention in its own right (Aigen, 2014).

Approaching research

As a methodological grounding, 'gentle empiricism' offered a congruent approach to this investigation of everyday practice (Ansdell and Pavlicevic, 2010; Ansdell and DeNora, 2016). Characterised by a commitment to exploring a phenomenon as it appears naturally and disturbing it as little as possible through research activity, the approach encourages investigative direction and theory to emerge from close attention to the phenomenon itself. As a music therapy research approach, it finds its roots in an attitude to practice developed by Paul Nordoff and Clive Robbins, most notably in a reverent, responsive attention to the ways in which 'people-in-musical-relationship' show themselves (Ansdell and Pavlicevic, 2010, 134). In my own practice, an equivalent openness to what each child, musical gesture or closing cadence might bring is central to my own understanding of improvisational music therapy. 'Gentle empiricism', as a methodological pillar, allowed a natural correspondence between my approaches both as practitioner and researcher.

Context-specific music therapy practice was the core focus of this study. As such, it was positioned within a strong tradition of music therapy practitioner-led research, by which I mean research concerned with, and driven by, the problems and conundrums posed within practice for the practitioner and others (Thompson, 2012; Strange, 2014; O'Neill and Crookes, 2018). Practitioner-led research has many strengths, including the researcher's knowledge and experience in a clinical area and existing relationships with parents, carers and professionals who have used, or are familiar with, a particular service.

The existing relationships with parents whose children had attended music therapy were crucial in developing the study. They enabled the involvement of those who were familiar with the service and whose experience could help to focus the study (INVOLVE, 2012). In its seminal stages, informal discussions with parents served to guide the definition of the research area. Subsequently, specific advice was sought in developing research materials and interview formats. Such involvement mirrored the participatory nature of music therapy itself and enriched the quality of the project.

14 Claire Flower

Ethical considerations

This study of everyday practice involving children, parents and music therapists within my own workplace brought with it specific ethical issues. Inequalities in power relations were a common thread, and cultivating an alertness to them and their potential impact was crucial (Procter, 2014; Muller and Gubrium, 2016). I needed to consider such relations in regard to the music therapists and other staff in the study and the degree to which my role as service manager might interfere with their wish, or capacity, to participate freely. Similarly, in inviting parents to take part, I needed to consider the extent to which my role might influence their decision. Might I, for instance, be perceived as someone with influence as to whether, or for how long, their child might receive music therapy? Ultimately, I responded directly to questions such as these when they were voiced during the study. For the issues that remained unspoken, I endeavoured to remain alert in keeping with a broader reflexive attitude.

Reflexivity can be understood as the researcher's awareness of the influence they may exert on what is being investigated, together with a continuing critical assessment of the ways in which the experience of research affects them (Stige, Malterud, and Midtgarden, 2009; Finlay, 2014; Probst, 2015). Finlay argues that it has become a fundamental aspect of qualitative research, the need for which is broadly accepted to ensure the quality and ethical robustness of research.

I understand reflexivity as an attitude that brings an expectation that the researcher and the research area will be mutually influential. Such a perspective is congruent with the ontological and epistemological foundations of this particular study in which both music therapy and knowledge are understood as co-created and context-dependent (Carter and Little, 2007). A reflexive attitude must, however, find practical outworkings. For me, the academic framework of doctoral study supported this in terms of writing, supervision and peer discussion opportunities. Beyond the academic, the situated nature of the study enabled ongoing dialogue between colleagues, families and others and me. Such dialogue offered ways by which to manage the underlying tensions of undertaking research in the practice environment, enriching the process and the subsequent learnings.

Partway through the study, I moved from a primarily clinical to a managerial role within the service. This brought new responsibilities for me in terms of managing the music therapy service within the wider CDS structure. It also brought in to focus the impact of research design decisions. I had decided at the outset of the study not to research my own practice specifically but rather focus on clinical work as practiced by music therapists within the service as a whole. This would, I felt, enable me to step back from my own practice, avoiding potential ethical complexities with the children and parents with whom I worked. In moving into a managerial role, however, researching music therapy as practiced by those I managed brought further complexity. One therapist, for example, voiced her concerns that a parent might say things about her child's therapy that she might not disclose to the therapist. How, she wondered, might I, as researcher and manager, deal with any difficult or, conversely, complimentary comments that I might hear? Concerns such as these, arising from the intertwining of research and practice, and from the choice of methods used, were very real and needed careful attention.

A further ethical consideration concerned children's involvement in the research. Participating parents and I talked with their child about whether they were happy for us to talk about the music therapy sessions they had had, and assent was understood to have been given by the child. It is important here to clarify why the child was not more of an active participant in the study. The majority of children attending music therapy within the CDS have significant difficulties with verbal communication and cognitive functioning. It was extremely unlikely that any child recruited to the study would be able to describe verbally their experiences of music therapy, and this was indeed the case. Given that the child could not participate directly, particularly in the interview phase, I was, however, concerned that the child's voice would be included as fully as possible in the study. This became one factor in using mixed methods, and one that I return to later in the chapter.

Finally, it is important to comment on the relationship between the study design and the institutional context in which it sat. As a broad methodological base, 'gentle empiricism' (Ansdell and DeNora, 2016) provided a suitably congruent fit with the practices investigated. The study as a whole, however, needed to be positioned in relation to the epistemological framework of the wider NHS institution. While it can be seen to be changing, the research culture of the NHS, as exemplified by the ethics approval documentation at the time, continues to privilege the experimental, interventionist study (Procter, 2014). There was a necessary and pragmatic reality to the design and methodological decisions in this study. My intention was to design a mixed-methods study that would successfully gain approval while remaining sufficiently anchored in my core research values. Crucially, this entailed pursuing a research approach that was suitably congruent with the improvisational nature of music therapy practice itself. It was this intention that informed both the overall study design and, more specifically, the use of video material as a tool within the investigation.

Summarising research

A single guiding question underpinned the whole study:

> How is music therapy with a child and parent enacted within a specific health-care context?

I use the term 'enactment' here as defined by social scientist Law (2004, 56) who describes it as 'the continuous practice of crafting'. Enactment, he suggests, is concerned with how things come into being. My interest lay in uncovering the ways in which music therapy with a child and parent came into being, considering it as dynamic crafting between people, objects and place. The study itself consisted of two discrete but linked studies, a preliminary and subsequent main study.

The preliminary study was a single case design exploration of what I termed the music therapy trio of child, parent and therapist. It utilised two main research methods: video elicitation interviews (VEIs; Henry, Forman and Fetters, 2011) and video microanalysis (Trondalen and Wosch, 2016) and drew on interpretative phenomenological analysis as the analytic frame (Smith, Flowers and Larkin, 2009). Key findings from the study pointed to the emergent nature of the trio and the permeable borders across which musicing happens between the therapy room and the everyday life of the family.

Based on these findings, the main study broadened in scope to explore the enactment of music therapy across the interlinked contexts of the wider CDS and family life beyond the clinic. Making use of differentiated focus groups with parents, music therapists and CDS staff, I used a Modified Grounded Theory approach to analysis (Charmaz, 2014; Krueger and Casey, 2015). This phase of study had a particular focus on the forms of expertise through which music therapy is enacted, adopting a symmetrical focus on the expertise of all involved (DeNora, 2006).

This chapter focuses on the use of video material as a research tool within the mixed-methods design of the preliminary study. While I am not discussing the findings of the study or their implications in depth in this chapter, I do, however, want to comment briefly on the key argument made at the conclusion of the thesis. In brief, the findings suggest that an understanding of music therapy practices that focuses only on events and relationships within the therapy room is, at best, partial, failing to account for the detailed work of child and parent beyond the room (Flower, 2019). I argue for the cultivation of an ecological attitude that brings a reconsideration of the borders between therapy room and everyday life. Such an attitude is expectant of the skilled crafting of child and parent in making use of what music affords them in relational and action terms.

This challenges an understanding of wellbeing in music therapy as being limited to the activity and place of the music therapy session. Rather, music therapy may engender a child and family's wellbeing beyond the therapy room and with only tenuous links to the activity of the session. Children and families draw on their own cultural resources, blending them with those afforded in music therapy. The means by which this occurs is a fertile area for future research.

It also carries implications for the ways in which music therapy practice within this and similar health-care contexts is conceptualised. It suggests the weight given to the events, relationships and place of the weekly session be balanced differently, with a greater focus of attention being given to the ongoing musical work of child, parent and others in everyday life. There has been, I argue, an understandable, but disproportionate, weight given to the craft of the therapist, with an imperative now to rebalance the scales with a sharper focus on the crafting of all involved in music therapy (Rolvsjord, 2015; Flower, 2019). This shift, I would suggest, will also contribute to the capacity for a health-care setting such as the CDS to broaden its understanding of wellbeing, seeing children and families as not only recipients of health care but also generators of wellbeing.

Using video in research

While the emphasis on the crafting forms part of the closing argument of my doctoral thesis, in retrospect, key methodological decisions made at the design stage appear crucial in reaching those conclusions. The use of clinical video material became a research tool through the study, ultimately being employed in three distinct ways. I focus in this chapter on its use in the two methods utilised in the preliminary study: the VEI and video microanalysis. To trace its use, it is necessary to outline further detail of the study.

The preliminary study was exploratory in nature. Familiar, as a practitioner, with my own experiences of working with a child and parent present, I wanted to step back from my everyday familiarity and approach the child, parent, therapist trio afresh (Ansdell and Pavlicevic, 2010). I set out then to explore the phenomenon of the trio as it showed itself in two particular ways: through interviewing participants on their experiences of being in music therapy and using microanalysis to elucidate the musical-social processes and events of the trio.

I adopted a single case design, recruiting to the study one parent who was attending music therapy with her child and the therapist working with them. The parent and I talked with the child about whether he was happy for us to talk about his music therapy sessions, and she felt he gave his assent.

There is a strong tradition of case study research both within psychology and the social sciences (Smith, Flowers and Larkin, 2009; Yin, 2014) and within music therapy (Holck, 2004; Gilboa and Roginsky, 2010; Pasiali, 2012). It allows a flexible design frame in which methods can be shaped to the specific area of interest. Given the exploratory nature of this phase, the depth and detail afforded by a single case approach reflected my intention to allow areas of interest to emerge. As Smith et al. (2009, 30) comment, 'At one level, single case studies simply show us that (or how) something *is*, and can unfold this in an insightful manner'. The question then was what specific research methods might enable this unfolding.

The answer came from everyday practice. As part of a child's music therapy in the CDS, and with the full consent of parents, therapists regularly video record sessions. This material is used by therapists and parents during or after a child's therapy to review sessions and plan ahead. Given the routine use of video in practice, and the wish to keep practice central, how, I wondered, might video be used as a research tool? Could watching video material with a parent and therapist provide impetus and direction to the more conventional semi-structured research interview?

Video use in the research interview

There has been a growing use of video technology within qualitative research in recent years (Heath, Hindmarsh and Luff, 2010; Knoblauch, 2012; Luff and Heath, 2012). Often, it serves as an adjunct to other qualitative methods in studies that investigate how events or interactions occur. For example, Heath, Luff and Svensson

18 Claire Flower

(2007) combined video and conversation analysis in an innovative study of interactions within health-care settings. The resulting method, they suggest, 'provides the opportunity to explore the ways in which health care is accomplished within everyday organisational environments' (p. 114).

Within music therapy research into work with children and young people, the use of video material has also developed significantly, primarily as a means to research their activity in therapy (Holck, 2007; Haslbeck, 2013; Vlachova and Collavoli, 2014). A number of studies have also reviewed video material with research participants as a means to generate further data (Sorel, 2004; Strange, 2014). Sorel, in a comparable study of music therapy with a mother and son pair, selected video extracts from sessions to incorporate into interviews with the parent and, in this case, two therapists. In this, and more generally across the literature, the selection and analysis of video material is the responsibility of the researcher.

This approach left me with a dilemma. It seemed to assume that, as the researcher, I was in a position to determine what video material might be significant. This was at odds with a research orientation that sought to privilege the knowledge of others, wishing to create an exploratory culture in which the investigative direction could be guided by that of participants. How, I wondered, could video material be used in such a way as to achieve this?

The solution seemed to be found in the VEI method (Henry, Forman, and Fetters, 2011; Henry and Fetters, 2012). Defined as 'a method in which participants are interviewed about an event while watching and reflecting on a video-recording of that event' (Henry, Forman, and Fetters, 2011, 934), VEI was developed largely as a tool for studying interactions between medical practitioner and patient. Henry and Fetters (2012, 119) document three main areas of participant experience that emerge through VEIs: (1) recalling, (2) reliving and (3) reflection. Participants, they suggest, might recall thoughts and feelings experienced during the recorded event; they may relive it, even displaying bodily or emotional responses to events shown, and they may also reflect on the actions and thoughts of themselves, or others, at the time of the event.

The VEI offered a creative and congruent method within this study. It expanded the scope of the conventional semi-structured interview, foregrounding everyday music therapy practice. It also meant that by viewing, in separate meetings with therapist and parent, video of the same session, differing perspectives on events in which both had participated might be heard.

The separate research meetings took place after the child's course of therapy had ended, each meeting being audio recorded. In keeping with the exploratory nature of the study, in both meetings, I invited participants simply to watch the video recording of one of their recent sessions with me, pausing the video at any point in order to comment freely. Neither parent, therapist nor I had watched the video prior to our meeting. From a research perspective, this meant that rather than pursuing events on video that sparked particular interest in me, potentially closing down areas of interest, I could remain open to what seemed of interest to participants. The direction of discussion was guided then by their responses to watching the video.

Methodological issues in researching everyday music therapy practice **19**

Any questions and comments from me were intended to clarify or draw out the participant's responses.

Interpretative phenomenological analysis (IPA) offered a congruent theoretical frame for data analysis (Smith, Flowers and Larkin, 2009; Smith, 2011). Working with the flexible analytic steps it offers, it was possible to identify key statements from the therapist and parent material. These were then synthesised to create five integrated themes through which the phenomenon of the child, parent, therapist trio could be understood. The five themes were articulated as follows (Table 1.1):

TABLE 1.1 Integrated themes

The trio appears through the following:
- The parent and therapist sharing a focus on the child
- The differing perspectives of parent and therapist
- The collaborative processes
- The parent and therapist sharing a focus on the finding of a parental role
- The changing forms, person and place

My intention here is not to delve further into these specific findings but to consider the impact of using VEI on the analytic process. To do that, I will make use of specific examples from the material.

Henry and Fetters (2012) identify 'reflecting' and 'recalling' as two of three distinctive types of response commonly noted in analysis of VEI material. Initially, these provided useful headings under which to organise analytic comments. The therapist, for instance, reflected on the parent's and child's possible experiences of music therapy and, from her own perspective, the events of therapy and her own decision-making at key points. The parent had a more keenly focused reflective attitude, wondering about, and commenting on, the child's experience. In terms of 'recalling', watching the video seemed to bring to mind thoughts and questions had by both the therapist and parent at the time.

The extract used as an introduction to this chapter offers a way of understanding the potency of recall through VEI. In summary, both therapist and parent laugh as the child turns towards the guitar, dropping his beaters and reaching for it. On the video, the therapist sings, 'Oh dear, have I distracted you?' During the interview, however, the therapist paused the video to comment:

> I remember feeling quite guilty at that point that there was potentially something quite nice that had been possible with Mum and then I just went for the guitar without really thinking about it…and as I watched myself do that just now I think I had the same impulse again which was, 'Oh look, something's happening that I can support, play more of a supportive role, sort of wanting to come underneath it'. But that's not the kind of effect, the immediate effect of what happens.

Viewing the events again brings to mind not only what happened but also how it was thought about at the time: 'I remember feeling quite guilty at that point'. The therapist's recollection is given further weight then by watching events from the past unfold again in the present: 'as I watched myself do that just now I think I had the same impulse again'.

VEI brings a temporal shift, drawing past events vividly into the present moment. This is one of its strengths as a research method. Had I adopted the more conventional semi-structured interview, with participants talking about experiences in the past, then not only might the level of detail have been blurred but also those past experiences would not have had the same quality of an intense present.

A further unexpected benefit of the VEI lay in the ambiguities of language that it revealed. This first became apparent in noticing occasional indistinctness about the use of personal pronouns. The parent, for instance, in watching her child on video play the drum, paused the video to comment, 'At home we've been practising this'. The therapist too, noting the child's increasing activity, said, 'Things have opened up a bit in terms of the way that we can play together'. I began to notice an inherent ambiguity in these and similar phrases. To whom, exactly, was the pronoun 'we' referring? Did the 'we' of which the therapist spoke include only herself and the child, or was it to be taken to mean the parent as well? Equally, who was included in the 'we' at home who had been practicing? It was unclear to me whether this included the father or only mother and child. Further contextual detail was needed in order to make the meaning explicit (Sawyer, 2003).

My suspicion is that such ambiguity arose in part through the act of commenting on the video. Certainly, it was clear that discussions circled fluidly around different relational groupings, including pairs and the three as a whole. Therapist and parent both spoke vividly of their own experiences, prompted by events on the video. But they also talked not only about the other individuals but also the three possible pairings within the therapy room: child/parent, child/therapist and parent/therapist. When the parent also drew her partner's musical activity and experience into the discussion, the narrative became more complex still.

Such complexity, which emerged through the analytic work, pointed towards the interweaving relationships, roles and events within the music therapy trio. VEI contributed significantly to this picture. As a method, it gave opportunities for recollection and reflection, bringing depth to the research encounter. The temporal blurring of past and present, together with people and relationships appearing and receding, brought a dynamic quality to the material, enriching this exploratory phase.

Video use within microanalysis

My use of video material in this phase was not yet complete, however. I was also curious to know the extent to which an investigation of musical-social events within the session could enlarge my understanding of how the music therapy trio 'worked' (Ansdell and DeNora, 2016). Using interviews alone could not adequately address these questions, and it became apparent that mixed methods, using video

Methodological issues in researching everyday music therapy practice **21**

as an underpinning thread, offered the best approach. I returned then to the same video with the intention of conducting a microanalysis of a selected section of it.

Microanalysis is widely used within music therapy research as a means of investigating microprocesses (Holck, 2007; Wosch and Wigram, 2007; Trondalen and Wosch, 2016). While the level of analytic detail employed will be study-dependent, music therapy microanalysis generally gives significant attention to musical events alongside a degree of focus on the actions and interactions through which they come about. In this study, microanalysis offered an appropriate research method through which 'the ways in which people do things together' might be understood (Holck, 2007, 30). My intention was to attend to the musical-social activities of the trio, as viewed on video, notating a selected extract of video and adding descriptive text, as necessary.

A contributory factor in choosing to use microanalysis in the mixed-methods approach was the wish to balance the range of voices heard in the study. VEI privileged the voices of both the parent and therapist. While perceptions of the child's experience and descriptions of their activity had been spoken of at length at interview, my intention was to build on the findings of the VEI in understanding the ways in which their activity shaped the emergent events of the trio. The detailed observational work of microanalysis provided a means to uncover that activity most vividly.

Microanalysis – of what?

Approaching microanalysis means solving a practical problem of data selection. In other words, what, or how much, material to analyse. It was unfeasible, given the constraints of the study, to analyse the entire 30-minute video at anything more than a superficial level. A degree of pragmatism was called for in selecting a short section of material to consider in sufficient depth. The question of selection was not practical alone, however, but ideological. It circled back to the epistemological groundings of the study which considered practice and knowledge as co-created. How, then, could the selection of video be guided by the participation to this point of the parent and therapist rather than being mine alone? Ultimately, a four-step process led to the selection of a 90-second section of video, which in itself became a frame for a detailed microanalysis of 50 seconds of material.

The first analytic step was for me to view the video of the complete music therapy session a number of times without making notes, familiarising myself with the material. Only then did I write a full narrative account of the session, viewing and pausing the video as I did so. This account included descriptions of the observable activity of each person and the timings of events or transitions between them.

Second, I partitioned the account into timed segments, by which I mean distinct periods of activity marked by moments of change (Abrams, 2007, 96). The segmented timings were presented in tabular form (Table 1.2), together with the length of each segment and brief, functional descriptors of the content.

Writing the narrative account and segmenting the activity into timed sections served a clear investigative purpose. As an overarching principle guiding the

22 Claire Flower

TABLE 1.2 Segmented timings with descriptors

Number of Segment	Start Time of Segment on Video	Duration of Segment (mm.ss)	Brief Descriptor of Main Activity in Segment
1	2.14	00.51	*Arrival.* Parent and therapist talk. Child strums guitar.
2	3.05	02.25	*Hello song.* Therapist and child use guitar and voice. Song extends to include further vocal and guitar play.
3	5.30	00.50	*Transition.* From guitar to tambourine.
4	6.20	02.57	*Tambourine play.* Therapist, child and parent use tambourine.
5	9.17	00.27	*Transition.* Therapist introduces floor drum, fetching beaters.
6	9.45	04.22	*Floor drum play 1.* Therapist, child and parent use floor drum with beaters and hands. Therapist also uses guitar.
7	14.07	01.49	*Floor drum play 2.* Therapist has moved guitar away. Therapist, child and parent use floor drum.
8	15.56	00.44	*Transition.* Therapist introduces box of small instruments. Therapist and parent talk. Remnants of therapist and child drumming.
9	16.40	06.38	*Small instrument play.* Therapist, child and parent use small instruments from box. Therapist uses flute.
10	23.18	01.44	*Tidy up time.* Therapist, child, and parent put instruments in box.
11	25.06	03.59	*Ocean drum play.* Therapist and child play, parent watches.
12	29.05	00.55	*Transition.* Therapist, child and parent move to piano.
13	30.00	05.19	*Piano play.* Therapist and child play piano, parent holds child on her lap and watches. Therapist sings and signs goodbye to child.
14	35.19	00.39	*Leaving.* Therapist and parent talk. Child continues to play.
15	35.58	–	Video stops.

selection of a specific extract, I had continued to keep to the foreground the phenomenon of the child, parent, therapist trio itself (Holck, 2007). At what points in the session, I wondered, were all three individuals most overtly musically active, and how might this illuminate an understanding of the ways in which music therapy with child and parent happens?

Methodological issues in researching everyday music therapy practice **23**

It was possible to identify such points occurring within Segment 6 (Table 1.2), an episode of play based around the floor drum. The richness of this section had become apparent in writing the narrative account. In contrast to more clearly dyadic interaction at other points, the complex, overlapping interplay of activity between all three people had been frustrating, necessitating repeated, slowed viewings in order to describe clearly. This was a useful frustration, suggesting that this episode might be brought to light more vividly through detailed microanalytic work.

A third analytic step, however, brought a sharp focus to the selection process. This entailed circling back to the VEI material. I wondered whether it was possible to find any overlaps in the pause points at which the therapist and parent had stopped the video to comment. Were there, I wondered, particular moments that had prompted both parent and therapist to stop the video, and if so, might the act of pausing the video suggest that those moments were potential hot spots to which I should pay attention?

Considered together, a prominent cluster of pause points emerged. Both parent and therapist, in their separate interviews, had paused the video twice within the same 90-second period. When correlated with the timing of Segment 6, the pause points sit within this section, occurring from 9:48. The overlap of timings and complex activity was striking and emphasised further by the IPA analysis, which confirmed the personal significance of these moments. Within that period, parent and therapist had commented on what were ostensibly the same events but from sharply differing perspectives. Taken together, these cumulative factors suggested the 90-second extract as a potentially rich section to analyse in detail.

Having selected the 90-second extract, I narrowed the analytic lens further to focus on a 50-second arc of clear musical activity. The analytic task now demanded I zoom in further to describe events in greater detail (Pavlicevic, 2010). Narrowing the analytic lens further to focus on a 50-second arc, within the larger whole, of clear music activity, I created a detailed narrative account. Events unfolded with such rapidity and intricacy that using video software with variable playback speed was essential, enabling a teasing out of the finest details. Writing such a detailed narrative provided an orienting basis from which to understand events, but it also prompted further consideration of method.

The act of writing highlighted the inherent limitations of written language as an adequate tool for the purpose of describing the simultaneity of emerging events within the trio. Nor, I found, was it possible to convey effectively the intricate interplay of sound, gesture and movement between each individual, pair and the whole. In order to capture and represent the multiple layers of concurrent and interlinked activities more closely, exploring graphic means of representation became necessary.

Music therapy literature provides a spectrum of approaches to describe, represent and analyse clinical material, for either clinical or research purposes (Cohen et al., 2012). This includes detailed verbal descriptions and analysis (Trondalen, 2007), conventional musical notation and graphic notation (Bergstrøm-Nielsen, 2009; Cohen et al., 2012). Key to the choice of method is the imperative of a good 'fit' for the needs of any particular project (Haslbeck, 2013). Having found verbal description

24 Claire Flower

wanting in catching the complexity of the material, I wondered whether graphic representation might align more closely with my intention.

As a starting point in creating a graphic score, I used a conventional Western classical music notation system. Notation allowed the representation of simultaneous activity, with therapy enabling a level of detail through which musical processes and structures could be investigated (De Backer and Wigram, 2007; Suvini, Apicella, and Muratori, 2017). The preliminary notation, completed manually, had the appearance of a conventional score, albeit with certain adaptations. At a technical level, for example, I did not specify a time signature or add bar lines, judging that their inclusion constrained, rather than contributed to, an understanding of the improvisation. In contrast, I included a key signature at a musically appropriate point, both to avoid the unnecessary use of accidentals and to reflect an emerging tonality in the improvisation.

Beyond the conventional musical notation, however, I added written text, recording a range of musical or extra-musical details. These included transcriptions of sung or spoken words and notes on instruments being passed between people. This text animated the preliminary notation, emphasising the emergent nature of the musical improvisation through additional detail of who did what, with whom and how. It was expanded further through the insertion, at the relevant points, of words spoken by participants in the pause points generated in our meetings.

This retrospective account may give the impression of a carefully and systematically executed process. This was not the reality. I began a first notated draft by hand on a large roll of wallpaper. In creating a rough draft in this way, my intention was to digitise it using a music software programme, such as Sibelius. As the rough draft became increasingly layered, however, with text, notation, symbols and other markings, it became clear that what I had thought of as a rough working document was actually the most faithful, congruent representation of the complex, messy events I could imagine. I would argue that the process of building the graphic score itself reflected the emergent nature of the study in which single steps influenced successive decisions. In this way, the detail of the eventual overall design followed, to some extent, the flow of the unfolding research material itself.

Once complete, it was possible to examine the score closely for discrete events, identifying both specifically musical patterns and what I termed relational events – that is, patterns of activity between one or more individuals. Fourteen discrete events were identified, with repetitions of the majority of them found across the score. Details of these can be found elsewhere (Flower, 2019). I want to focus briefly here though on one anomalous event within the analysed extract. Three seconds in duration, and occurring towards the start of the extract, the event is notable for being the longest passage in the entire session in which therapist, child and parent play simultaneously. I want to describe this in some musical detail, partly to outline the research interest in the microprocesses revealed here as the three negotiate a musical-social space but also as an argument for the use of video microanalysis as a method.

The example that follows (Figure 1.1) is taken from the graphic score between 10:03 and 10:10. Therapist, child and parent each have their own line of manuscript,

FIGURE 1.1 Example from graphic score

which includes musical and textual detail describing their activity. An additional line is added to the therapist's activity towards the end to include the vocal line.

The primary, generative activity is between parent and child, with the parent encouraging the child's use of the beater on the drum by singing, 'Barney [not his real name] do it' (10:03). As he begins to beat, she voices an affirming, 'That's it' (10:05). The parent's vocalising culminates in an expansive upward and downward sweeping, 'Good boy!' The child stops drumming as the parent's vocalisation ends.

This episode, as described, unfolds as a shared, cohesive event, appearing swiftly between them before fading away. The microanalysis, however, reveals how the event is expanded through the therapist's activity. Tracing the lines of child and therapist, it is possible to see the therapist mirroring the child's activity by beating the drum in time with him. A further mirroring is evident, however, as the therapist matches the parent's vocal phrase 'Good boy!', picking up the parent's higher-pitched 'boy…' and tracing with her its downward swoop. When both parent and child stop, the therapist adds a further three drumbeats, reinforced vocally by singing 'boom, boom, boom', as though bringing the episode to a close before pausing herself (10:10).

As a whole this episode can be understood as a finely tuned, collaborative event, emerging initially from the parent offering rhythmic and melodic impetus to the child's drumming. In turn, the therapist appears alert and responsive to the actions of both parent and child in their own right, as well as that of the parent/child pair. By mirroring the child's drumming and the parent's vocalising, the therapist affirms their separate activity. It is in the sounding of the parent/therapist pair through a shared, if fleeting, vocalisation that a novel element is shown to appear. At this moment, a greater whole emerges in which all three pairs sound at once.

Identifying this microprocess was key in shining new light on the finely tuned collaborative processes between child, parent and therapist. As such, it signalled a need to conceptualise music therapy with a child and parent differently. While activity has been previously understood as being predominantly between child and therapist, the microanalysis demonstrated not only the degree and quality of a parent's participation but also the musical manifestation of the therapist's attention to both child and parent. The process of microanalysis allowed such fine-grained detail to come to light, confirming it as a method of choice for researchers keen to unearth unfolding practices between people, musical or otherwise.

26 Claire Flower

Reflections

Integrating the use of clinical video material, by way of the VEI and microanalysis, brought both richness and complexity to the study. Aspects of that complexity were unexpected and, perhaps in keeping with the unpredictable, emergent nature of music therapy itself, could not have been anticipated prior to the event. I had not anticipated, for example, the wide array of responses that watching the video material during the interview would trigger in me. As a music therapy practitioner, watching the material for the first time, I was immediately drawn to the clinical content itself; on the child, his physical and musical presence; the parent's participation and expertise; and the therapist's activity in response to both. This in itself provided reflective material that was ultimately woven into the findings.

Perhaps most significantly, the VEI triggered a growing awareness of the multiple ways of looking which the method engendered. Layers of activity and interactivity appeared in the video, in the research meeting and in the interplay between the two. This multiplicity was most apparent in the meeting with the parent. I found myself, for example, noting from the video how closely the parent watched the child while also observing the parent in the interview tapping her foot and smiling as she watched her child on the screen.

The parent's response was animated and fulsome, but also sounded a note of caution in me about the ethical implications of viewing video in research. Video material is not neutral, and the ways in which it is viewed may not be foreseeable. Being alert to the deeply personal responses its use may bring is a clear ethical responsibility for the researcher and should not be underestimated (Stige, Malterud, and Midtgarden, 2009).

Using clinical video material brought richness but was not without its challenges. For instance, the quality of the video used in the study, recorded by the therapist as part of ongoing clinical work, was questionable. Prior to sessions, therapists attach a camera to a fixed point in the room. In positioning it, the intention is to capture as much of the session's activity in the visual field as possible. Unfortunately, on this particular occasion, the parent, therapist and child had positioned themselves in such a way that their faces were not always fully in view of the camera and therefore of the viewer! This was an unforeseen consequence of using pre-existing clinical material which certainly kept the research process true to the realities and glitches of everyday practice.

On reflection, the value of combining the VEI with microanalysis was that it made possible multiple ways of approaching the same video material. It gave the opportunity to drill further into the detailed activity of a short section, understanding emergent events, actions and interactions differently. Developing a graphic score illuminated the finely interwoven work of child, parent and therapist together in music therapy moments. Such moments could not be known only through the words of participants, nor would microanalysis itself be a sufficiently full narrative without the words of those participants. It is in combining the two that the possibilities of utilising video in music therapy research become evident.

Methodological issues in researching everyday music therapy practice **27**

My intention in this study was to balance a research design that served the practices I sought to investigate with hearing and representing as faithfully as possible the voices of those between whom those practices appeared (Stige and Aarø, 2012; Ansdell and DeNora, 2016). The wish was to hear the voices of all involved in music therapy brought its own dilemmas. This was most apparent in terms of the difficulty of including the child's voice directly. The inherent difficulties of including children in research are currently a focus of cross-disciplinary attention and certainly not confined to this study (Carroll and Sixsmith, 2016; Jacobsen and Thompson, 2017; Lees et al., 2017). Children with little or no spoken language, as was the case in this study, may present particular challenges for researchers in terms of inclusion. In addressing this difficulty, I sought to pay particular attention to the child's activity through the development of the graphic score and microanalysis. The child, one might argue, was also kept central through the meanings others made of their experiences, actions and interactions, although this inevitably brought a certain interpretative distance. Looking ahead, I believe there are challenges to be addressed in terms of developing creative research approaches through which children's greater participation can be enabled. Through the very nature of their practice, music therapists and other arts practitioners are well placed to propel this conversation forward.

Concluding thoughts

In this chapter, I have described two distinct ways in which clinical video material was used in this mixed-methods study. First, its use within the VEI brought a methodological congruence to this practice-led study, reflecting the everyday use therapists and parents make of video. As a method, its use was instrumental in uncovering the divergent perspectives of parent and therapist. Second, microanalysis extended the investigative value of the same video, bringing a specific methodological lens through which to articulate and understand events. This enabled the finely grained musical detail through which music therapy is enacted to be brought to light. As an integrated whole, I would suggest that together they offered an investigative grounding. They impelled me to keep practice central, retaining a focus on what people do in music therapy together, and kept the research process aligned as closely as possible to the fabric of everyday practice.

This study arose from questions about practice, and its outcomes have been intended to circle back into practice, both at the local and broader levels. Foregrounding practice, the ways in which people do music therapy together has given the study particular impetus. The research design and methodological approaches have followed this drive, seeking to explain practice as it shows itself.

I have outlined in this chapter a number of the dilemmas posed by researching music therapy practice in context. Tussling with these dilemmas has, I would argue, strengthened the study itself. I hope it has also contributed to future thinking both in music therapy and, more broadly, about approaches to researching practice. The practice arena, with all its complexities, offers optimal environments, relationships and events for investigating how the actions and interactions of health care are

28 Claire Flower

understood and by whom. Practices such as music therapy may then develop in ways that correspond to the realities of those co-creating health care together.

Questions for discussion and further reflection

What are the competing demands that Claire considered in the context of researching music therapy within an NHS CDS?

What are the challenges she highlights that are associated with the role of practitioner/researcher?

How has Claire adopted a robust and methodologically credible way to research emergent/improvisatory practice?

Are there other contexts in which video methods could usefully be applied?

References

Abrams, B. (2007). The use of assessment profiles (IAPs) and RepGrid in microanalysis of clinical music improvisation. In T. Wosch and T. Wigram (eds.), *Microanalysis in music therapy: methods, techniques, and applications for clinicians, researchers, educators and students*. London: Jessica Kingsley Publishers, pp. 92–106.

Aigen, K. (2014). *The study of music therapy: current issues and concepts*. New York: Routledge.

Aked, J., Marks, N., Cordon, C. and Thompson, S. (2008). *Five ways to wellbeing: a report presented to the Foresight Project on communicating the evidence base for improving people's well-being*. London: New Economics Foundation.

Allgood, N. (2005). Parents' perceptions of family-based group music therapy for children with autism spectrum disorders. *Music Therapy Perspectives*, 23, 92–99.

Ansdell, G. (2014). *How music helps in music therapy and everyday life*. Farnham, UK: Ashgate Publishers.

Ansdell, G. and DeNora, T. (2016). *Musical pathways in recovery: community music therapy and mental wellbeing*. London: Routledge.

Ansdell, G. and Pavlicevic, M. (2010). Practising 'gentle empiricism' – the Nordoff-Robbins research heritage. *Music Therapy Perspectives*, 28, 131–139.

Bergstrøm-Nielsen, C. (2009). Graphic notation in music therapy: a discussion of what to notate in graphic notation, and how. *Approaches: Music Therapy and Special Music Education*, 1 (2), 72–92.

Carroll, C. and Sixsmith, J. (2016). Exploring the facilitation of young children with disabilities in research about their early intervention service. *Child Language, Teaching, and Therapy*, 32 (3), 313–325.

Carter, S.M. and Little, M. (2007). Justifying knowledge, justifying method, taking action: epistemologies, methodologies, and methods in qualitative research. *Qualitative Health Research*, 17 (10), 1316–1328.

Charmaz, K. (2014). *Constructing grounded theory*. London: SAGE Publications.

Chelsea and Westminster Hospital NHS Foundation Trust. (2017a). *Cheyne Child Development Service*. Available at: http://www.chelwest.nhs.uk/services/childrens-services/community-services/cheyne-child-development-service (Accessed 4 June 2017).

Chelsea and Westminster Hospital NHS Foundation Trust. (2017b). *Music therapy*. Available at: http://www.chelwest.nhs.uk/services/therapy-services/childrens-therapy/music-therapy (Accessed 4 June 2017).

Chiang, J.Y.K. (2008). *Music therapy for young children who have special needs: The music therapy experience from the perspectives of carers and professionals* [Unpublished MMT Dissertation]. Wellington, NZ: New Zealand School of Music.

Cohen, S., Gilboa, A., Bergstrøm-Nielsen, C., Leder, R. and Milstein, Y. (2012). A multiple-perspective approach to graphic notation. *Nordic Journal of Music Therapy*, 21 (2), 153–175.

De Backer, J. and Wigram, T. (2007). Analysis of notated music examples selected from improvisations of psychotic patients. In T. Wosch and T. Wigram (eds.), *Microanalysis in music therapy: methods, techniques, and applications for clinicians, researchers, educators and students*. London: Jessica Kingsley Publishers, pp. 120–133.

DeNora, T. (2006). Evidence and effectiveness in music therapy: problems, power, possibilities and performances in health contexts (a discussion paper). *British Journal of Music Therapy*, 20 (2), 81–93.

Edwards, J. (ed.) (2011). *Music therapy and parent-infant bonding*. Oxford: Oxford University Press.

Edwards, J. (2012). We need to talk about epistemology: orientations, meaning, and interpretation within music therapy research. *Journal of Music Therapy*, 49 (4), 372–394.

Finlay, L. (2014). Engaging phenomenological analysis. *Qualitative Research in Psychology*, 11 (2), 121–141.

Flower, C. (2008). Living with dying: reflections on family music therapy with children near the end of life. In A. Oldfield and C. Flower (eds.), *Music therapy with children and their families*. London: Jessica Kingsley Publishers, pp. 177–189.

Flower, C. (2019) *Music therapy with children and parents: toward an ecological attitude*. Unpublished PhD Dissertation. Goldsmiths, University of London.

Gilboa, A. and Roginsky, E. (2010). Examining the dyadic music therapy treatment (DUET): the case of a CP child and his mother. *Nordic Journal of Music Therapy*, 19 (2), 103–132.

Haslbeck, F.B. (2013). Creative music therapy with premature infants: an analysis of video footage. *Nordic Journal of Music Therapy*, 23 (1), 5–35.

Heath, C., Luff, P. and Svensson, M.S. (2007). Video and qualitative research: analysing medical practice and interaction. *Medical Education*, 41, 109–116.

Heath, C., Hindmarsh, J. and Luff, P. (2010). *Video in qualitative research: analysing social interaction in everyday life*. London: SAGE Publications.

Henry, S.G., Forman, J.H. and Fetters, M.D. (2011). "How do you know what aunt Martha looks like?" a video elicitation study exploring tacit clues in doctor-patient interactions. *Journal of Evaluation in Clinical Practice*, 933–939.

Henry, S.G. and Fetters, M.D. (2012). Video elicitation interviews: a qualitative research method for investigating physician–patient interactions. *Annals of Family Medicine*, 10 (2), 118–125.

Holck, U. (2004). Turn-taking in music therapy with children with communication disorders. *British Journal of Music Therapy*, 18 (2), 45–54.

Holck, U. (2007). An ethnographic descriptive approach to video microanalysis. In T. Wosch and T. Wigram (eds.), *Microanalysis in music therapy: methods, techniques and applications for clinicians, researchers, educators and students*. London: Jessica Kingsley Publishers, pp. 29–40.

INVOLVE (2012) *Briefing notes for researchers: involving the public in NHS, public health and social care research*. INVOLVE. Eastleigh.

Jacobsen, S.L., McKinney, C.H. and Holck, U. (2014). Effects of a dyadic music therapy intervention on parent-child interaction, parent stress, and parent-child relationship in families with emotionally neglected children: a randomized controlled trial. *Journal of Music Therapy*, 51 (4), 310–332.

Jacobsen, S.L. and Thompson, G. (eds.) (2017). *Music therapy with families: therapeutic approaches and theoretical perspectives*. London: Jessica Kingsley Publishers.

30 Claire Flower

Knoblauch, H. (2012). Introduction to the special issue of *Qualitative Research*: video-analysis and videography. *Qualitative Research*, 12 (3), 251–254.

Krueger, R.A. and Casey, M.A. (2015). *Focus groups: a practical guide for applied research*. 5th ed. Thousand Oaks, CA: SAGE Publications.

Law, J. (2004). *After method: mess in social science research*. London: Routledge.

Lees, A., Payler, J., Ballinger, C., Lawrence, P., Faust, S.N. and Meads, G. (2017). Positioning children's voice in clinical trials research: a new model for planning, collaboration, and reflection. *Qualitative Health Research*, 27 (14), 2162–2176.

Luff, P. and Heath, C. (2012). Some 'technical challenges' of video analysis: social actions, objects, material realities and the problems of perspective. *Qualitative Research*, 12 (3), 255–279.

MacDonald, R. A. R., Kreutz, G. and Mitchell, L. (2012) *Music, health, and wellbeing*. Oxford: Oxford University Press.

Misselbrook, D. (2014). W is for wellbeing and the WHO definition of health. *British Journal of General Practice*, 64 (628), 582.

Muller, A. E. and Gubrium, E. (2016). Researcher linguistic vulnerability: a note on methodological implications. *Qualitative Health Research*, 26 (1), 141–144.

O'Neill, N. and Crookes, L. (2018). *Music therapy: The carryover – an evaluation of specialist music therapy practice with 2 year olds with complex needs in an educational session*. Paper presented at the *3rd British Association for Music Therapy Conference*, 16–18 February, London.

Oldfield, A. and Flower, C. (eds.) (2008). *Music therapy with children and their families*. London: Jessica Kingsley Publishers.

Pasiali, V. (2012). Resilience, music therapy, and human adaptation: nurturing young children and families. *Nordic Journal of Music Therapy*, 21 (1), 36–56.

Pavlicevic, M. (1999). *Music therapy: intimate notes*. London: Jessica Kingsley Publishers.

Pavlicevic, M. (2010) Because it's cool. Community music therapy in Heideveld, South Africa. In B. Stige, G. Ansdell, C. Elefant and M. Pavlicevic (eds.), *Where music helps: community music therapy in action and reflection*. Surrey: Ashgate Publishing Limited, pp. 93–98.

Probst, B. (2015). The eye regards itself: benefits and challenges of reflexivity in qualitative social work research. *Social Work Research*, 39 (1), 37–48.

Procter, S. (2014). *Music therapy: what is it for whom? An ethnography of music therapy in a community mental health resource centre* [Unpublished PhD dissertation]. Exeter University.

Rolvsjord, R. (2015). What clients do to make music therapy work: a qualitative multiple case study in adult mental health care. *Nordic Journal of Music Therapy*, 24 (4), 296–321.

Sawyer, R.K. (2003). *Group creativity: music, theater, collaboration*. New York: Psychology Press.

Smith, J.A., Flowers, P. and Larkin, M. (2009). *Interpretative phenomenological analysis: theory, method and research*. London: SAGE Publications.

Smith, J.A. (2011). Evaluating the contribution of interpretative phenomenological analysis. *Health Psychology Review*, 5 (1), 9–27.

Sorel, S. (2004). *Presenting Carly and Elliot: exploring roles and relationships in a mother-son dyad in Nordoff-Robbins music therapy*. Unpublished PhD dissertation. New York University.

Stige, B., Malterud, K., and Midtgarden, T. (2009). Towards an agenda for evaluation of qualitative research. *Qualitative Health Research*, 19 (10), 1504–1516.

Stige, B., Ansdell, G., Elefant, C., and Pavlicevic, M. (eds.) (2010). *Where music helps: community music therapy in action and reflection*. Surrey: Ashgate Publishing Limited.

Stige, B. and Aarø, L.E. (2012). *Invitation to community music therapy*. London: Routledge Publishers.

Strange, J. (2014). *Improvised music to develop interaction between teenagers with profound and multiple learning disabilities and learning support assistants in group music therapy* [Unpublished PhD Dissertation]. Cambridge: Anglia Ruskin University.

Suvini, F., Apicella, F. and Muratori, F. (2017). Music therapy microanalysis of parent-infant interaction in a three-month-old infant later diagnosed with autism. *Health Psychology Report*, 5 (2), 151–161.

Thompson, G. (2012). *Making a connection: randomised controlled trial of family centred music therapy for young children with autism spectrum disorder* [Unpublished PhD Dissertation]. University of Melbourne.

Thompson, G. and McFerran, K.S. (2013). 'We've got a special connection': qualitative analysis of descriptions of change in the parent-child relationship by mothers of young children with autism spectrum disorder. *Nordic Journal of Music Therapy*, 1–24.

Trondalen, G. (2007). A phenomenologically inspired approach to microanalysis of improvisation in music therapy. In T. Wosch and T. Wigram (eds.), *Microanalysis in music therapy: methods, techniques and applications for clinicians, researchers, educators and students*. London: Jessica Kingsley Publishers, pp. 198–210.

Trondalen, G. and Bonde, L.O. (2012). Music therapy: models and interventions. In R. MacDonald, G. Kreutz and L. Mitchell (eds.), *Music, health, and wellbeing*. Oxford: Oxford University Press, pp. 40–64.

Trondalen, G. and Wosch, T. (2016). Microanalysis in interpretivist research. In B.L. Wheeler and K.M. Murphy (eds.), *Music therapy research*, 3rd ed. Gilsum, NH: Barcelona Publishers, pp. 589–598.

Vlachova, Z. and Collavoli, G. (2014). *Microanalysis research for autistic children*. Paper presented at the *14th World Congress of Music Therapy*. Krems, Austria.

Walworth, D.D. (2009). Effects of developmental music groups for parents and premature or typical infants under two years on parental responsiveness and infant social development. *Journal of Music Therapy*, 46 (1), 32–52.

Williams, K.E., Berthelsen, D., Nicholson, J.M., Walker, S. and Abad, V. (2012). The effectiveness of a short-term group music therapy intervention for parents who have a child with a disability. *Journal of Music Therapy*, 49 (1), 23–44.

Wood, J., Sandford, S. and Bailey, E. (2016). "The whole is greater". Developing music therapy services in the National Health Service: a case study revisited. *British Journal of Music Therapy*, 30 (1), 36–46.

Wosch, T. and Wigram, T. (eds.) (2007). *Microanalysis in music therapy: methods, techniques, and applications for clinicians, researchers, educators and students*. London: Jessica Kingsley Publishers.

Yin, R.K. (2014). *Case study research: design and methods*. London: SAGE Publications.

2

USING A MIX OF QUALITATIVE METHODS TO INVESTIGATE VULNERABILITY IN THE MEDICAL PROFESSION

Rachel Locke, Jane Bell and Samantha Scallan

Background

In general, doctors are not seen as vulnerable but are commonly thought of as being 'high-flyers' and even invincible, not usually in need of support. There has been a shift in more recent years, however, with doctors increasingly being able to acknowledge and discuss a range of vulnerabilities (Malterud and Hollnagel, 2005; Bochner, 2009; Malterud, Fredriksen and Gjerde, 2009; Epstein and Krasner, 2013; Ofri, 2013; Balme, Gerada and Page, 2015; Gerada, 2016; Woolf et al., 2016; Gerada, 2017; Kay, 2017; Lyons, Gibson and Dolezal, 2018; Miles, 2020). This chapter reflects on the use of a mix of methods that provide qualitative data from a number of different studies to research the experiences of these doctors who may otherwise not have a voice in research and whose situations could otherwise remain unexplored.

We have adopted a qualitative approach to carry out our investigations of vulnerability in the medical profession. We have done this for two reasons: the first is that as academics on an MA in medical education programme at the University of Winchester, we are strongly committed to the endeavour of exploring 'situated' practice by the use of qualitative data in situations which are complex, contextual and involve human interactions and experience (Fish and Coles, 1998; Golby and Parrott, 1999; Elmer, 2001; Bell, 2012; Bell et al., 2012; Lake and Bell, 2016; MA Medical Education Tutor Team, 2017). The second is that there is a gradual, growing (but still tentative) acceptance of qualitative data within the medical profession (Bunniss and Kelly, 2010; Illing, 2013; Varpio, Martimianakis and Mylopoulos, 2015). The existence and nature of this debate are evident, for example, in a series of articles and letters published by the *British Medical Journal* in 2016 (Greenhalgh et al., 2016; Loder et al., 2016).

As authors, we have employed a mix of methods within a qualitative research design because they provide deeper, richer understandings of a situation or phenomenon

DOI: 10.4324/9780429263484-3

than one method alone. This fits with the focus of this book on the responsive and sensitive application and adaption of research design to investigate aspects of wellbeing and health that may not be suited to a traditional mixed-methods approach – that is, a combination of quantitative and qualitative approaches. We allow, and argue for, a broader definition of mixed methods that applies a mix of methods, each collecting qualitative data within a qualitative design. The purpose of this chapter is to help researchers, and interested practitioners, appreciate the value of the use of qualitative mixed methods in this and similar fields. To this end, the benefits and challenges that we found with such an approach are explored in depth throughout the chapter.

We start by saying more about what we mean by vulnerability in relation to the medical profession and our approach to the research. We then draw on a body of published work, across a decade, conducted by the authors with colleagues to reflect on the things we see now as the priorities for research exploring wellbeing and health.

Vulnerability and the medical professional

Individuals may be vulnerable because of a specific trait or situation that they find themselves in that can leave them exposed and potentially pose a risk to their physical or mental wellbeing. The research in this chapter relates to vulnerability in terms of harmful stress, learning difficulties and clinical practice performance issues. We have chosen to use the term 'vulnerability', although we acknowledge there are other terms we could have employed to characterise our areas of investigation, including weakness, problem, difficulty or struggle.

Our appreciation of vulnerability as a sensitising concept is shaped by multiple influences, including Brown, who perceives 'vulnerability' as something that should be recognised and acknowledged rather than swept under the carpet (Brown, 2012). It is not something to be navigated out of but comes with doing significant work and opening ourselves up to emotional risks and uncertainty as a key role in the development of our self-esteem (Brown, 2012). It is therefore something potentially transformative: 'vulnerability is the core, the heart, the centre of meaningful human experiences' (Brown, 2012, 244). For us, this raises fundamental issues about the place of 'vulnerability' in the medical profession.

Professionals working in the field of medicine are expected to be strong; indeed, patients need doctors to be strong (Atkinson, 1995; Sinclair, 1997; Gawande, 2002; Montgomery, 2006). It is an intrinsic part of the doctor/patient relationship that patients, in a vulnerable position themselves, are able to rely on their doctors. There are a number of popular recent accounts of being a junior doctor that illustrate this well (for example, Clarke, 2017; Kay, 2017). Historically, doctors have not admitted to vulnerability, and there is a stigma to doing so amongst this professional group. Within the espoused medical culture of the National Health Service (NHS), coping and surviving despite pressure and stress are held up as necessary and admirable qualities. As a result, explicit recognition of vulnerability as a lens in research is currently limited, though developing.

34 Rachel Locke et al.

However, more recently, there has been heightened attention on the importance of the wellbeing and health of caring professionals and the resulting benefits (or risks) to patient care (Department of Health, 2009; Maben et al., 2012; Francis, 2013; Elton, 2019; West and Coia, 2019). Doctors in the UK, like all NHS staff, need to work longer due to a raised retirement age, and in certain medical specialties, there are additional recruitment and retention issues (Campbell et al., 2015). There is evidence of large numbers of experienced doctors leaving the profession to take early retirement (Moberley, 2019). To reflect the growing recognition of doctors who may need help, postgraduate medical training organisations (formerly known as deaneries) have worked to identify them and provide support where it is needed. Consequently, there has been a growing interest in 'resilience' (Peters, 2006; Epstein and Krasner, 2013; McCann et al., 2013; Balme, Gerada and Page, 2015; Stacey, 2018; McKinley et al., 2019), and literature has appeared in recent years on various aspects of vulnerability: physical illness (e.g. Harrison and Sterland in Cox et al., 2006), mental health (e.g. Kinman and Teoh, 2018; Riley et al., 2018) and dyslexia (e.g. Shrewsbury, 2012; Locke et al., 2017).

Our view is that vulnerability is not about an individual's weakness (or deficit) but a recognition and response to a complex interplay between the individual, system and working environment that will lead to different experiences and outcomes for doctors (Department of Health, 2000; Farmer et al., 2002; Dekker, 2007). A systemic approach drives our research that is concerned, in the main, with how the system can and should support doctors.

Approach to research

Research within medical practice has, until recently, been equated with a positivist, quantitative approach. The randomised control trial has been frequently referred to as the 'gold standard' and other methods compared, usually unfavourably, with that standard (Montgomery, 2006). The move to evidence-based medicine has reinforced the emphasis upon large-scale research producing numerical, statistically significant data, and medical journals have historically published predominantly quantitative studies (see, for example, the *British Medical Journal* and the debate in 2016 around qualitative research). Few would disagree that such trials are appropriate to the investigation of medicine, and indeed, medical science is often held up as an exemplar of progress through high-quality research. However, the limitations of this approach to the investigation of the social and educational aspects of medical practice have been recognised in more recent years. Qualitative research approaches are now usually included within both undergraduate and postgraduate curricula (see, for example, GMC, 2018a), and medical journals have begun to publish some qualitative work (O'Brien et al., 2014; BMJ, 2020). Such studies, however, remain the exception and may be viewed as less valuable, being unsuitable for inclusion within the meta-analyses of evidence-based medicine.

As well as resulting in qualitative research being regarded as inferior, the emphasis on such large-scale, statistically analysed research has another consequence. Research

Vulnerability in the medical profession **35**

is regarded as something that is conducted at a distance from medical practice. As Schön described it,

> Research is institutionally separate from practice, connected to it by carefully defined relationships of exchange. Researchers are supposed to provide the basic and applied science…. Practitioners are supposed to furnish researchers with problems for study.
>
> (Schön, 1983, 26)

This view of research, and the nature of high-quality research, favours the investigation of areas amenable to quantitative measurement and statistical analysis. It discourages consideration of aspects of experience which are contextual, individual and can only be adequately described in words and investigated with qualitative, or at least mixed, methods. Traditionally, the field of medicine has lacked the cultural capital and language to explore questions that could not be framed quantitatively. Thus, vulnerability would not historically have been a subject considered suitable for investigation, and the tools available for researching it would not have been available or acceptable to most of the medical profession.

We argue that methods from the qualitative paradigm provide the means to be sensitive to vulnerability and are able to do justice to this important topic. Further, we advocate not just a single method rather the employment of several methods in the same study to provide deeper, richer understandings. We recognise that mixed methods can involve different methods from just one paradigm rather than a traditional quantitative/qualitative mix (Morse, 2016). We adopted a mixed-method design of multiple methods within the qualitative paradigm. The collection of data from different sources in this way is perceived as a means of enhancing rigour or validity by checking one source of data against another – i.e. triangulation. This assumes a single truth exists and can be identified by investigating a particular phenomenon from different perspectives. However, this claim in itself derives from a positivistic perspective (Bressers, Brydges and Paradis, 2020). We argue, rather, that the strength of mixed methods is that they can highlight any nuances and differences that exist around a particular phenomenon from different stakeholders' perspectives (Hammersley and Atkinson, 2007; Melia, 2010; Paradis, Leslie, and Gropper, 2016; Bressers, Brydges and Paradis, 2020). In this way, our research responds to the shifting context of wellbeing and health and particularly to the growing recognition of vulnerability amongst medical professionals.

Our case studies

We have looked back at our body of research in the following areas:

- the prevention of harmful stress,
- the impact of dyslexia and 'workarounds', and
- the identification of performance issues.

The revisiting of these studies has given us an opportunity to share our current thinking about the approaches and issues in mixed-methods research about the wellbeing of doctors. This reappraisal has resulted in the identification of three principles that cut across each of the individual projects: (1) inclusivity and concern for the under-researched, (2) methodological and analytical rigour and (3) experience and voice. These reflect broader commitments in carrying out research generally and are explored next in relation to three case studies. We are sensitive in our discussion to what may help other researchers thinking about or planning on using mixed methods. We reflect on the value of mixed methods and what we would do differently in future research, a discussion that is further developed in the conclusion.

In writing the chapter, we also wanted to revisit the literature that linked to our case study topics, as well as the wider contextual literature that positions our arguments. For the former, an iterative approach was taken that balanced general keyword searches to identify papers via the main databases accessed through OpenAthens and Google Scholar with focused 'pearl growing' (Ramer, 2005; Booth, 2008) – a strategy that examines relevant papers for references and citations for other sources of relevance. Search saturation was reached when papers were encountered more than once. Papers identified as relevant were read and matched to the appropriate chapter section. For the latter, we drew on familiar literature used in our teaching and research practice.

We now discuss our three studies in turn, beginning with an investigation into ways to help prevent harmful stress.

Prevention of harmful stress amongst doctors

In this case study, we considered excessive work-related stress as a potential cause of vulnerability (Locke and Lees, 2020). Here we refer to chronic stress as being harmful, as, whilst some stress can be beneficial, work demands that are too onerous may cause harmful physical or psychological reactions for those concerned. It has serious consequences for the individuals themselves but also doctors' standards of performance may fall, which means they may need time off or may even leave the profession. Significantly poor performance can have implications for patient safety. All of this can have a detrimental effect on patients who need the appropriate number of doctors working consistently at a good standard.

Practising doctors are generally left to their own devices to cope with stress. Although activities outside work are important to maintain and enhance wellbeing, doctors also need to engage with work in a 'nourishing' way (Epstein and Krasner, 2013) and strive for 'fulfilment' (Bohman et al., 2017). The stigma of mental health and the need for doctors to be 'strong' for their patients and having a fear of being exposed has meant doctors have not always sought help as issues arise. They are a group that is under-researched, so we sought to find out more.

Our research was concerned with identifying the mechanisms of intervention available to doctors before the harmful consequences identified earlier manifest themselves. We focused on educational interventions intended to help practising doctors learn ways to prevent, recognise and manage the harmful effects of stress. Such interventions are increasingly offered as a part of continuing professional development (Fortney et al., 2013; Platt et al., 2015). We wanted to ascertain successful educational interventions, the features of these interventions and any factors that may affect outcomes. The aim was to be able to inform professional practice by generating knowledge about strategies for workforce stress reduction of relevance to employing health-care organisations.

In the study, we chose two complementary data collection techniques – a literature review and focus groups. These different techniques were employed because they allowed us to investigate different aspects of the research aim to generate knowledge about strategies for reduction of harmful stress amongst the medical workforce. The literature indicated what 'successful' interventions were being used and their key features, thus giving us a broad view. The focus groups enabled us to explore doctors' experience of workplace stress and interventions.

We searched for papers published between 1990 and 2017 on the themes of stress that included an education-based intervention and practising doctors. One area of inclusion/exclusion that was subjected to especial scrutiny was how to determine whether an intervention was 'successful'. We selected studies based on primary research using quantitative and/or qualitative measures that revealed some positive outcomes relating to the impact of the intervention on doctors' stress and related concepts relevant to the subject matter because of a found benefit to wellbeing. In this way, our approach was appreciative and inclusive. This departed from other reviews that have focused on quantitative empirical research and the exclusion of studies that we argued brought useful learning and enabled us to see different things. EPPI-Reviewer 4 software was used for the purposes of the research synthesis. Review criteria were met in 31 studies of 1,356 originally retrieved.

Two focus groups were conducted with participants who were medical educators. The rationale for the focus on educators here was they shared their experience of medical practice and education where interventions may have been introduced. Focus group 1 had five participants and focus group 2 had six participants. In qualitative enquiry, it is always important to know something about the facilitator (Mays and Pope, 1995). In this study, they were an experienced researcher and educator. They were familiar with the importance of these focus groups as the opportunity for dialogue and co-construction of meaning and narrative or 'voice' rather than just a means of eliciting information. The participants were asked the following questions:

- Is stress a problem in the NHS, and does it affect your working life?
- Have you taken part in, or organised, any interventions to help you recognise or manage stress? Please describe them and say what you thought about them.
- How would you describe the impacts of these interventions? (what difference did they make to whom)?
- Do you feel these interventions may be better suited to certain settings or professional groups? Please say why.

38 Rachel Locke et al.

The focus groups were recorded and transcribed. The analysis used the process of induction to derive themes from the data (Braun and Clarke, 2006), with qualitative data analytical package NVivo used to manage the process. The research team was involved in coding the data, and any differences in perspective were discussed and resolved.

Our commitment to methodological and analytic rigour included our ethical ways of working, particularly because of the sensitivity of the topics under consideration. Sharing personal experiences of stress is potentially difficult. Participants may have been reluctant to discuss this topic in front of their peers in a focus group. In running the focus groups, the researcher made it clear that what was discussed would not be attributable to them as individuals in any subsequent use of the data and dissemination of the findings. Participants were given an information sheet that explained the purpose of the research and asked to provide written consent. They talked about the guilt they felt for even feeling stress (and therefore would not want to mention it to colleagues) because of the pressure all staff are under in the NHS. *'It's the same for everybody so you can't put your hand up and say 'this is hard' because everybody has got it the same so you can't whinge'* (FG1). Participants were open and honest in these groups. The fact that the focus group participants knew each other may have helped. They were all part of the same university postgraduate cohort of medical educators.

The use of mixed methods revealed what single-method research would not have done: participants generally had not tried the interventions evaluated in the literature. The descriptive literature review (Grant and Booth, 2009) enabled us to identify three broad categories of interventions that were utilised in our research: (1) mindfulness type, (2) coping and solutions focused and (3) reflective groups. The nature of these interventions and examples are detailed in Table 2.1.

TABLE 2.1 Types of educational interventions to help manage harmful stress in doctors

	Mindfulness-type	*Coping and solution focused*	*Reflective groups*
Nature of intervention	Calming physiological effects achieved via mindful awareness, meditation, relaxation and yoga exercise	Adoption of positive coping strategies (e.g. problem-solving, seeking social support) and behaviour change	Support of colleagues, sharing concerns and learning new techniques
Examples of intervention	Mindful awareness, meditation, relaxation and yoga exercise	Cognitive behavioural therapy/coaching, motivational interviewing	Balint groups

By and large, participants had little experience of the types of interventions identified in the literature. Focus group participants generally had no experience of mindfulness-type activity, one trainee psychiatrist had participated in a Balint group and participants mentioned scales and tools used on educational training days for general practitioners (GP) to manage stress and foster resilience, mostly coping and solution-focused activities. Differences between specialities arose – so there was supervision for trainees in psychiatry that explored the psychological aspects of patient encounters but 'more hit and miss' in general practice than hospital medicine, despite a history of Balint groups. Analysis of the focus group discussions yielded an understanding of stress as a major issue. The quotes in Box 2.1 illustrate this and exemplify broader patterns of data that were foregrounded through the analytic process. There remains a reluctance to seek support, as there continues to be stigma with mental health issues amongst doctors. Doctors are perceived by themselves and others as invincible and expected to cope – '*if you can't cope, then you just clearly weren't a very good doctor, so man up and suck it up really*' (FG1).

The gap revealed between what the literature suggests and what is actually happening in practice meant that the use of mixed methods enabled us to identify a pattern of divergence, whereas the mixed-methods literature refers more commonly to convergence in this manner. Without the voice of the doctors here, we would not have been able to identify this aspect, and for us, this emphasises the importance of this characteristic for any study. We reflect on the absence of voice later on in the discussion about our research on the identification of poor performance in NHS organisations.

It is interesting to reflect too on the order in which data collection techniques were applied. As our literature search was undertaken first, we had findings from the literature we could share with the focus groups' participants in terms of which educational interventions were found to work to manage stress. In this way, it benefitted the medical profession and indirectly patients and members of the public in relation to the quality of care received. We felt we were providing the participants something 'in return' for them giving up their time to participate in the research, a core tenet of educational research (Golby and Parrott, 1999). Conducting a literature review

---

BOX 2.1 FOCUS GROUP PARTICIPANTS' VIEWS OF HARMFUL STRESS

- *Now I feel like everything's so stretched. There are fewer resources, or there's the same resources but a greater demand, and I think for me that's what makes people stressed* (FG2)
- *You feel like you're in a losing battle, sometimes don't you* (FG2)
- *Having a team member who's highly stressed affects whole team because everyone's trying to compensate…. Knock-on negative effects of stress* (FG1)
- *We all agree that it's a major issue. We're all seeing doctors losing their lives, potentially because of stress levels. Junior doctors…consultants* (FG2)

first is a conventional approach in research. Indeed, it is the approach we have adopted in all three case studies. However, this may feel a little top-down, rather than referring to what is going on in practice first (more bottom-up). On reflection, this feels like a tension in the process to us.

We now move on in our second case study to reflect upon the research we carried out about doctors with dyslexia.

Doctors with dyslexia: Impact and 'workarounds'

In this case study, we consider dyslexia as a potential vulnerability (Locke et al., 2017). Doctors, like anyone with dyslexia, can have difficulties which affect the way in which they undertake their work. The sorts of challenges they may face relate to written work, reading and poor short-term memory (Shrewsbury, 2012; Shrewsbury, 2016). It is important to recognise that each doctor with dyslexia will be different in terms of the difficulties they experience. A commonality, however, is that individuals are likely to have developed ways to overcome the challenges presented by dyslexia. In the context of the workplace, these are referred to as 'workarounds'. In this way, they have attempted to address any vulnerability and overcome any risk to wellbeing and health that dyslexia may have presented.

In the study, we wanted to be able to explore and account for how qualified doctors (i.e. post-medical school training) across primary and secondary care manage their dyslexia and whether and how they are supported in the workplace. This is an area where there is little existing research (Locke et al., 2015) as the majority of studies have focused upon medical students or doctors in training (Gibson and Leinster, 2011; McKendree and Snowling, 2011; Newlands, Shrewsbury and Robson, 2015; Shaw, Malik and Anderson, 2017; Shaw and Anderson, 2018; Asghar et al., 2019). In the case study, we employed three data collection techniques: (1) interviews, (2) surveys and (3) Freedom of Information (FOI) requests. The research questions that this study sought to answer were as follows:

1. What is the impact of dyslexia on clinical practice?
2. What are the coping strategies used by doctors with dyslexia to minimise the effect?

Generally, people who struggle, whether it is because of dyslexia or other difficulties, are not going to volunteer and engage with research. The challenges of recruitment to this research reflected the stigma associated with doctors having dyslexia. The negative assumptions resulted in doctors keeping dyslexia hidden, as they want to appear professional and competent. As such, they are at risk of not having a voice in research and so being marginalised. This is contrary to the popular belief that doctors are 'high-flyers' and not in need of support. Providing a choice of methods was a way of finding a way of including this hard-to-reach group.

We needed to be responsive to the likely needs of doctors with dyslexia and so encouraged participation through a combination of different data collection techniques, from which participants (i.e. the doctors with dyslexia) could choose. We offered semi-structured interviews and an online survey as means to take part in the study. For those who did not want to take part in a face-to-face interview, the option of a survey sent by email meant they could remain more anonymous. The research employed quite an innovative use of methods as it allowed participants (i.e. the doctors with dyslexia) a choice of the way in which they participated and the sort of data that they chose to provide. The data collection techniques with the doctors with dyslexia explored impact and 'workarounds'.

Twenty-four doctors who had received support for dyslexia from the Professional Support Unit (PSU) or were known to the PSU as being dyslexic were invited to take part in the study. (PSUs are regionally based organisations that provide short-term, solution-focused interventions for trainee doctors and dentists who are having difficulty in progressing in training.) Even with a choice of methods, the process of recruitment of doctors to the study of doctors was lengthy. There were repeated requests for participants for the study from the population of 24 identified by the PSU. The final sample number was 14: six doctors took part in interviews, six in an online survey and two doctors were interviewed 'in situ' to allow for discussion and the observation of strategies in clinical practice in real time (White, 2007).

We cannot say definitively that more doctors came forward because of the use of a choice of methods but we do know we had a larger number participate compared to other studies. We advocate moving forward the offering of different methods to suit participants and applying this innovative approach to research those who may be hard to reach and whose experiences have been under-researched.

Existing research tends to be self-reported, based on the views and experiences of individual doctors with dyslexia (Shrewsbury, 2012; Newlands, Shrewsbury and Robson, 2015; Shaw, Anderson and Grant, 2016; Shaw and Anderson, 2017). In wanting to fully explore this area, we also sought the perspectives of educators and employers who have responsibility for accommodating the needs of this group. In so doing, we were looking beyond dyslexia being an individual doctor's issue and one that requires adjusting a working environment to better serve the needs of doctors with dyslexia. Effective means of support were framed in this research on the basis of 'the social model' of disability (Goffman cited in Riddick, 2001). In this model, the way society is structured frames experience of and response to the disability. This contrasts with a view of disability whereby an individual with a disability differs from the norm in a significant way and interventions must correct any deficiencies (i.e. 'the deficit model'). In the social model, support is provided for doctors with dyslexia through the removal of 'disabling' barriers in the workplace (Oliver, 2009). In seeking to protect people from discrimination, the Equality Act (2010) requires employers in the UK to make 'reasonable adjustments' for disability to create 'enabling' working environments (Morris and Turnbull, 2006; the Equality Act, 2010).

Again, the PSU indicated who may be appropriate to include due to their knowledge about the assistance available for doctors with dyslexia or their support of doctors with dyslexia in an educational role. Hospital Trusts (i.e. hospital- or community-based, health-care providers), in the same locality as the PSU, were contacted and responded to FOI requests about the support that they provided in the workplace as employers of doctors with dyslexia. Such requests are permitted in the UK under the FOI Act, 2000 that entitles the public to request access to information held by public authorities. The information provided covers policies and standards as applied to all UK NHS staff with disabilities. The use of FOI requests aligned with our view of the importance of an organisation's part in the support of doctors.

Interestingly, but perhaps not surprisingly, a finding of the research derived from a thematic analysis of the data was that doctors with whom we talked had not all had a diagnosis but were self-diagnosed. Even where they had a diagnosis, they often did not disclose their dyslexia to their employer (Newlands, Shrewsbury and Robson, 2015). One of our recommendations was therefore that doctors with dyslexia need to be helped to feel comfortable enough to disclose and to seek help in achieving a formal diagnosis (Locke et al., 2017). Educators need to challenge any negative assumptions that exist, as well as promote understanding about the elements that contribute to a positive working environment.

Study participants reported having developed individual ways of coping and devised useful strategies, although from our data we cannot be sure that such adjustments contributed to an 'enabling' work environment. Supportive characteristics included the opportunity to shadow others and extra time and space to complete paperwork on a busy ward.

An ethical issue was the fear participants may have of being exposed. There has been a shift in the educational view of circumstances that might affect learning, meaning that dyslexia is now recognised earlier, with a corresponding increase in the numbers of medical students declaring dyslexia as a specific learning difficulty upon entry into undergraduate training (BMA, 2009). Whilst there has been a shift resulting in less stigmatisation of doctors with dyslexia than there once was, experiential accounts suggest further work is needed (Shaw, 2018). For us, it was important that participants were not identifiable, so the interviewers gave assurances of confidentiality to those that participated. In the study, no personal data was requested; rather, they were asked to provide a context to their training and work experience, and for the survey, for example, they were not required to record their names.

The collective expertise of the research team in qualitative data analysis was drawn upon to gather, interpret and synthesise the data. To assist with methodological and analytical rigour, this mixed-methods research was a collaborative type of practitioner research with the academic research team working with professionals. This approach, with its origin and methodological basis in education research and teacher development (Stenhouse, 1975; Schön, 1983), provides a valuable and well-tested approach for those wanting to carry out enquiries into their area of work or study (Locke, 2019). More recently, such an approach to research has been recognised as 'engaged scholarship', and through such an approach the relevance and impact of research can be broadened (Scallan, 2014). A GP on the multi-disciplinary team provided access to participants and played the role of an 'insider' to interpret the medical world for the rest of the research team. A dyslexia specialist brought their 'insider' expertise about how dyslexia presents and means of support, as well as an awareness of the need to challenge the narrative around doctors with dyslexia being unsafe in their clinical practice. As 'outsiders', the researchers questioned any assumed knowledge and ways of seeing that may otherwise have resulted in an over-familiarity with people, places and events.

Our work about the means of identifying poor performance is now reviewed as the third and final case study in this chapter.

Identification of poor performance in NHS amongst doctors

We consider poor performance a symptom of vulnerability as it usually arises from multiple causes and can be seen as a manifestation of a variety of issues (Locke et al., 2013). Performance that is deemed 'poor' includes when doctors do not meet the standards for practice that are set out by the regulatory body, the General Medical Council (GMC). It may relate to conduct, performance or capability. Clinical performance issues may include

- out-of-date or incompetent clinical practice,
- inappropriate clinical practice arising from a lack of knowledge or skills which put patients at risk,
- inability to communicate effectively,
- inappropriate delegation of clinical responsibility,
- inadequate supervision of delegated clinical tasks, and
- ineffective clinical team-working skills.

There are only ever a few doctors who give cause for concern, although performance issues are particularly problematic in health care because of the potential for serious harm to patients. Between January and December 2018 (the most recent figures), there were 298,538 doctors registered with the GMC, 8,573 'enquiries' were made regarding fitness to practise, and just 247 went through the stages of investigation to a tribunal (GMC, 2018b). The factors that influence a doctor's performance, for example, mental health issues and alcohol and drug misuse, have been studied and reported upon (see, for example, Cox et al., 2006). Poor performance can, however, be difficult to detect because it is not necessarily a one-off, serious clinical error that exposes the poor performer; more typically it is a 'rising tide' of poor practice, ongoing possibly for months or years that is eventually in some way formally recognised (Berrow et al., 2007). Low-level poor performance relies more on the reports of colleagues and other NHS staff than one-off clinical errors. There continues to be a reluctance amongst the medical profession to raise concerns about colleagues. It also has been difficult to identify because of a historical culture of loyalty within the medical profession and a general reluctance to report colleagues who are poorly performing (Cowan, 2007; Thistlewaite and Spencer, 2008). Such professional loyalty may be indicative of NHS organisations as 'professional bureaucracies' in which doctors, with their 'formal' or specialist knowledge, exercise a high degree of control (Mintzberg, 1979; Friedson, 1986). Doctors are not willing to report other doctors, as by speaking out they do not want to jeopardise somebody's career. Where concerns are raised informally, so-called soft intelligence, this presents challenges as it often lacks a well-defined evidence base to act upon in disciplinary proceedings or is considered 'gossip'.

There have not traditionally been methods of picking up early indicators of poor performance and addressing the issues individually and systemically. Poor performance has sometimes been picked up late when patient safety may be a risk and so action at that stage has been forceful, resulting in serious consequences for a doctor's livelihood. This has impeded colleagues picking up and acting on early indicators, as there was no way of intervening without risking serious long-term and irreversible consequences. However, since 2002, doctors have been required to take part in annual peer appraisal, a process that may provide the opportunity to detect the possibility of poor performance at an early stage and introduce preventive strategies. Since 2012, all medical practitioners must take part in a process of revalidation (normally over a five-year cycle) to demonstrate they are up to date and fit to practise. Revalidation and appraisal are closely linked, as supporting evidence from annual appraisals feeds into the revalidation process. A benefit of the appraisal conversation is that it is helpful in identifying learning or career development needs, although this 'formative' view is perceived as incompatible with the 'summative' or performance-related assessment that underlies revalidation (Scallan et al., 2016). In reality, perhaps discussions about development and performance cannot (or should not) be neatly separated (Launer, 2019).

Our research was concerned with the way in which poor performance is identified and the effectiveness of the methods to do so. There is little knowledge in the UK about this across the primary, secondary and tertiary care sectors in a range of organisations that comprise the NHS (e.g. primary care, mental health, foundation and acute Trusts). The situation is the same internationally (WHO, 2010). The research questions were as follows:

- How do NHS organisations identify poor performance amongst career doctors?
- What is the effectiveness or otherwise of the methods of identifying poor performance?
- How can existing processes be strengthened?

In this investigation, we employed three data collection techniques – a literature review, FOI requests and interviews. This enabled us to provide a fuller picture of the ways in which poor performance is reported. Primarily identification happened after an event (for example, adverse event reports, complaints). Clinical audit was used proactively but more robustly in the acute sector rather than in primary care. Techniques were not found to be consistently applied, and there were limitations in the capacity for sharing information. Supervision was found to have the potential to pick up poor performance at the team level, although its use was variable in practice.

The search of existing literature identified what was already known about identifying current practice in the identification of performance issues amongst doctors in the UK. This review of existing work kick-started the study. This exercise generated over 10,000 published references, and a sifting process resulted in a set of 35 core articles that discussed and, in some cases, evaluated a method or process for identification of poor performance amongst doctors.

The policy review gave us insight into the intentions of Trust organisations in this area. This involved requests for information from local Trusts about documents related to the current state of practice relating to the identification of doctors with performance issues. Fifteen out of 20 Trusts approached went on to supply information under the FOI Act (2000).

Interviews with those holding responsibility for managing poor performance and insight into what was happening in practice comprised questions about the key enablers and challenges of identification of poor performance. Fourteen semi-structured interviews were conducted to deepen understandings about what had been found in the literature and accounted for whether different processes were considered effective and whether they could be strengthened. Interviewees were recruited purposively so as to include individuals with an overview of processes and tools in use and experience or insight that may be significant at a practice level. Most informants in the sample had multiple clinical and management roles, bringing a breadth of experience to the research. As a strategy to validate the data, interviewees were asked to read the transcripts of their interviews and an initial draft of the findings to check they reflected their experiences. The analytic process was thematic as in the other two case studies discussed in this chapter.

Underpinning the rationale for a mixed-methods approach was an acknowledgement of the importance of systems and the complex interplay between the individual doctor and their environment. Rather than seeing poor performance as a 'deficit' in the individual doctor, we recognised that poor practice may be suggestive of broader problems in a team or organisation within which the doctor works. That is, systemic problems can expose a doctors' vulnerability, resulting eventually in the symptom of poor performance. Such a perspective enables the 'root cause' of a problem to be investigated and issues addressed in a wider system (Department of Health, 2000; Farmer et al., 2002; Dekker, 2007). This has parallels with how we viewed dyslexia, not as an individual doctor's issue but how it requires adjusting a working environment to better serve the needs of doctors with dyslexia. Also, as with the dyslexia study, in investigating this area, the data collection needs to include representation from different areas of the 'system'.

One of the challenges of this work was that an initial aim to provide examples of good practice could not be met. The literature review did not provide such examples, and the policy review highlighted 'standard' practice rather than any variation thereof. What the use of mixed methods gave us was agreement between data sources that provided us with confidence in our conclusion that there were no cases of good practice. Rather, issues were raised about the effectiveness of current tools for

46 Rachel Locke et al.

identification of poor performance, and there was evidently still a lot of work to be done in evaluating the current tools and developing stronger, more robust processes.

As with all the case studies presented in this chapter, the research was undertaken and managed in accordance with the University of Winchester's ethics policy. The literature searches and policy review drew upon papers, policies and other documentary information already in existence in the public domain, so these data collection strategies posed no ethical implications regarding the content of the material sought. For the interviews, potential interviewees were informed that participation in the project was voluntary, and opportunities for withdrawal were provided at various stages of the research process as part of informed consent.

One of our commitments is to reach out to doctors who may otherwise not have a voice in research and whose situations could otherwise remain unexplored. With the opportunity to revisit our research about the identification of the poor performance of doctors, we now see that we did not seek the views of the doctors themselves about the ways in which they had been identified. Those doctors about whom concerns had been raised were not included in the sample. The reason for this was the work was commissioned by the Revalidation Support Team that, as part of the Department of Health, was at the time responsible for introducing and rolling out medical revalidation. The concern was to find out about how NHS organisations identified poor performance and for the research team to find out about how these processes may be strengthened in light of revalidation. Getting the perspective of doctors who had been 'identified' was not a priority at the time.

The sample *should* have included doctors who were considered to be performing poorly. They may have been hard to reach because, as is the case with other difficulties like those presented by dyslexia, they are not necessarily going to step forward and confidentially engage with research. However, now it seems an oversight that this group was effectively marginalised from the research, and because of this, their voices were not heard. Doctors themselves do not like to be seen to have a problem which impacts their clinical ability, and those who do risk being stigmatised. There is, therefore, little incentive for doctors to refer themselves for help. This poses a dilemma for the researcher trying to investigate issues that are by their nature hidden and to which people are reluctant to admit. With the benefit of hindsight, it seems by not including this cohort of doctors in the research, we may have only been serving to reinforce any stigma and the culture of silence surrounding poor performance. We feel there are wider lessons here for researching sensitive areas that we come onto next.

Reflecting further on this study, another concern was the use of the term 'poor performance'. This was a phrase employed by the commissioner of the research at the time the project started. By the end of the work, however, thinking had shifted, as this terminology was seen as negative, suggesting a need for performance management and disciplinary action. This reflected a move towards being more supportive of doctors about whom there are concerns about their practice. There was some discussion at the time about what would be more appropriate terminology (although we did not reach any firm conclusions), and more recently in research about the remediation of doctors, a similar term is still being used – i.e. 'underperformance' (Price et al., 2018).

In revisiting three studies, we have started to point to the value and some of the challenges of mixed methods, which we now develop further in the conclusion to the chapter.

Conclusion

In this chapter, we have explored vulnerability in the medical professional and the impact this can have on the physical and mental wellbeing of individuals, as well as the potential wider consequences for patients. Whilst we appreciate doctors are not usually thought of as 'marginalised', we accounted for how this can be an appropriate description in some situations, and vulnerability can and does occur in this professional group. We carried out our exploration of vulnerability by using a qualitative research approach, employing a variety of methods. Medicine has traditionally relied on a quantitative approach epitomised by the randomised control trial. We have discussed how there has been increased recognition within medical practice of the value of a qualitative approach to the investigation of aspects of experience that are contextual, as well as personal. We described our research design for each of the studies as mixed methods. Our employment of qualitative data collection techniques and the use of more than one technique in each study enabled us to explore in detail the topic of vulnerability in a number of areas. It meant we could explore the complex interplay that we recognise between individual doctors and the systems within which they work.

A reframing of our work in this chapter highlighted some key principles (i.e. inclusivity, methodological and analytical rigour and experience and voice) that guided the discussion of each of the case studies and reflected more generally these commitments in our research. Here we seek to draw out some of the wider lessons from this chapter for researchers contemplating the use of mixed methods to carry out research with other groups, particularly those involving wellbeing and health.

In conducting research with similar groups, researchers need to recognise the fear that participants may have over being 'outed' about a perceived vulnerability. We have discussed the stigma to doctors caused by dyslexia, stress and poor performance and the steps that were taken in our research to mitigate such fear. We acknowledged that this may have provided a barrier to individuals participating in the first place or positioned them as 'hard to reach'. We have found that the use of mixed methods can afford participants a choice of methods (something that could not be considered within the traditional positivist paradigm of the randomised control trial) and in this way responds to the needs of a cohort, as they can select the way in which they participate and the type of data that they would like to provide. So where there are challenges in recruitment to a study because of the nature of the topic being investigated and/or the characteristics of the participants themselves and as such the cohort is 'hard to reach', this approach gives voice to those not traditionally heard in mainstream research. We take seriously the idea of personalising research and offering different methods to suit participants and apply this novel approach to other research where (would-be) participants may be difficult to recruit. As a methodology, this area should be explored further in the development of mixed methods research more generally.

The complexities of carrying out mixed-methods research require researchers to work in nuanced ways. We highlighted the in-method ethical challenge of handling focus group discussions sensitively. Researchers need to balance this with a tenacity in recruitment where groups are hard to reach. As mixed-methods research is not just an add-on of different data collection techniques, to be able to carry out this type of enquiry well, a high level of resources and skills are needed on the part of researchers. On top of the code of practice that applies in terms of achieving methodological and analytical rigour in single-method qualitative research, researchers must be responsive to the implications of a mix of methods across the stages of a study from design, data collection and interpretation to dissemination. They are required to be accomplished in being able to explore the experiences of different participants via different methods and engage in sense making to be able to create a narrative that is then brokered or shared more widely. They will have to respond to where, for example, there is difference about the phenomenon of wellbeing from different stakeholders' views. This is a possible characteristic of mixed-methods research within the qualitative paradigm but not always an easy aspect to manage. We experienced differences in data sources in our study investigating the ways in which to manage harmful stress amongst doctors. We advocate acting in an open and honest way about it and seeing it as a valued feature of mixing methods within the qualitative paradigm.

Researchers engaging in mixed methods need to consider the order in which methods are best used. In each of the case studies reported in this chapter, we started with a literature review. This is a recognised approach, but an alternative would be to consider what is going on in practice first. The qualitative approach stems from a belief that practice is primary, and theory should stem from practice (Schön, 1983). This notion demonstrates an appreciation of the value of practitioners' knowledge of the field rather than a view of knowledge as external with theory formed away from practice. In our first case study, looking at the prevention of harmful stress, we showed how the employment of two methods produced findings that led us to consider whether beginning with a literature review is necessarily the most effective start to the investigation of these complex, contextual situations.

We are reminded that all research takes place in a political arena, and the choice of projects that are funded, and subsequently researched, is necessarily influenced by current thinking, policy and practice. As researchers, we need to work hard to appreciate and take into account any external agenda. Our commissioned research about the identification of poor performance raised issues in this regard. In this chapter, we have highlighted the use of terminology and how to refer to 'poor performance' given its potentially negative connotations. Reviewing this research with the benefit of hindsight also made us aware that we could (and perhaps should) have included the relevant doctors in the research – i.e. doctors about whom concerns had been raised. As researchers, we are now all much more aware of the voices that

Vulnerability in the medical profession **49**

are/are not being included in a study. We argue that research, ideally, needs to be multi-perspectorial to reflect the complexities of a given situation whilst at the same time recognising that there are real challenges in the nature of such participation. On reflection, however, as researchers, we do not want to be reinforcing the marginalisation of groups. We believe that mixed methods can be used to ensure that the narratives of appropriate groups are included and the different aspects of a research study are explored sufficiently.

Finally, there is a need for researchers and non-researchers to collaborate in the study of and enquiry into professional practice. In this chapter, we have described how the use of mixed-methods research has brought people together, which has meant different expertise could be drawn upon in medical education and development to address different aspects of the research, from planning and designing to data collection and analysis. Through collaboration and inclusivity, that the application of qualitatively driven mixed methods promotes, future researchers can facilitate the emergence of different perspectives and in so doing address inequality and social injustice in wellbeing and health. In this way, researchers will not only make a difference to the way in which research is carried out but also achieve transformative outcomes. We look forward to seeing this impact in future research projects.

Questions for discussion and further reflection

What are some of the challenges associated with exploring vulnerability in the medical profession?

Traditionally, what are some of the challenges associated with qualitative approaches within medical research?

How have the authors designed their mixed-methods research studies in response to these challenges?

What reflections do the authors make on how they may adapt future research to further enhance inclusivity, and what challenges could this pose?

References

Asghar, Z., Williams, N., Denney, M. and Siriwardena, A. N. (2019). Performance in candidates declaring versus those not declaring dyslexia in a licensing clinical examination. *Medical Education*, 53 (12), 1243–1252.

Atkinson, P. (1995). *Medical talk and medical work*. London: SAGE Publications.

Balme, E., Gerada, C. and Page, L. (2015). Doctors need to be supported, not trained in resilience. *BMJ Careers*, 351, h 4709.

Bell, J. (2012). *How is practice learnt? The professional development of medical educators undertaking an MA education* [Doctoral Dissertation]. Winchester: University of Winchester.

Bell, J., Hutchison, A., Rea, T. and Richards, P. (2012). Transformative pedagogies and the professional learning of educators. In P. Rabensteiner and P. Ropo (eds.), *European dimensions in education and teacher training*. Baltmannsweiler: SVHG., 46–92.

Berrow, D., Humphrey, C., Field, R., Jobanputra, R. and Faw, L. (2007). Clarifying concerns about doctors' clinical performance. What is the contribution of assessment by the

National Clinical Assessment Service? *Journal of Health Organization and Management*, 21 (3), 333–343.

BMJ.com (2020). *BMJ website*. Available at: https://www.bmj.com/specialties/qualitative-research.

Bochner, A. P. (2009). Vulnerable medicine. *Journal of Applied Communication Research*, 37 (2), 159–166.

Bohman, B., Dyrbye, L., Sinsky, C. A., Linzer, M., Olson, K., Babbott, S., Murphy, M. L., deVries, P. P., Hamidi, M. S. and Trockel, M. (2017). Physician well-being: the reciprocity of practice efficiency, culture of wellness, and personal resilience. *NEJM Catalyst*, 3 (4). https://catalyst.nejm.org/doi/full/10.1056/CAT.17.0429.

Booth, A. (2008). Unpacking your literature search toolbox: on search styles and tactics. *Health Information and Libraries Journal*, 25 (4), 313.

Braun, V. and Clarke, V. (2006). Using thematic analysis in psychology. *Qualitative Research in Psychology*, 3 (2), 77–101.

Bressers, G., Brydges, M. and Paradis, E. (2020). Ethnography in health professions education: slowing down and thinking deeply. *Medical Education*, 54, 225–233.

British Medical Association (BMA) (2009). *Equality and diversity in UK medical schools.* London: British Medical Association.

Brown, B. (2012). *Daring greatly: how the courage to be vulnerable transforms the way we live, love, parent, and lead.* New York: Gotham Books.

Bunniss, S. and Kelly, D. R. (2010). Research paradigms in medical education research. *Medical Education*, 44 (4), 358–366.

Campbell, D., Siddique, H., Kirk, A. et al. (2015). NHS hires up to 3,000 foreign-trained doctors in a year to plug staff shortage. *The Guardian*, 28 (January). Available at: https://www.the-guardian.com/society/2015/jan/28/-sp-nhs-hires-3000-foreign-doctors-staffshortage.

Clarke, R. (2017). *Your life in my hands: a junior doctor's story.* London: Metro Publishing.

Cowan, J. (2007). Good medical practice should improve patient safety. *Clinical Governance: An International Journal*, 12 (2), 136–141.

Cox, J., King, J., Hutchinson, A. and McAvoy, P. (eds). (2006). *Understanding doctors' performance.* Abingdon: Radcliffe Publishing Limited.

Dekker, S. (2007). *Just culture: balancing safety and accountability.* Farnham: Ashgate.

Department of Health (DOH). (2000). *An organisation with a memory.* London: The Stationery Office.

Department of Health. (2009). *The Boorman review of NHS health and wellbeing: final report.* London. Department of Health Product No. 299039. Available at: https://webarchive nationalarchives.gov.uk/20130124052413/http://www.dh.gov.uk/prod_consum_dh/groups/dh_digitalassets/documents/digitalasset/dh_108910.pdf.

Elmer, R. (2001). Reconstruction of medical educators' practice by way of an MA (Ed). *Teacher Development*, 5 (3), 297–308.

Elton, C. (2019). Doctors can't care for patients if the system doesn't care for them – an essay by Caroline Elton. *BMJ*, 364.

Epstein, R. M. and Krasner, M. S. (2013). Physician resilience: what it means, why it matters, and how to promote it. *Academic Medicine*, 88 (3), 301–303.

Farmer, E. A., Beard, J. D., Dauphinee, W. D., LaDuca, T. and Mann, K. V. (2002). Assessing the performance of doctors in teams and systems. *Medical Education*, 36, 942–948.

Fish, D. and Coles, C. (1998). *Developing professional judgement in healthcare.* Oxford: Butterworth-Heinemann.

Fortney, L., Luchterhand, C., Zakletskaia, L. et al. (2013). Abbreviated mindfulness intervention for job satisfaction, quality of life, and compassion in primary care clinicians: a pilot study. *Annals of Family Medicine*, 11 (5), 412–420.

Francis, R. (2013). *Report of the Mid Staffordshire NHS Foundation Trust public inquiry executive summary*. London: The Stationery Office HC947.

Friedson, E. (1986). *Professional powers: a study of the institutionalization of formal knowledge*. Chicago: The University of Chicago Press.

Gawande, A. (2002). *Complications: A surgeon's notes on an imperfect science*. London: Profile Books Limited.

Gerada, C. (2016). Healing doctors through groups: creating time to reflect together. *British Journal of General Practice*, 66 (651), e776–e778.

Gerada, C. (2017). Doctors and mental health. *Occupational Medicine*, 67 (9), 660–661.

Gibson, S. and Leinster, S. (2011). How do students with dyslexia perform in extended matching questions, short answer questions, and observed structured clinical examinations? *Advances in Health Science Education*, 16 (3), 395–404.

GMC (2018a). *Outcomes for Graduates 2018*. Available at: https://www.gmc-uk.org/-/media/documents/dc11326-outcomes-for-graduates-2018_pdf-75040796.pdf.

GMC (2018b). *Fitness to practise statistics 2018*. London: GMC.

Golby, M. and Parrott, A. (1999). *Educational research and educational practice*. Exeter: Fairway Publications.

Riddick, B. (2001). Dyslexia and inclusion: time for a social model of disability perspective? *International Studies in Sociology of Education*, 11, 223–236.

Grant, M. J. and Booth, A. (2009). A typology of reviews: an analysis of 14 review types and associated methodologies. *Health Information and Libraries Journal*, 26 (2), 91–108.

Greenhalgh, T. et al. (2016). An open letter to The BMJ editors on qualitative research. *BMJ*, 352, i563.

Hammersley, M. and Atkinson, P. (2007). *Ethnography: principles in practice*. London: Routledge.

Harrison, J. and Sterland, J. (2006). The impact of health on performance. In J. Cox, J. King, A. Hutchinson and P. McAvoy (eds.), *Understanding doctor's performance*. Oxford: Radcliffe Publishing Ltd, 10–33.

Illing, J. (2013). Thinking about research: theoretical perspectives, ethics and scholarship. In T. Swanwick (ed.), *Understanding medical education: Evidence, theory and practice* (2nd ed.). Oxford: The Association for the Study of Medical Education/Wiley Blackwell, 329–347.

Kay, A. (2017). *This is going to hurt: secret diaries of a junior doctor*. London: Picador.

Kinman, G. and Teoh, K. (2018). *What could make a difference to the mental health of UK doctors? A review of the research evidence. Technical Report*. London: Society of Occupational Medicine and The Louise Tebboth Foundation.

Lake, J. and Bell, J. (2016). Medical educators: the rich symbiosis between clinical and teaching roles. *The Clinical Teacher*, 13, 43–47.

Launer, J. (2019). In defence of appraisal. *Postgraduate Medical Journal*, 95 (1122), 235–236.

Locke, R. (2019). Showcasing insider research. *The Clinical Teacher*, 16 (3), 1–2.

Locke, R. Alexander, G. Mann, R. Kibble, S. and Scallan, S. (2017). Doctors with dyslexia: strategies and support. *The Clinical Teacher*, 14 (5), 38–53.

Locke, R. and Lees, A. (2020). A literature review of interventions to reduce stress in doctors. *Perspectives in Public Health*, 140 (1), 38–53.

Locke, R. Scallan, S. Leach, C. and Rickenbach, M. (2013). Identifying poor performance among doctors in NHS organizations. *Journal of Evaluation in Clinical Practice*, 19 (5), 882–888.

Locke, R. Scallan, S. Mann, R. and Alexander, G. (2015). Clinicians with dyslexia: a systematic review of effects and strategies. *The Clinical Teacher*, 12 (6), 394–398.

Loder, E. et al. (2016). Qualitative research and the BMJ. *BMJ*, 352, i641.

Lyons, B., Gibson, M. and Dolezal, L. (2018). Stories of shame. *The Lancet*, 391 (10130), 1568–1569.

MA Medical Education Tutor Team. (2017). *Philosophy of the programme*. Winchester: University of Winchester.

Maben, J., Peccei, R., Adams, M. et al. (2012). *Exploring the relationship between patients' experiences of care and the influence of staff motivation, affect and wellbeing (final report)*. London: NIHR Service Delivery and Organisation programme.

Malterud, K. and Hollnagel, H. (2005). The doctor who cried: a qualitative study about the doctor's vulnerability. *The Annals of Family Medicine*, 3 (4), 348–352.

Malterud, K., Fredriksen, L. and Gjerde, M. H. (2009). When doctors experience their vulnerability as beneficial for the patients: a focus-group study from general practice. *Scandinavian Journal of Primary Health Care*, 27 (2), 85–90.

Mays, M. and Pope, C. (1995). Rigour and qualitative research. *BMJ*, 311 (6997), 109–112.

McCann, C. M., Beddoe, E., McCormick, K. et al. (2013). Resilience in the health professions: a review of recent literature. *International Journal of Wellbeing*, 3 (1), 60–81.

McKendree, J. and Snowling, M. J. (2011). Examination results of medical students with dyslexia. *Medical Education*, 45 (2), 176–182.

McKinley, N., Karayiannis, P. N., Convie, L., Clarke, M., Kirk, S. J. and Campbell, W. J. (2019). Resilience in medical doctors: a systematic review. *Postgraduate Medical Journal*, 95 (1121), 140–147.

Melia K. (2010). Recognizing quality in qualitative research. In I. Bourgeault, R. Dingwall and R. de Vries (eds.), *The SAGE handbook of qualitative methods in health research*. Thousand Oaks: SAGE Publications Ltd, 559–574.

Miles, S. (2020). Addressing shame: what role does shame play in the formation of a modern medical professional identity? *British Journal of Psychiatry Bulletin*, 44 (1), 1–5.

Mintzberg, H. (1979). *The structuring of organisations*. Englewood Cliffs: Prentice-Hall.

Moberley, T. (2019). Doctors' early retirement triples in a decade. *BMJ*, 365, 14360.

Montgomery, K. (2006). *How doctors think: clinical judgement and the practice of medicine*. Oxford: Oxford University Press.

Morris, D. and Turnbull, P. (2006). Clinical experience of studies with dyslexia. *Journal of Advanced Nursing*, 44, 633–642.

Morse, J. (2016). *Essentials of qualitatively-driven mixed-method designs*. London: Routledge.

Newlands, F., Shrewsbury, D. and Robson, J. (2015). Foundation doctors and dyslexia: a qualitative study of their experiences and coping strategies. *Postgraduate Medical Journal*, 91, 121–126.

O'Brien, B. C., Harris, I. B., Beckman, T. J. et al. (2014). Standards for reporting qualitative research: a synthesis of recommendations. *Academic Medicine*, 89 (9), 1245–1251.

Ofri, D. (2013). *What doctors feel: how emotions affect the practice of medicine*. Boston: Beacon Press.

Oliver, M. (2009). *Understanding disability: from theory to practice*. 2nd ed. Tavistock: Palgrave Macmillan.

Paradis, E., Leslie, M. and Gropper, M. A. (2016). Interprofessional rhetoric and operational realities: an ethnographic study of rounds in four intensive care units. *Advances in Health Science Education*, 21, 735–748.

Peters, D. (2006). Doctor's resilience: can physicians heal themselves. *Journal of Holistic Healthcare*, 3 (1), 3–6.

Platt, D., Chinn, J., Scallan, S. and Lyon-Maris, J. (2015). Fostering resilience with GPs: a workshop approach. *Education for Primary Care*, 26 (5), 328–331.

Price, T., Brennan, N., Cleland, J., Prescott-Clements, L., Wanner, A., Withers, L., Wong, G. and Archers, J. (2018). Remediating doctors' performance to restore patient safety: a realist review protocol. *BMJ Open*, 8 (10), e025943.

Ramer, S. L. (2005). Site-ation pearl growing: methods and librarianship history and theory. *Journal of the Medical Library Association*, 93 (3), 397.

Riley, R., Spiers, J., Chew-Graham, C. A., Taylor, A. K., Thornton, G. A. and Buszewicz, M. (2018). 'Treading water but drowning slowly': what are GPs' experiences of living and working with mental illness and distress in England? A qualitative study. *BMJ Open*, 8 (5), 276–290.

Scallan, S. (2014). Educating for complexity and professional judgement: whither the role of practice-based research? *Education for Primary Care*, 25 6, 299–301.

Scallan, S., Locke, R., Eksteen, D. and Caesar, S. (2016). The benefits of appraisal: a critical (re) view of the literature. *Education for Primary Care*, 27 (2), 94–97.

Schön, D. A. (1983). *The reflective practitioner: how professionals think in action*. New York: Basic Books, Inc.

Shaw, S. C., Malik, M. and Anderson, J. L. (2017). The exam performance of medical students with dyslexia: a review of the literature. *MedEdPublish*, 6 (3), 2.

Shaw, S. C. and Anderson, J. L. (2018). The experiences of medical students with dyslexia: an interpretive phenomenological study. *Dyslexia*, 24 (3), 220–233.

Shaw, S. C., Anderson, J. L. and Grant, A. J. (2016). Studying medicine with dyslexia: a collaborative autoethnography. *Qualitative Report*, 21 (11), 2036–2054.

Shaw, S. C. K. and Anderson, J. L. (2017). Doctors with dyslexia: a world of stigma, stonewalling and silence, still? *MedEdPublish*, 6. https://doi.org/10.15694/mep.2017.000029.

Shaw, S. C. K. (2018). Learned helplessness in doctors with dyslexia: time for a change in discourse? *Nurse Education in Practice*, 32, 99–100.

Shrewsbury, D. (2016). Dyslexia in general practice education: considerations for recognition and support. *Education for Primary Care*, 27 (4), 267–270.

Shrewsbury, D. (2012). Trainee doctors with learning difficulties: recognising need and providing support. *British Journal of Hospital Medicine*, 73 (6): 345–349.

Sinclair, S. (1997). *Making doctors: An institutional apprenticeship*. Oxford: Berg.

Stacey, M. R. (2018). How to be a resilient doctor: skills to maximize your antifragility. *British Journal of Hospital Medicine*, 79 (12), 704–707.

Stenhouse, L. (1975). *An introduction to curriculum research and development*. London, UK: Heinemann.

The Equality Act. (2010). Her Majesty's Stationery Office. Available at: https://www.legislation.gov.uk/ukpga/2010/15/contents. (Accessed 29 July 2020).

The Freedom of Information Act. (2000). Her Majesty's Stationery Office. Available at: https://www.legislation.gov.uk/ukpga/2000/36/contents. (Accessed 29 July 2020).

Thistlewaite, J. and Spencer, J. (2008). *Professionalism in medicine*. Oxford: Radcliffe Publishing.

Varpio, L., Martimianakis, M. and Mylopoulos, M. (2015). Qualitative research methodologies: embracing methodological borrowing, shifting and importing. In J. Cleland and S. Durning (eds.), *Researching medical education*. Oxford: The Association for the Study of Medical Education/ Wiley Blackwell, 231–244.

West, M. and Coia, D. D. (2019). *Caring for doctors caring for patients*. London: GMC.

White J. (2007). Supporting nursing students with dyslexia in clinical practice. *Nursing Standard*, 21, 35–42.

Woolf, K., Rich, A., Viney, R., Rigby, M., Needleman, S. and Griffin, A. (2016). *Fair training pathways for all: understanding experiences of progression (final report)*. London: UCL Academic Centre for Medical Education (ACME).

World Health Organization (WHO). (2010). *Assessing and tackling patient harm: a methodological guide for data-poor hospitals*. Available at: https://apps.who.int/iris/handle/10665/77100. (Accessed 29 July 2020).

3

QUALITATIVE METHODS TO OPTIMISE DESIGN AND CONDUCT OF RANDOMISED CONTROLLED TRIALS WITH CLINICAL POPULATIONS

Andrew Mitchelmore

Setting the scene

Research into the areas of human health and wellbeing forms the backbone of the prevention and treatment of the entire spectrum of physical and mental illness. The definition of health has remained unchanged for many decades. Health is a state of physical, mental and social wellbeing – not merely the absence of disease or infirmity (World Health Organisation, 1946). Wellbeing, which forms part of this definition, has been defined and described by a variety of authors, with little consistency in the literature as to a prominent definition. One frequently adopted definition, by Dodge et al. (2012), is that wellbeing is the balance point between an individual's resource pool and the challenges faced.

Interventional research studies primarily aim to assess methods of preventing or treating physical or mental health conditions (such as depression and anxiety disorders). Whilst improvements in the acute treatment of heart disease and stroke have led to increased long-term survival, this has placed extra pressure on those who treat these conditions chronically. The prevalence of cancer is increasing, with one in five men and one in six women now developing cancer worldwide in their lifetime (World Health Organisation, 2018a). As a result, the economic impact of cancer is significant and increasing (World Health Organisation, 2018b). Within the UK, the consistent increase in life expectancy previously observable has recently stalled. There has also been a sudden and sustained overall increase of people at older ages (Institute of Health Equity, 2017). Changes in life expectancy and quality of life cannot be attributed purely to the health services and state of medical knowledge, as political and socio-economic factors impinge heavily on the health of a population at any given moment. There is an urgent need for research into clinical populations for myriad reasons, but this includes identifying the reasons for this potential slowing (and even reversal) of life expectancy.

DOI: 10.4324/9780429263484-4

Design and conduct of randomised controlled trials with clinical populations **55**

As well as physical diseases taking their toll on the population at ever-decreasing ages, mental health disorders (e.g. depression, anxiety, panic disorder) are a significant focus of health and wellbeing research. The reported prevalence of these disorders in the United Kingdom has increased by around a fifth in the past 25 years (House of Commons Library, 2018) and, in 2014, 17.5% of working-age adults (16–64 years old) had symptoms of common mental health problems (Mental Health Foundation, 2016). Over the course of a lifetime, 19% of adults report being diagnosed with depression, and the prevalence of depression is projected to increase by 43%, severe depression by 49% and dementia by 70% between 2017 and 2035 (Royal College of Psychiatrists, 2018). Mental health conditions are observed across the lifespan. A recent report described how one in five university students have a current mental health diagnosis, around half of students report thoughts about self-harm and more than three-quarters of these students have hidden their symptoms because of fears about stigma (Pereira et al., 2019).

The complex and continually changing nature of physical and mental health issues mean that there is a clear need for continuing interventional studies to prevent and treat ill health in the United Kingdom. The completion of many trials in one research area allows for the creation of a pool of evidence, potentially to be collated in systematic reviews and meta-analyses. Eventually, this can lead to changes in evidence-based practice. These trials collect quantitative data ('how many?' and 'how much?'), qualitative data ('why?' and 'how?'; Green and Thorogood, 2013) or a combination of the two (mixed methods) to answer specific research questions.

Clinical trials continue to be the gold standard for answering clinical research questions, with randomised controlled trials (RCT) the most effective way of demonstrating the safety and effectiveness of interventions (Elliott et al., 2017). The success of these trials is dependent on recruiting enough patients and retaining them through follow-up (Berge et al., 2016). All trials rely on the willingness of the public to volunteer to participate (Locock and Smith, 2011). Recruiting and retaining adequate numbers of participants is important to ensure the robustness of the study and minimise costs (Thayabaranathan et al., 2016) and trials which are less robust may be so because of a lack of statistical power. The failure to recruit participants may reduce this statistical power and compromise both internal and external validity (Sun et al., 2017). Poor recruitment and a consequent low sample size also increase the risk of an investigation into a potentially effective intervention ending prematurely (Treweek et al., 2010), slowing the development of promising treatments into real practice.

Although researchers should be aware of the importance of recruiting well to research studies, Lasagna's law reports that researchers regularly overestimate the number of available participants for recruitment (Blanton et al., 2006). As a result, difficulties recruiting to research studies are common. Efforts to recruit participants frequently fail (Sussman, Cordova and Burge, 2018), leading to around a quarter of RCTs being prematurely discontinued, with 253 of 1017 examined trials being discontinued in one review (Kasenda et al., 2014). The most common reason for this discontinuation was poor recruitment. It is therefore crucial to understand the

56 Andrew Mitchelmore

barriers to recruitment, before trying to implement strategies to improve it (Bartlett, Milne and Croucher, 2018).

This chapter is written as the result of reflecting on a programme of doctoral research which involved research trials with stroke patients and the assessment of their cardiovascular health. The research included recruiting and working with 'healthy' adults but also extended time working with patients and participants in both acute (in the hospital) and chronic (in the laboratory) stages of their stroke journey. Throughout these trials, a range of unexpected situations continued to arise (e.g. deteriorations in patient health, daily in-patient routines, equipment malfunctions, participant drop out). Research experiences, particularly in the clinical environment, led me to discover that when working with clinical and vulnerable populations, I was expected to have a responsive and sensitive relationship with participants, which goes above and beyond what my experience had been to date. A number of the situations during data collection required quick decisions on the best course of action, as there were real consequences if the wrong decisions were made. With hindsight, some of these decisions were correct but others could have been better. Reflection on my work and action has been vital in my development as an early career academic and researcher, and I have taken the lessons from my doctoral studies into the academic world as both a lecturer and researcher. These lessons have included reflections on whether the inclusion of qualitative research could allow for the exploration of subjective participant feelings and emotions, alongside the objective measures provided by quantitative data collection. Whilst it is extremely important to measure changes in statistical variables, pure numbers are not always able to answer the follow-up questions posed by initial findings. Why have we found these findings? How much does this size of change really influence the feelings of individuals and their attitude towards life?

The chapter from this point takes the following structure: it first outlines the importance of reflective practice (which led to the content of this chapter) and gives examples of two main approaches to this. Then, based on the reading and discussion which followed the reflective process, the chapter sets out the ways in which qualitative methods can be incorporated into clinical trials to form mixed-methods designs. The chapter goes on to discuss a range of issues that can arise for trialists, prompted by personal research experiences, and reflects on strategies, including the use of qualitative techniques that may be useful in addressing these.

Reflective practice

The continual development of practical skills is essential in any field of work, and this development is particularly important in clinical research. Health professionals are able to draw on relevant knowledge to apply professional responsibilities and ethical principles in the midst of these changing work environments (Olckers, Gibbs and Duncan, 2007). The ability to confidently navigate difficult situations in research is gained by learning from mistakes and recognising successes. Rather than finishing a session and moving on to the next one, it is advisable to sit down and reflect on what went right, what went wrong and how performance could be improved in the future. To do this formally after every session may be unrealistic but to complete fortnightly or after a particularly positive or difficult session may be more viable.

Reflection has been considered good practice in medical education for many years (Jayatilleke and Mackie, 2013), with the process seen as a key skill in nursing and a skill that is expected of nursing students throughout their programmes (Wilding, 2008). Producing reflective practice is an important aspect of compiling evidence for continuing professional development. There has also been a focus on the necessity of it during the appraisal and revalidation process of doctors (Davies, 2012). There are some overlaps in situations experienced by clinicians or nurses and health researchers. As such, reflective practice should form part of the professional development of health researchers, particularly those in the early career stage.

There are a variety of different methods of reflective practice. Two of the most commonly cited methods were created by Kolb (1984) and Gibbs (1988). Kolb's model incorporates four stages (Figure 3.1):

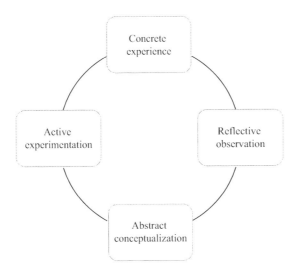

FIGURE 3.1 Kolb's reflective cycle

This cycle begins with the process of having an experience, represented by 'concrete experience'. In the case of topics covered in this chapter, this may involve a recruitment drive, a single data collection session, an experience in a classroom or even the first experience of the publication process. Once an event has taken place to be reflected upon, 'reflective observation' can take place. This involves reflecting on and reviewing the experience at hand and will include both positive and negative reflections. The 'abstract conceptualisation' here refers to learning from these experiences before the 'active experimentation' stage allows you to implement changes to your practice on a future occasion. The next concrete experience then occurs, allowing you to reflect on the successes or failures of changes you made, and the cycle continues.

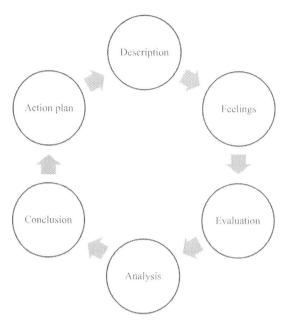

FIGURE 3.2 Gibbs' reflective cycle

Gibbs' cycle is another frequently adopted method of critical reflection. The five stages forming this cycle can be seen in Figure 3.2.

The description here refers to a specific experience before feelings and thoughts about this experience are reflected on. An overall evaluation of the experience incorporates both positive and negative aspects before an analysis makes sense of the situation as a whole and the conclusion outlines key lessons and what could have been done differently. The action plan here is where we can prepare for similar situations of a similar nature and outline which of our actions we would repeat and what new actions could be incorporated to improve the situational outcomes.

As an undergraduate or postgraduate student or even an early career academic, group reflective practice can greatly benefit personal development and improve confidence as a researcher. If there is already a group that meets, it is worth getting involved. If not, creating a research community looks great on a curriculum vitae. Those who view themselves as quantitative researchers can learn lessons from predominantly qualitative researchers, and vice versa. Growing and adapting one's work thanks to the experiences of others allows the integration of a mixed-methods approach more comfortably into any planned research, thereby strengthening it from several angles discussed in this chapter.

This chapter will take a broadly reflective structure and is designed to highlight the realities of trying to recruit, work with and retain clinical populations. It will also touch on what can go wrong during data collection, some of which are unavoidable when working with a clinical population. Parts of this chapter are

Design and conduct of randomised controlled trials with clinical populations **59**

academically underpinned, whereas others are based on personal experiences when things have not gone as planned during the data collection process.

The use of qualitative techniques to enhance trials research

Whereas quantitative techniques employed in clinical trials are vital in showing the efficacy of interventions such as drugs or other treatment regimes, qualitative research is focused on understanding meanings, experiences and perspectives. Qualitative methods such as interviews, observations or documentary analysis can be employed at different stages of clinical trials research to different ends, as shown in the following list based on the work of Lewin, Glenton and Oxman (2009):

LIST 1   PURPOSE OF QUALITATIVE RESEARCH IN TRIALS (LEWIN, GLENTON, AND OXMAN, 2009, P. 2)

Before a trial

- To explore issues related to the health-care question of interest or context of the research
- To generate hypotheses for examination in the RCT
- To develop and refine the intervention
- To develop or select appropriate outcome measures
- To develop effective recruitment strategies

During a trial

- To examine whether the intervention was delivered as intended, including describing the intervention as delivered (process evaluation)
- To 'unpack' processes of implementation and change
- To explore deliverers' and recipients' responses to the intervention

After a trial

- To explore reasons for the findings of the trial
- To explain variations in effectiveness within the sample
- To examine the appropriateness of the underlying theory
- To generate further questions or hypotheses

Caitlin et al. (2013) found that qualitative research holds potential to optimise interventions and the running of trials, to facilitate the interpretation of findings and to help trialists to be sensitive to the needs of the human beings involved in

60 Andrew Mitchelmore

trials, allowing faster recruitment and, overall, via ensuring effective designs, saving money. As we work through the identified set of issues that follows, I make some comments about how qualitative research could be (and has been) used to enhance understandings and address difficult issues in clinical trials. In the words of Mason (2006, p. 9), it appears that

mixing methods…offers enormous potential for exploring new dimensions of experience…and intersections between these. It can encourage researchers to see differently, or think 'outside the box' if they are willing to approach research problems with an innovative and creative palette of methods of data generation.

Issues for trialists to consider before data collection

Protocol development

A detailed and extensive proposal allows for the creation of appropriate and accurate hypotheses and/or research questions before the necessary step of ethical approval can be broached. The creation of both experimental and null hypotheses is a key step in producing clinically relevant results (Farrugia et al., 2010). At this stage, the required sample size can be calculated using computer software (a number of options are available for this) – this is referred to as an a priori sample size calculation. These power and sample size estimations measure how many participants are needed in a study (Jones, Carley and Harrison, 2003) for the study to detect a clinically relevant treatment effect (Hickey et al., 2018). Errors in statistical analysis can be categorised into two categories (Jones, Carley and Harrison, 2003):

- Type I errors involve incorrectly rejecting the null hypothesis (i.e. finding difference when there is not one).
- Type II errors involve incorrectly accepting the null hypothesis (i.e. finding no difference where there is one).

Recruiting a sufficient number of participants reduces the risk of either type of error taking place after data analysis. In health-related environments, these errors could potentially lead to interventions being applied which are ineffective or extensive delays to interventions which could have been effective if implemented sooner. As a result, many academic journals now require a paragraph relating to sample size calculations to be included before an article can be published.

Recruitment

The importance of recruitment is clear to see, but efforts to identify and recruit participants are often unsuccessful (Sussman, Cordova and Burge, 2018). Low recruitment is one of the most commonly cited barriers in clinical research (Arigo et al.,

Design and conduct of randomised controlled trials with clinical populations **61**

2018) and can lead to the extension of the time it takes to complete a research study, drops in staff and participant morale (Thayabaranathan et al., 2016), issues with feasibility and statistical power (Feldman et al., 2016) or even the premature termination of a trial (Gu and Ali, 2010).

Statistics relating to the discontinuation of research trials vary, but figures as high as a quarter have been reported (253 of 1,017 trials) in the literature (Kasenda et al., 2014), with the most commonly cited explanation being poor recruitment. One in ten cancer research trials has been reported to close prematurely because of poor participant accrual (Moorcraft et al., 2016). Even those trials which do complete struggle to do so on time. Fewer than 20% of clinical trials are reported to finish on time, with around half of these delays due to difficulties recruiting (Topolovec and Natarajan, 2016). Another review (Walters et al., 2017) suggests that only 56% of trials successfully recruit to their initial participant target, with 34% of trials having to revise their sample size (with 79% of these revisions being downward). The importance of research studies being well powered statistically has already been highlighted earlier, so the fact that such a proportion of published research studies are forced to be content with lower sample sizes is an area of concern.

Are things getting better? Between 1990 and 2014, trial efficiency and recruitment rates had not improved; if anything, they had declined (Kim and Chiong, 2017). In the past five years, poor patient recruitment and barriers to recruitment have been reported in trials investigating stroke (Polese et al., 2017), cancer (Zaharoff and Cipra, 2018), bowel disease (Herfath et al., 2017), kidney function and disease (Selewski, Herreshoff and Gipson, 2016), Parkinson's disease (Picillo et al., 2015) and mental health conditions (Bucci et al., 2015).

Watson (1999) reports that there are six key stages of recruitment:

1. Identifying eligible patient populations
2. Adequately explaining the study
3. Recruiting an adequate, representative sample
4. Obtaining true, informed consent
5. Maintaining ethical standards
6. Retaining patients until study completion
7. Optimising the cost-benefit ratio

From the statistics cited earlier, these stages are not always being successfully completed. As such, survey results from directors of the National Institute for Health Research Clinical Research Network have identified the top-three priorities of research into trial methodology to be (1) improving recruitment, (2) choice of outcomes and (3) improving retention (Smith et al., 2014). However, before any strategies to improve recruitment to studies can be created and implemented, it is vital to understand why people choose to take part in research and what barriers they face (Bartlett, Milne and Croucher, 2018).

What are the key reasons for lack of participation?

A range of reasons for poor recruitment to trials has been cited in the literature. As these are described next, try to envisage how having a patient-centred, relational and responsive approach to research could impact these barriers.

Obtaining consent from research participants is one of the cornerstones of ethical practice in research. However, consent is not easy to come by. For example, stroke can cause aphasia or cognitive incapacitation (Feldman et al., 2016), meaning that proxy decision-makers are needed (usually a family member). Proxy decision-makers may be less willing to enrol relatives into clinical research (Kesner et al., 2009), meaning researchers face a struggle to recruit these populations.

Another vital part of the research process is participant randomisation. Randomisation is the most critical feature of an RCT (Yelland et al., 2018), and for participants to be truly randomised in clinical trials, clinicians must be genuinely uncertain about whether a treatment will be beneficial. This is known as clinical equipoise (Jones and Cipriani, 2019). However, this aspect of trial preparation does not tend to sit well with participants themselves. Believing that a trial offers the best available treatment is one of the most commonly cited reasons for research participation (Moorcraft et al., 2016), and under the rule of clinical equipoise, patients cannot be certain that the trial will benefit their health. As a result, eligible patients can dislike the idea of being randomised by a computer to a treatment arm (Blazeby et al., 2014). One interviewee in research by Locock and Smith (2011) described how she would have gone ahead with her participation in an RCT but 'would have felt cheated' if randomised into the control group. The concept of randomisation was not well understood by many participants in this study. Morris and Nelson (2007, p. 943) say that being in research trials 'confronts research participants and/or their families with the inadequacy of current medical knowledge, which may be upsetting'. The act of randomisation, by definition, informs patients of this fact, which may be uncomfortable for them. Is it possible that by incorporating a qualitative arm into studies that involve randomisation, the subsequent building of a rapport and discussion with participants could lead to a greater understanding of the randomisation process from a participant's point of view? Could this qualitative education, in turn, reduce the feeling of 'being cheated' by randomisation into a control group?

It is also common for recruiters to find it challenging to explain trial design in simple and fair terms – leading to a poorly balanced presentation of treatment options (Griffin et al., 2016). This, combined with pre-existing negative feelings towards the randomisation process, can make recruitment extremely difficult. Even if the study is described clearly and concisely, visual representations of treatments may discourage participation, with graphic descriptions of surgery reported to put patients off taking part in studies containing surgical arms (Griffin et al., 2016).

Barriers to recruitment can affect investigators, as well as participants. Many investigators (52%) and centres (41%) are too busy with clinical and other work or have a poor research agenda or infrastructure (46%; Berge et al., 2016). Interventions can be complicated, time-consuming and costly (Berge et al., 2016), leading to slow

Design and conduct of randomised controlled trials with clinical populations **63**

recruitment on-site. To combat this, a variety of research has been conducted to try to isolate the key reasons for slow or difficult recruitment to clinical research studies. As academics, having an awareness of the difficulties we are likely to face allows us to prepare more efficiently for the challenge ahead. Some challenges to recruitment will be condition-specific, whereas other challenges will appear as a recurring theme across clinical groups. For example, Hadidi et al. (2012) identified three key challenges to stroke studies: (1) being accommodative to survivors' schedules, (2) establishing realistic inclusion and exclusion criteria and (3) providing incentives to the study participants in control groups. As discussed previously, randomisation is a scary concept to a potentially vulnerable and unwell participant, so providing a clear benefit of even being in a control group may widen the participation of those in a demographic who were previously unsure about the decision.

Alexandrov (2006) identified six key reasons for slow recruitment (specifically in stroke research – but these reasons can be applied to other conditions):

1. A slow start (insufficient site recruitment, unforeseen obstacles, etc.)
2. More complex protocols
3. Trial fatigue by investigators
4. Patients less willing to participate
5. Excessive (though necessary or often unavoidable) and lengthy regulatory work
6. Regulatory issues with drugs and devices, their combinations and evolving technologies

The Institute of Medicine (2012) reported another four key factors contributing to the failure of participant recruitment to clinical trials as a whole:

1. Lack of awareness amongst physicians and patients that relevant trials are available
2. Lack of awareness of the benefits of clinical trials
3. Maintaining clinical equipoise, especially when treatment arms are very different and patients or physicians have strong preferences for one therapy over another
4. Maintaining equipoise for pragmatic trials when the treatment evaluated is widely available and covered by outside payers

When planning a protocol, it is important to bear these reasons in mind, including strategies and contingency plans for when things do not go to plan. Most reasons for recruitment failure seem preventable with a pilot study applying a planned informed consent procedure (Briel et al., 2016) so it is always worth conducting a pilot study to identify major issues with a current protocol. When thinking about participant recruitment rates, it is also important to remember that there are a number of clinical trials being undertaken at any one time, and these trials are likely to be competing for participants. Even with a relatively simple protocol, reasonably relaxed inclusion and exclusion criteria and a large demographic group to recruit from, there is likely to be competition with other trials trying to recruit to similar samples. As such, it is important to be realistic about how long it will take to recruit the sample size that gives you an appropriate statistical power.

Some barriers will require time and effort to overcome (e.g. the necessary regulatory work), but the impact of many can be minimised through preparation, approaching research participants with an appropriate demeanour, gaining trust and working efficiently through a well-rehearsed protocol.

Research in this area conducted by Elliott et al. (2017) suggests that strong recruitment to RCTs can occur if certain factors are considered, including the following:

- Addressing clinically important questions at a timely point,
- Employing dedicated research staff,
- Ensuring all staff are trained about trial processes and interventions and
- Having straightforward data collection.

If data collection is taking place in a clinical environment, the importance of supportive research staff who are on board and well versed with the study protocol cannot be overestimated. An excellent clinician or research nurse who conducts the initial approach to a patient before the external researcher can gain official consent can make or break a research study. If researchers can work alongside a clinician or research nurse who is interested in a study, is aware of inclusion and exclusion criteria and knows what the study really involves, our lives are much easier. As such, creating strong relationships with these clinical staff as an external researcher is vital. A recurring theme throughout this chapter is the crucial importance of being amicable and warm to everyone we interact with in the research process to foster positive relationships. This includes academic colleagues, clinicians and patients. Bucci et al. (2015) describe how, when working in mental health, it is important to have a flexible, tailor-made approach for each clinical team to ensure a collaborative relationship is developed between research staff and clinicians, but this translates to a variety of health conditions – not just mental health itself.

When it comes to patients as research participants, we need to remember that these individuals may feel obligated to help by participating in research trials (Thayabaranathan et al., 2016). Alongside this obligation, participants may feel a range of other emotions. Some participants will approach research with a fearless 'treat me as a guinea pig' attitude in which they are content to participate without any worries, whereas others may feel extremely nervous about the experience. Another recurring theme throughout this chapter is the importance of assessing each participant and treating him or her as an individual rather than a participant code who will provide data. This may sound like an easy thing to do, but when collecting data from the 50th participant, it is naturally difficult to act with exactly the same enthusiasm as with the first or second participant.

Design and conduct of randomised controlled trials with clinical populations   **65**

Trust

Participants take part in research for both altruistic reasons and personal benefit. Most patients feel that participants should be informed of trial results after completion (Moorcraft et al., 2016) – something that benefits participants whatever their motivation and may convince unsure individuals that they gain some benefit. Research aiming to understand the motivations of potential research participants has concluded that trust is extremely important in the consent process. Some participants in work by Locock and Smith (2011) stated that they had not really read information sheets and purely trusted the verbal discussions with their doctors. Mistrust has also been noted as a patient barrier, specifically in minority patients, alongside the fear of experimentation (Amorrortu et al., 2018). Why is this the case?

A lack of trust may exist due to either a lack of knowledge about how research works or the presence of knowledge relating to how research has been conducted poorly in the past. Ethics are the backbone of research, and every research study must be approved by an ethics panel before data collection can take place. The earliest expression of medical ethics in the west (the Hippocratic Oath) states, 'I will do no harm or injustice to my patients'. However, there are multiple well-known examples of poor ethical practice that may inevitably lead potential participants to be reluctant to give consent. Whilst this is not a chapter on ethics, it is important to take the time to research examples where the ethical ball has been catastrophically dropped to understand why participants may be reluctant. This includes examples such as the 'Tuskegee study of untreated syphilis in the negro male', which ran for a quarter of a century and resulted in the death of around 100 participants who had not been informed as to the true nature of the research, and the 'Monster Study' of 1939, involving a protocol which resulted in a number of child participants developing life-long speech impediments.

These are just two relatively well-known examples which demonstrate why trust between participants and researchers or clinicians may be low and why participants may be consequently reluctant to consent to being recruited to a research study. If, as researchers, we can act in a way which increases trust and understanding, it is likely to produce improvements in participant recruitment and retention. To reduce levels of concern in research participants, different strategies can be used. Issues of terminology can be important – research suggests that using the term 'medical research' rather than 'clinical trial' may reduce negative connotations amongst community members (Amorrortu et al., 2018). We should also focus on making participants fully aware of the processes that form the data collection process. It is not always easy to explain trial design in simple terms, so the careful construction of information sheets and consent forms is key.

Trial documentation

Before taking part in research studies, potential participants are expected to read large amounts of information that is often complicated (Locock and Smith, 2011), but a third of older adults in England have difficulty reading and understanding basic health-related information (Bostock and Steptoe, 2012). This is an issue particularly relevant in clinical research, as a number of participant groups may suffer from some cognitive deficits, even if they are able to give consent without proxy. Even those without official cognitive deficits, including children, may lack attention or be unable to reach a reading level that would normally be comfortable due to their ill health and situational distress. Some clinical trial patient information sheets may, therefore, not be fit-for-purpose (Moorcraft et al., 2016). Long leaflets can be problematic, and more summarised information may be beneficial to potential participants when combined with the ability to verbally clarify points of misunderstanding with trusted professionals (Locock and Smith, 2011). Shortening and simplifying information and consent paperwork has been reported to result in significantly better understanding (Rogers et al., 1998), but how do we go about doing this?

The Gunning-Fog Index (Gunning, 1968) is one method of quantifying the reading level required to comprehend a body of text. The index is calculated using the average sentence length, percentage of hard words (words ≥ 3 syllables in length that are not pronouns or two-syllable words with –es and –ed endings). The formula used is 0.4 x (average sentence length + percentage hard words).

There are several websites which will do the calculation after the copy and pasting of a passage greater than 100 words in length. The number calculated gives an indication as to the complexity of the passage. For example, a score of 4.9 or lower would mean the text could be understood by someone in year 5, a score of 7 would mean a passage is well suited to a reader in year 8, whereas a score of 17 would imply that a passage is suited to a postgraduate individual. Being able to adapt the wording of information sheets to a specific audience may greatly increase your ability to recruit to a research study.

When explaining a protocol to a participant verbally and seeking consent for their participation, it is crucial to describe the process as simply and chronologically as possible. It may be a good idea to have the protocol as a memorised and rehearsed script, as this allows the preparation of a concise description of the research study. Prospective participants also need sufficient time to think about the study, as they may not feel they understand exactly what taking part in a trial involves if they make the decision too quickly (Stryker et al., 2006). As such, all potential participants should be given at least 24 hours to consider their options and think of any questions they may want to ask before providing or declining consent. Participants should also be given the opportunity to air any concerns they have before the study begins, as this may reduce the likelihood of drop out. Practical considerations are also an important part of improving recruitment and retention rates – for example, transportation may be the most critical non-medical recruitment concern (Blanton et al., 2009). If data collection is taking place in a clinical setting, then this consideration is irrelevant, but for studies expecting clinical groups to travel to data collection sessions, alternative arrangements should be considered in advance to avoid drop out or unexpected increases in the cost of the study.

Use of qualitative techniques at the pre-trial phase

In the preceding section, a number of issues for trialists to grapple with at the pre-trial stage have been identified, including difficulties with recruiting, explaining trials and related concepts (such as randomisation) in understandable and acceptable terms both verbally and within documentation. These issues are linked to a need to establish trust and rapport and recognise the human vulnerability of potential trial participants. One way in which qualitative research can be used is to identify reasons why a trial may not be recruiting as well as expected. For example, in research into the reasons for slow recruitment to a three-armed RCT offering either radiation, surgery or monitoring following diagnosis of prostate cancer, Donovan et al. (2002) used in-depth interviews to investigate potential participants' interpretation of study information. They found that clinicians struggled to explain the concept of equipoise to participants within the design of an RCT. It was also found that recruiters unwittingly used terminology which was off-putting to describe one of the arms of the trial. This arm was known as the 'watchful waiting' arm, which some respondents took to mean that doctors would watch and wait for them to die. As a result of the findings, the wording of trial information was changed, with an increased emphasis on the equivalence of all arms, resulting in improved recruitment. Whilst Donovan's study actually took place during the conduct of a trial due to low response rates, it is becoming increasingly common to incorporate qualitative research into the feasibility stage of a trial to enhance the likelihood that trial information and recruitment processes will be acceptable and effective for participants during the main trial.

During data collection

The data collection process is something that is difficult to learn realistically in a classroom environment. A large proportion of what is described in the rest of this chapter is based on personal experiences collecting data in clinical and academic environments. It is important to accept that some lessons in data collection are mainly learned through trial and error, so it is completely normal for things not to go to plan when working with clinical groups. It is how we react and learn as researchers that moulds our ability to cope with unexpected and potentially difficult situations.

When working with clinical populations, we must remember that we are seeing individuals in an extremely small cross-section of their lives and in a cross-section which may be the most difficult they will ever travel through. As such, maintaining a responsive and relational approach is key. Particularly when working with in-patient populations, a particularly positive or negative experience with research can certainly play a part as to the mindset towards other aspects of recovery that a patient adopts during their hospital stay. Some stroke survivors who have participated in my previous work have provided information as to how they felt after their strokes (Figure 3.3).

FIGURE 3.3 How does it feel to have a stroke and then be a participant in research?

Most clinicians encounter older patients with depression in their day-to-day practice, with a higher proportion of people aged over 65 committing suicide than any other age group (Rodda, Walker and Carter, 2011). Depression is common after stroke, with around 30% of survivors experiencing the condition (NHS, 2017), and also prevalent in people with cancer, with 24% of patients having reported depression after an initial cancer diagnosis (Cardoso et al., 2016). In this demographic, being female, being older and having a more advanced stage of cancer were all independent risk factors for the presence of depression. Depression is also remarkably common in chronic obstructive pulmonary disease (Tselebis et al., 2016), and clinically significant depressive disturbances are observed in 40%–50% of patients with Parkinson's disease (Marsh, 2013). It is important to remember that a proportion of any clinical research participants are likely to be presenting with depressive symptoms or anxiety, and their perception of researcher interactions with them is key.

We should also be ready to encounter widely varying emotions. Emotionalism is a condition common after stroke, with individuals having difficulty controlling their emotional behaviour (including crying and laughing; Allida et al., 2019). As a result, good preparation involves an awareness that if data collection takes place over multiple days (even consecutive days), the mental state of a participant may be liable to be different between visits (potentially influencing the data collected). Although measures of psychological state can potentially be used as a covariate in statistical analysis, any reduction in the consistency of sessions weakens a study. It is also important to remember that it is not always just the participant who may be experiencing symptoms of mental health issues. In conditions such as motor neurone disease (amyotrophic lateral sclerosis [ALS]), major depression even in the later stages is rare (Rabkin et al., 2005), but there may be an increase of burden and

Design and conduct of randomised controlled trials with clinical populations **69**

depression in caregivers. In fact, Gauthier et al. (2007) observed significant changes in the depressive state of caregivers over a nine-month time period. Any interaction with family and caregivers of participants from a clinical population should be conducted with this in mind.

Another important consideration when interacting with participants is that they may even be having suicidal thoughts. Suffering a stroke increases the risk of suicide ideation and death due to suicide (Pompili et al., 2012), whereas an increased risk of suicide in the six months after a cancer diagnosis has also been observed (Henson et al., 2019). Making the most of training opportunities from your workplace can prepare you for knowing how to react when someone is honest with you about their suicidal feelings. As an early career researcher, I was confronted with this situation, as a research participant informed me of their intention to take their own life after discharge from hospital. This type of situation highlights why it is so important for researchers to have a positive relationship with clinical staff and to have discussed in advance how any issues (e.g. suicidal thoughts, sudden drops in blood pressure) should be reported.

This example leads to a discussion about what sort of relationship exists between a researcher and a participant. A common response from research participants is the reinforcing of the 'I am a person, not a number' mantra. Relationships are key to helping recruitment run smoothly (Bartlett, Milne and Croucher, 2018). Blanton and colleagues (2006) describe how the importance of characteristics such as friendliness and responsiveness to create an atmosphere of trust cannot be overestimated. Bartlett, Milne and Croucher (2018) discuss how it is important to engage a person with dementia by beginning every encounter with an act of kindness, even if it something as small as a smile and a compliment. However, this approach should apply to all research participants – not purely those with dementia. Using acts of kindness to form a positive rapport with study participants also allows for better communication. As part of this book chapter, recently graduated students and stroke patients who have recently taken part in research studies were asked what traits they thought were important in a researcher in a clinical setting.

What key traits should a clinical researcher have?

We asked some recently graduated undergraduate students and previous research participants what the key traits they feel are necessary in a researcher (Table 3.1).

Poor communication between clinicians and patients can contribute to a lack of understanding of a patient's problems, meaning the patients feel unable to access, understand and utilise health information (Shaw et al., 2009). As researchers, if we foster a healthy relationship with participants involving strong communication, we may even be asked by a patient to clarify the meaning of terms that they have misunderstood from a clinician. It is extremely important, however, that we ensure that we are not taking on the role of a doctor in an in-patient setting. As suggested previously, this is a situation where having a pre-agreed plan of action makes life much simpler. Whether it is as simple as entering into ward notes that the patient needs

TABLE 3.1 What do recent students and stroke research participants think are the most important traits in a researcher?

Recent students	Clinical research participants
'The ability to demonstrate empathy towards those you are working with and a sound understanding of the issues being faced'	'Good communication with understanding and a sympathetic approach to the patient'
'Time management, empathy, an understanding of the population, and being prepared'	A personable, friendly approach to engage in a working partnership'
'The ability to recognise the need to consult in events where patient wellbeing may be compromised'	'A friendly and helpful approach with patience'
'Confidence and an ability to deal with unexpected situations'	
'The ability to recognise the need to consult in events where patient wellbeing might be compromised'	

some clarification or even having a discussion with a nurse or doctor, we should not put ourselves in a position where we may have to be accountable for comments made to the patient regarding their welfare. In addition, we must remember that our work may even give participants a feeling of purpose at a time when they may feel extremely let down by their bodies, so a reiteration of gratitude for their participation can go a long way to improving patient morale.

It is also inevitable that, during the data collection process, practical difficulties will arise during testing sessions and when trying to collect follow-up data from participants. When collecting patient-reported outcomes, one review by Fielding et al. (2008) found that 18% of research studies had between 11% and 20% missing data, and another 18% of studies had >20% missing data. After a priori sample size calculations have been completed, even reaching the number required for strong statistical power can be difficult. To have missing data from participants greatly weakens statistical analysis further down the line. This missing data may be due to the loss of participants during follow-up procedures.

Practical difficulties are particularly frequent when working with clinical populations in acute treatment settings. Sudden dips in health do happen, and two recent examples come to mind from personal experience. One participant on a hyper-acute stroke ward with an approximate blood pressure of ~145/90 mmHg was making conversation, but within the space of one-two minutes, he started to become quieter and looked slightly clammy. His blood pressure had dropped to 88/50 mmHg and heart rate from ~80b min^{-1} to 35b min^{-1}. A second example involved a participant who was a chronic stroke patient but who had difficulties with thermoregulation. After two hours of seated data collection, he announced that he felt slightly too warm and needed to move, proceeding to lean forward from his chair and collapse, gripping onto a massage table. His back was soaked with sweat; he was barely conscious, and his blood pressure dropped to a dangerously

Design and conduct of randomised controlled trials with clinical populations **71**

low level. What was the common denominator between these two events? The participants did not verbalise any feeling of discomfort or unease before it was too late to avoid a potentially dangerous situation. It is common for participants to keep pushing through a difficult moment to try to avoid being inconvenient. As a researcher, it is so important to keep our focus on patient welfare as a priority over our own data collection.

As researchers in clinical environments, we are likely going to come face-to-face with blood, sweat, tears and urine on a regular basis. After a stroke, around half of patients suffer from bladder problems, and approximately a third lose bowel control (Stroke Association, 2012). Researchers cannot be squeamish or repulsed by any of these fluids! Reacting negatively to the realities of the life of a patient is likely to make them feel extremely uncomfortable and result in an elevated risk of low patient morale and, less importantly, study withdrawal.

Other practical issues include equipment failure and unexpected changes to a patient's routine (e.g. diagnostic imaging, physiotherapy), resulting in clashes with a data collection session. It is documented that investigators must balance the need for valid data with the protection of a patient's best interests (Blanton et al., 2006), but patient welfare is *always* the priority. As such, a research session is extremely unlikely to be the priority for the patient or the clinicians compared to other events in a hospital.

Maintaining this positive relationship with participants relies on being flexible and adaptable. Remember that to research participants in a clinical setting, research-ers are one of the faces of the hospital. Those participants without any knowledge of academia may even consider us as part of their treatment team. As such, we have a responsibility to minimise how unpleasant their time as an in-patient is. Particularly within a repeated measures study, there is a good chance that we will spend more time with them on these days than the clinicians or nursing staff will have time to, who are balancing their time around a larger number of patients on an individual ward. Listen attentively and do the little things that make a difference. One example from my own experience was a participant who had no family or friends visiting who told me that they were really struggling with the hospital food. They added that what they most missed from the outside world was tinned peaches. I checked with nursing staff that there were no dietary reasons, that peaches were not an option and then provided a couple of cans for them. If a patient wants to feel like they are giving something back to the researcher, why not admit you enjoy cup-cakes and accept them when they appear at your next session? If a patient wants lifestyle advice, why not give some of your own time at the end of the session to discuss the importance of physical activity and not smoking or drinking to excess (taking into account the earlier comments regarding not taking on the role of the doctor). If we give participants our time outside of the minimum required for their data, they are far more likely to give us extended periods of their time in return.

As mentioned earlier, it is crucial to individualise the research experience for every participant. I have had experiences where every step of the protocol needs to be described in detail to avoid anxiety, and participants feel the need to know

72 Andrew Mitchelmore

exactly how data collection will feel, *exactly* what their data is suggesting, before not being eager to ever see me again. I have had other experiences where participants are happy to be a guinea pig and happy to just get on with it so I can stay after the data collection has finished and sit on the corner of a hospital bed watching rugby. We must never go into a session with any preconceptions as to what the session will involve, or it becomes a lot more difficult to react well to any situation that arises.

People of all ages, creeds and socio-economic backgrounds have a variety of opinions on controversial topics, with a certain percentage of any population having discriminatory beliefs or prejudices. The filtering of prejudice, however, appears to be more problematic for older adults (Castillo et al., 2014). If you have fostered a positive rapport with your participant and are having a relaxed and open conversation, it may therefore be the case that you come across political or racial views that surprise you or leave you unsure how to respond. In seven years of studying, I never attended a session that prepared me for how to respond to an uncomfortable situation of this type or that it was even likely to occur. The awareness in advance that this situation may arise will give you the opportunity to plan responses in advance, depending on what your conscience dictates and what you deem appropriate. It is certainly important to be aware that you are likely to face this uncomfortable situation during data collection.

After initial data collection is complete, you may require participants to attend follow-up sessions to measure changes in a variable over time. The failure to retain patients is a common challenge for trials (Kearney et al., 2017). These high attrition rates increase the risk of bias, particularly if participants lost to follow-up are isolated to either an intervention or control group, compared to those who were retained (Abshire et al., 2017). Berge et al. (2016) identified key methods of improving retention:

- Regular and personal contact with patients and families or with general practitioner (GP)
- Monetary or other incentives
- Simple and regular follow-ups using multiple ways of contact
- Entry criteria that select patients who can be expected to be compliant

A combination of adequate study preparation and creating positive, as well as personal relationships with participants, has the potential to maximise the effectiveness of these methods and reduce participant data loss in follow-up visits. If we can create a sensitive and amicable rapport with our research participants, the likelihood of our research study as a whole being successful is greatly increased.

Use of qualitative techniques to enhance the running of the trial

In view of the previous comments about the likelihood of 'unanticipated' events, it is perhaps useful to flag here that qualitative research can be used as a form of 'process evaluation' to investigate if the trial is actually running as anticipated. As highlighted

Design and conduct of randomised controlled trials with clinical populations **73**

here, life 'on the ground' of a clinical trial is often very different from that envisaged at the protocol stage, and this may influence outcomes. Qualitative process evaluation using methods including observation can be very helpful in determining if there are elements of context or implementation that are impinging on the trial and its outcomes. For example, the *Footprints in Primary Care Study* (Thomas, 2017) investigated an intervention aimed at improving the care of frequent attenders in primary care via GPs' use of a psycho-social telephone consultation technique with an identified cohort of patients. The intervention was developed by staff within one GP practice and showed promising findings in an in-service evaluation; however, when this was rolled out to a larger-scale evaluation, results proved disappointing, with no increase in telephone consultations amongst frequent attenders and only 10% of GPs saying that they were using the psycho-social approach. Researchers used a mix of qualitative methods, including recording and conducting conversation analysis on GP/'frequent attender' telephone conversations. The process evaluation revealed that patients were often resistant to telephone consultations and that GPs found the intervention 'script' difficult to follow with 'real patients' who often took conversations in unanticipated directions. These findings, with examples of potentially problematic areas, were incorporated into training for GPs to use the intervention moving forwards.

Looking forwards

If we prepare well, approach research participants with a sensitive and relational approach and reflect on our professional practice, working with research participants can be a rewarding and enjoyable experience. There are extraneous variables that will take place. Mistakes will happen, participants will get sicker, participants will withdraw, equipment will break, but we can minimise the disruption caused to our work by approaching these studies in a professional and appropriate manner. This chapter has highlighted the potential benefits of a mixed-methods approach to intervention studies as a holistic and proactive way of identifying and dealing with potential issues. As a traditionally quantitative researcher, including appropriate qualitative measures into your work has the potential to improve participant recruitment, retention and experience, all whilst potentially allowing you to answer more 'why' questions relating to your quantitative findings. If you are a traditionally qualitative researcher, adopting quantitative methods also allows for a broadening of your skill set and a different angle when interpreting your findings.

Incorporating this mixed-methods approach also allows us to maximise our development as researchers and optimise participant experience. We should never underestimate the amount we can learn from our participants outside of the data they provide. One advantage of incorporating a mixed-methods research approach into your work is a large reduction in the risk of inadvertently treating participants as a number rather than a name, as the purpose of qualitative research is to understand personal attitudes, beliefs and perspectives. By definition, qualitative and mixed-methods research strategies allow participants to have a voice and not be

74 Andrew Mitchelmore

purely defined by the data they are offering. All methods of research have particular strengths and specific limitations (Kelle, 2006), so combining these methods can lead to optimal research strategies in terms of data collection and participant.

Questions for discussion and further reflection

What are the challenges associated with recruiting to clinical trials amongst Andrew's population of interest?

What is the value of reflective practice with regard to clinical trials research?

How does Andrew suggest the inclusion of qualitative techniques within mixed-methods designs could enhance the conduct of clinical trials?

Are you surprised by any of the key traits that students and participants suggest that clinical researchers should possess? Would you agree with these and/or add any other desirable characteristics?

References

Abshire, M., Dinglas, V. D., Cajita, M. I. A., Eakin, M. N., Needham, D. M. and Himmelfarb, C. D. (2017). Participant retention practices in longitudinal clinical research studies with high retention rates. *BMC Medical Research Methodology*, 17, 30.

Alexandrov, A. V. (2006). Slow recruitment in clinical trials: failure is not an option!. *International Journal of Stroke*, 1 (3), 160.

Allida, S., Patel, K., House, A. and Hackett, M. L. (2019). Pharmaceutical interventions for emotionalism after stroke (review). *Cochrane Database of Systematic Reviews*, 3, CD003690.

Amorrortu, R. P., Arevalo, M., Vernon, S. W., Mainous III, A. G., Diaz, V., McKee, M. D. et al. (2018). Recruitment of racial and ethnic minorities to clinical trials conducted within specialty clinics: an intervention mapping approach. *Trials*, 19 (1), 115.

Bartlett, R., Milne, R. and Croucher, R. (2018). Strategies to improve recruitment of people with dementia to research studies. *Dementia*, 18 (7–8), 2494–2504.

Berge, E., Stapf, C., Salman, R. A. S., Ford, G. A., Sandercock, P., van der Worp, H. B. et al. (2016). Methods to improve patient recruitment and retention in stroke trials. *International Journal of Stroke*, 11 (6), 663–676.

Blazeby, J. M., Strong, S., Donovan, J. L., Wilson, C., Hollingworth, W., Crosby, T. et al. (2014). Feasibility RCT of definitive chemoradiotherapy or chemotherapy and surgery for oesophageal squamous cell cancer. *British Journal of Cancer*, 111 (2), 234–240.

Bostock, S. and Steptoe, A. (2012). Association between low functional health literacy and mortality in older adults: longitudinal cohort study. *BMJ*, 344, e1602.

Briel, M., Olu, K. K., von Elm, E., Kasenda, B., Alturki, R., Agarwal, A. et al. (2016). A systematic review of discontinued trials suggested that most reasons for recruitment failure were preventable. *Journal of Clinical Epidemiology*, 80, 8–15.

Bucci, S., Butcher, I., Hartley, S., Neil, S. T., Mulligan, J. and Haddock, G. (2015). Barriers and facilitators to recruitment in mental health services: care coordinators' expectations and experience of referring to a psychosis research trial. *Psychology and Psychotherapy: Theory, Research and Practice*, 88, 335–350.

Cardoso, G., Graca, J., Klut, C., Trancas, B. and Papoila, A. (2016). Depression and anxiety symptoms following cancer diagnosis: a cross-sectional study. *Psychology, Health and Medicine*, 21 (5), 562–570.

Design and conduct of randomised controlled trials with clinical populations **75**

Castillo, J. L. A., Equizabal, A. J., Camara, C. P. and Gonzalez, H. G. (2014). The fight against prejudice in older adults: perspective taking effectiveness. *Revista Latinoamericana de Psicologia*, 46 (3), 137–147.

Davies, S. (2012). Embracing reflective practice. *Education for Primary Care*, 23, 9–12.

Dodge, R., Daly, A. P., Huyton, J. and Sanders, L. D. (2012). The challenge of defining wellbeing. *International Journal of Wellbeing*, 2 (3), 222–235.

Donovan, J., Mills, N., Smith, M., Brindle, L., Jacoby, A., Peters, T., Frankel, S., Neal, D. and Hamdy, F. (2002) Improving design and conduct of randomised trials by embedding them in qualitative research: (ProtecT) study. *BMJ*, 325, 766–770

Elliott, D., Husbands, S., Hamdy, F. C., Holmberg, L. and Donovan, J. L. (2017). Understanding and improving recruitment to randomised controlled trials: qualitative research approaches. *European Urology*, 72 (5), 789–798.

Farrugia, P., Petrisor, B. A., Farrokhyar, F. and Bhandari, M. (2010). Research questions, hypotheses and objectives. *Canadian Journal of Surgery*, 53 (4), 278–281.

Feldman, W. B., Kim, A. S., Josephson, A., Lowenstein, D. H. and Chiong, W. (2016) Effect of waivers of consent on recruitment in acute stroke trials. *Neurology*, 86 (16), 1543–1551.

Fielding, S., Maclennan G., Cook, J. A. et al. (2008). A review of RCTs in four medical journals to assess the imputation to overcome missing data in quality of life outcomes. *Trials*, 9, 51.

Gauthier, A., Vignola, A., Calvo, A., Cavallo, E., Moglia, C., Sellitti, L. et al. (2007). A longitudinal study on quality of life and depression in ALS patient-caregiver couples. *Neurology*, 68 (12), 923–926.

Gibbs, G. (1988). *Learning by doing: A guide to teaching and learning methods.* Further Education Unit. Oxford Polytechnic: Oxford.

Green, J. and Thorogood, N. (2013). *Qualitative methods for health research.* London: SAGE Publications.

Griffin, D., Wall, P., Realpe, A., Adams, A., Parsons, N., Hobson, R. et al. (2016). UK FASHIoN: feasibility study of a randomised controlled trial of arthroscopic surgery for hip impingement compared with best conservative care. *Healthy Technology Assessment*, 20 (32), 1–172.

Gunning, R. (1968). *The technique of clear writing.* New York: McGraw-Hill.

Hadidi, N., Buckwalter, K., Lindquist, R. and Rangen, C. (2012). Lessons learned in recruitment and retention of stroke survivors. *Journal of Neuroscience and Nursing*, 44 (2), 105–110.

Henson, K. E., Brock, R., Charnock, J., Wickramasinghe, B., Will, O. and Pitman, A. (2019). Risk of suicide after cancer diagnosis in England. *JAMA Psychiatry*, 76 (1), 51–60.

Herfath, H. H., Jackson, S., Schliebe, B. G., Martin, C., Ivanova, A., Anton, K. et al. (2017). Investigator initiated IBD trials in the US: facts, obstacles and answers. *Inflammatory Bowel Diseases*, 23 (1), 14–22.

Hickey, G. L., Grant, S. W., Dunning, J. and Siepe, M. (2018). Statistical primer: sample size and power calculations – why, when and how?. *European Journal of Cardio-Thoracic Surgery*, 54 (1), 4–9.

House of Commons Library. (2018). *Mental health statistics for England: prevalence, services and funding.* Available at: https://researchbriefings.files.parliament.uk/documents/SN06988/SN06988.pdf. (Accessed 14 July 2019).

Institute of Health Equity. (2017). *Marmot indicators briefing.* Available at: http://www.instituteofhealthequity.org/resources-reports/marmot-indicators-2017-institute-of-health-equity-briefing/marmot-indicators-briefing-2017-updated.pdf. (Accessed 8 July 2019).

Institute of Medicine. (2012). *Public engagement and clinical trials: new models and disruptive technologies: Workshop summary.* Washington, DC: The National Academies Press.

Jayatilleke, N. and Mackie, A. (2013). Reflection as part of continuous professional development for public health professionals: a literature review. *Journal of Public Health*, 35 (2), 308–312.

Jones, H. and Cipriani, A. (2019). Barriers and incentives to recruitment in mental health clinical trials. *Evidence Based Mental Health*, 22, 49–50.

Jones, S. R., Carley, S. and Harrison, M. (2003). An introduction to power and sample size estimation. *Emergency Medicine Journal*, 20, 453–458.

Kasenda, B., von Elm, E., You, J., Blumle, A., Tomonaga, Y., Saccilott, R. et al. (2014). Prevalence, characteristics, and publication of discontinued randomized trials. *JAMA*, 311, 1045–1051.

Kearney, A., Daykin, A., Shaw, A. R. G., Lane, A. J., Blazeby, J. M., Clarke, M. et al. (2017). Identifying research priorities for effective retention strategies in clinical trials. *Trials*, 18, 406.

Kelle, U. (2006). Combining qualitative and quantitative methods in research practice: purposes and advantages. *Qualitative Research in Psychology*, 3 (4), 293–311.

Locock, L. and Smith, L. (2011). Personal experiences of taking part in clinical trials – a qualitative study. *Patient Education and Counseling*, 84 (2011), 303–309.

Marsh, L. (2013). Depression and Parkinson's disease: current knowledge. *Current Neurology and Neuroscience Reports*, 13 (12), 409.

Mason, J. (2006) Mixing methods in a qualitatively driven way. *Qualitative Research* 6 (1), 9–25.

Mental Health Foundation. (2016). *Fundamental facts about mental health 2016.* Available at: from https://www.mentalhealth.org.uk/sites/default/files/fundamental-facts-about-mental-health-2016.pdf. (Accessed 15 July 2019).

Moorcraft, S. Y., Marriott, C., Peckitt, C., Cunningham, D., Chau, I., Starling, N. et al. (2016). Patients' willingness to participate in clinical trials and their views on aspects of cancer research: results of a prospective cancer survey. *Trials*, 17, 17.

Morris, M. C. and Nelson, R. M. (2007). Randomized, controlled trials as minimal risk: an ethical analysis. *Critical Care Medicine*, 35 (3), 940–944.

NHS. (2017). *Guideline to the provision of psychological support following stroke.* Available at: https://www.england.nhs.uk/mids-east/wp-content/uploads/sites/7/2018/04/10-stroke-psychological-support.pdf. (Accessed 1 August 2019).

Olckers, L., Gibbs, T. J. and Duncan, M. (2007). Developing health science students into integrated health professionals: a practical tool for learning. *BMC Medical Education*, 7, 45.

Pereira, S., Reay, K., Bottell, J., Walker, L., Dzikiti, C., Platt, C. and Goodrham, C. (2019). *University student mental health survey 2018.* Available at: https://uploads-ssl.webflow.com/561110743bc7e45e78292140/5c7d4b5d314d163fecdc3706_Mental%20Health%20Report%202018.pdf. (Accessed 17 July 2019).

Picillo, M., Kou, N., Barone, P. and Fasano, A. (2015). Recruitment strategies and patient selection in clinical trials for Parkinson's disease: going viral and keeping science and ethics at the highest standards. *Parkinsonism and Related Disorders*, 21 (9), 1041–1048.

Polese, J. C., Faria-Fortini, I., Basilio, M. L., Faria, G. S. and Teixeira-Salmela, L. F. (2017). Recruitment rate and retention of stroke subjects in cross-sectional studies. *Cien Saude Colet*, 22 (1), 255–260.

Pompili, M., Venturini, P., Campi, S., Seretti, M. E., Montebovi, F., Lamis, D. A. et al. (2012). Do stroke patients have an increased risk of developing suicidal ideation or dying by suicide? An overview of the current literature. *CNS Neuroscience Therapy*, 18 (9), 711–721.

Rabkin, J. G., Albert, S. M., Del Bene, M. L., O'Sullivan, I., Tider, T., Rowland, L. P. and Mitsumoto, H. (2005). *Prevalence of depressive disorders and change over time in late-stage ALS*, 65 (1), 62–67.

Rodda, J., Walker, Z. and Carter, J. (2011). Depression in older adults. *BMJ*, 343, d5219.

Rogers, C. G., Tyson, J. E., Kennedy, K. A., Broyles, R. S. and Hickman, J. F. (1998). Conventional consent with opting in versus simplified consent with opting out: an exploratory trial for studies that do not increase patient risk. *The Journal of Pediatrics*, 132, 606–611.

Royal College of Psychiatrists. (2018). *Suffering in silence: age inequality in older peoples' mental health care*. Available at: https://www.rcpsych.ac.uk/docs/default-source/improving-care/better-mh-policy/college-reports/college-report-cr221.pdf. (Accessed 13 July 2019).

Selewski, D. T., Herreshoff, E. G. and Gipson, D. S. (2016). Optimizing enrolment of patients into nephrology research studies. *Clinical Journal of the American Society of Nephrology*, 11 (3), 512–517.

Shaw, A., Ibrahim, S., Reid, F., Ussher, M. and Rolands, G. (2009). Patients' perspectives of the doctor-patient relationship and information giving across a range of literacy levels. *Patient Education and Counseling*, 75 (1), 114–120.

Smith, T. C., Hickey, H., Clarke, M. et al. (2014). The trials methodological research agenda: results from a priority setting exercise. *Trials*, 15, 32.

Stroke Association. (2012). *Continence problems after stroke*. Available at: https://www.stroke.org.uk/sites/default/files/continence_problems_after_stroke.pdf. (Accessed 1 August 2019).

Stryker, J. E., Wray, R. J., Emmons, K. M., Winer, E. and Demitri, G. (2006). Understanding the decisions of cancer clinical trial participants to enter research studies: factors associated with informed consent, patient satisfaction, and decisional regret. *Patient and Education Counseling*, 63 (1–2), 104–109.

Sun, Z., Gilbert, L., Ciampi, A. and Bsaso, O. (2017). Recruitment challenges in clinical research: Survey of potential participants in a diagnostic study of ovarian cancer. *Gynecologic Oncology*, 146 (2017), 470–476.

Sussman, A. L., Cordova, C. and Burge, M. R. (2018) A comprehensive approach to community recruitment for clinical and translational research. *Journal of Clinical and Translational Science*, 8 (2), 249–252.

Thayabaranathan, T., Cadilhac, D. A., Srikanth V. K., Fitzgerald, S. M., Evans, R. G., Kim, J. et al. (2016). Maximizing patient recruitment and retention in a secondary stroke prevention clinical trial: lessons learned from the STAND FIRM study. *Journal of Stroke and Cerebrovascular Diseases*, 25 (6), 1371–1380.

Thomas, C. (2017). *Qualitative research in process evaluation: Intervention fidelity*. Presented at 'Qualitative Research to Optimise Design and Conduct of Randomised Trials', School of Social and Community Medicine Short Course, March 14, Bristol.

Treweek, S., Pitkethly, M., Cook, J. et al. (2010). Strategies to improve recruitment to randomised controlled trials. *Cochrane Database Systematic Reviews*, 2010 (4), MR000013.

Tselebis, A., Pachi, A., Ilias, I., Kosmas, E., Bratis, D., Moussas, G. and Tzanakis, N. (2016). Strategies to improve anxiety and depression in patients with COPD: a mental health perspective. *Neuropsychiatric Disease and Treatment*, 12, 297–328.

Walters, S. J., Henriques-Cadby, I. B. A., Bortolami, O., Flight, L., Hind, D., Jacques, R. M. et al. (2017). Recruitment and retention of participants in randomised controlled trials: a review of trials funded and published by the United Kingdom Health Technology Assessment Programme. *BMJ Open*, 7, e015276.

Watson, P. D. (1999). Patient recruitment: US perspective. *Pediatrics*, 104, 619–622.

Wilding, P. M. (2008). Reflective practice: a learning tool for student nurses. *British Journal of Nursing*, 17 (11), 720–724.

World Health Organisation. (1946). *Preamble to the constitution of the World Health Organization as adopted by the International Health Conference*. New York: World Health Organisation,

19–22 June 1946. Available at: https://www.who.int/about/who-we-are/frequently-asked-questions (Accessed 19 July 2019).

World Health Organisation. (2018a). *Latest global cancer data: cancer burden rises to 18.1 million new cases and 9.6 million cancer deaths in 2018.* Available at: https://www.who.int/cancer/PRGlobocanFinal.pdf. (Accessed 13 July 2019).

World Health Organisation. (2018b). *Cancer.* Available at: https://www.who.int/news-room/fact-sheets/detail/cancer. (Accessed 13 July 2019).

Yelland, L. N., Kahan, B. C., Dent, E., Lee, K. J., Voysey, M., Forbes, A. B. and Cook, J. A. (2018). Prevalence and reporting of recruitment, randomisation and treatment errors in clinical trials. A systematic review. *Clinical Trials*, 15 (3), 278–285.

Zaharoff, B. and Cipra, S. (2018). Improving oncology clinical trial participation and experience. *Science and Society*, 4 (12), 793–796.

4

MIXED METHODS AND WELLBEING

Issues emerging from multiple studies into mentoring for doctors

Alison Steven and Gemma Wilson

Introduction

This chapter outlines our experiences of using mixed methods in 'real–world' wellbeing research, through reflecting on a series of issues arising across a number of research studies exploring mentoring for doctors' wellbeing.

Over the past two decades, Professor Alison Steven (AS) has worked on several mentoring initiatives and studies with Dr Nancy Redfern, a consultant anaesthetist with a lifelong interest in mentoring. This duo became a team when joined by Dr Val Larkin a senior lecturer in midwifery with a long-standing interest in mentoring and staff support methods and Dr Gemma Wilson (GW) a registered health psychologist with expertise and interest in preventative health and staff wellbeing. Over the years, our combined experience indicated that mentoring did indeed seem to have a beneficial impact on doctors' wellbeing, and unanticipated findings from studies exploring and evaluating mentoring activities linked to wellbeing gradually emerged from each project. As each study was completed, links to wellbeing crystallised further, culminating in the most recent study, which responded to these emerging insights by specifically aiming to explore relationships between mentoring activities and doctors' wellbeing.

The chapter aims to achieve the following:

*   Introduce the context of mentoring in medicine research;
*   Surface and discuss a series of methodological, practical and ethical issues related to 'doing' mixed-methods research in the field of wellbeing. These are issues for researchers and students to think about when embarking on, and undertaking, such research; and

DOI: 10.4324/9780429263484-5

- Illustrate the ways in which the research context, and the mix of methods and designs employed, facilitated the emergence of unanticipated findings related to wellbeing.

Before describing and discussing the studies, we will set the scene by giving a brief introduction to mentoring in medicine and provide methodological context. We will also identify the notions and conceptions of wellbeing employed in the later studies.

Background/context

Mentoring in medicine

The terms 'mentor' or 'mentoring' are used across many professions and occupations and have a range of meanings and definitions (Johnson, 2002; Sambunjak, Straus and Marusic, 2006; Connor and Pokora, 2007; Crisp and Cruz, 2009; Driessen, Overeem and van der Vleuten, 2011; Polley, Cisternino and Gray, 2021). The origins of the term 'mentoring' lie in the apprenticeship model of work, where an experienced person passed on their knowledge and skills to an inexperienced and usually younger individual.

In medicine, an influential and commonly used definition of mentoring comes from the UK's 1998 Standing Committee on Postgraduate Medical and Dental Education (Standing Committee on Postgraduate Medcial and Dental Education, 1998):

> The process whereby an experienced, highly regarded, empathic person (the mentor), guides another individual (the mentee) in the development and re-examination of their own ideas, learning, and personal and professional development. The mentor who often, but not necessarily, works in the same organisation or field as the mentee, achieves this by listening and talking in confidence to the mentee.
>
> (Oxley, 1998, p. 1)

In health and social care, the term 'mentor' has also occasionally been used to signify a practitioner who supervises and assesses students in a practice setting (Harrington, 2011).

Although the term mentoring is commonly used, there are actually many conceptualisations or 'types' of 'mentoring'. A range of implicit and explicit philosophies underpin the various types of mentoring and influence how mentoring is undertaken. In addition, there are several roles or functions (including career and psychosocial functions) which a mentor may take on depending on the type of mentoring being offered (Kram, 1988). Mentoring types range from the traditional patron/protégé model, through to the mentor as advisor and/or problem solver, educator, or facilitator/empowerer (Sambunjak, Straus and Marusic, 2006; Connor and Pokora, 2007).

Mixed methods and wellbeing **81**

While mentoring may be useful and beneficial, doctors can be reluctant to seek out and use a mentor due to the stigma often attached to accessing such support. Doctors can misinterpret mentoring as being for the 'needy', those who have problems or are underachievers.

Research into mentoring

Much research has been undertaken into mentoring across a wide range of disciplines (Buddeberg-Fischer and Herta, 2006; Nowell et al., 2015; Geraci and Thigpen, 2017; Yoon et al., 2017; Liao et al., 2020) and using a variety of methods and methodologies (Frei, Stamm and Buddeberg-Fischer, 2010; Gong et al., 2020; Kow et al., 2020; Ng et al., 2020b). However, in medicine, studies have tended to focus on mentoring schemes, programmes and initiatives (Buddeberg-Fischer and Herta, 2006; Frei, Stamm and Buddeberg-Fischer, 2010; Kurré et al., 2012; Efstathiou et al., 2018; Ortega et al., 2018; Sheri et al., 2019); mentoring relationships and processes (Cheong, 2014; Sng et al., 2017; Heeneman and Grave, 2019); career development or progression (Stamm and Buddeberg-Fischer, 2011; Garr and Dewe, 2013; Pethrick et al., 2017; Efstathiou et al., 2018; Ong et al., 2018); and the mentoring of students (Mann, 1992; Buddeberg-Fischer and Herta, 2006; Frei, Stamm and Buddeberg-Fischer, 2010; Kalen et al., 2012; Farkas et al., 2019a; Skjevik et al., 2020; Ng et al., 2020a). It seems that much of the research has focused on academic medicine (Sambunjak, Straus and Marusic, 2006; Kashiwagi, Varkey and Cook, 2013; Geraci and Thigpen, 2017; Cross et al., 2019; Farkas et al., 2019b; Huggett et al., 2020), with fewer studies related to individual specialties (Lee et al., 2019; Sayan et al., 2019; Ng et al., 2020b) or indeed covering multiple medical specialties (Oxley et al., 2003; Cheong et al., 2020).

Although some studies in this field exclusively use qualitative methods (Sambunjak, Straus and Marusic, 2010; Kalen et al., 2012; Garr and Dewe, 2013; Loosveld et al., 2020), there are few of them. Rather in line with the predominant traditional 'science' approach in health care, quantitative approaches with 'realist' orientated ontological underpinnings and positivist/post-positivist epistemological orientations are, instead, commonplace (Sambunjak, Straus, and Marusic, 2006; Yoon et al., 2017; Efstathiou et al., 2018; Ortega et al., 2018; Cross et al., 2019; Heeneman and Grave, 2019; Sheri et al., 2019; Ng et al., 2020b). The significance given to quantitative approaches is illustrated in a much-cited systematic review of mentoring in academic medicine (Sambunjak, Straus and Marusic, 2006) – which purposefully excluded qualitative designs. This is typical of a systematic review, or meta-analytic design; however, given this exclusion, it is not possible to know how qualitative studies compared to quantitative studies, and any use of mixed-methods designs in the studies included is unclear. Indeed, in this systematic review, survey approaches predominated with 34 (87%) of the 39 studies including the use of cross sectional self-report surveys (Sambunjak, Straus and Marusic, 2006).

More recent reviews in diverse topic areas of medicine still seem to echo the spread of these research characteristics. For example, a review of mentor training programmes

(Sheri et al., 2019), which included all study designs and types, described only 6 (9%) of 68 included articles as mixed-methods studies, with a predominance of quantitative, survey-based studies. Another review of the benefits, barriers and enablers of mentoring female health academics (encompassing both medical and health professions literature) included 27 studies (Cross et al., 2019), of which only 3 were described as mixed methods, and 14 (52%) were deemed 'cross-sectional survey' studies.

Finally, we carried out a systematic narrative review in 2018 which explored links between mentoring and wellbeing (Wilson et al., 2017). Within this review, there were far fewer articles, and only ten empirical studies were relevant for inclusion. Of these, five were qualitative studies (involving interviews or focus groups), three were quantitative (all using questionnaires) and three were mixed methods. By highlighting the presence of qualitative research in this area, the systematic narrative review conducted by our research team highlights the potential bias of past reviews which exclude qualitative research. Other methodological insights from these reviews (Wilson et al., 2017; Cross et al., 2019; Sheri et al., 2019) illustrate that of the studies described as 'mixed methods', some appear to only use multiple surveys (Steiner et al., 2004; Feldman et al., 2009; Dutta et al., 2011; Welch et al., 2012), while others employed surveys and reflective writing (Pfund et al., 2013), surveys and analysis of curriculum vitae (Kirsch et al., 2018) and a mix of questionnaires, with other data collection methods, such as focus groups and interviews (Mann, Ball and Watson, 2011; Steele, Fisman and Davidson, 2013; Eisen et al., 2014). This highlights the variability in what is deemed to constitute 'mixed methods', and rather than utilising a mixed-methods design, integrating qualitative and quantitative methodologies, many of these studies are using several methods while being led only by a qualitative or quantitative design. Studies using a mixed-method design and several methods are advantageous in enabling complex social research questions to be answered from different sources (Greene, 2015).

Mentoring and wellbeing

There is a growing evidence base in medicine and health care which suggests being involved in mentoring programmes and relationships has benefits for both mentees and mentors (Oxley et al., 2003; Steven, 2008; Steven, Oxley and Fleming, 2008; Swann, Ramsay and Bijlani, 2008; Overeem et al., 2010; Stamm and Buddeberg-Fischer, 2011). Such benefits have been conceptualised by AS, as stretching across the professional and personal worlds that doctors inhabit (Steven, Oxley and Fleming, 2008). However, as noted previously, medical and health care research has predominantly been concerned with the benefits of mentoring to student development, career advancement, specialty choices, job satisfaction and performance (Buddeberg-Fischer and Herta, 2006; Frei, Stamm and Buddeberg-Fischer, 2010; Kalen, Ponzer and Silen, 2012; Kashiwagi, Varkey and Cook, 2013; Cheong, 2014; Cruz-Correa, 2014; Drolet et al., 2014; Ortega et al., 2018; Prendergast et al., 2019; Blanco and Qualters, 2020; Ng et al., 2020b).

Little attention has been paid to the impact of mentoring on wellbeing in the research literature, with few studies actually dealing explicitly with this area and

Mixed methods and wellbeing   **83**

many studies focusing on mentoring and wellbeing as only a small part of a wider project (Wilson et al., 2017). The impact of mentoring on wellbeing includes improved employee wellbeing (Department of Health, 2010), working relationships (Steven, Oxley and Fleming, 2008), sense of collegiality (Steven, Oxley and Fleming, 2008; Overeem et al., 2010; Kalen, Ponzer and Silen, 2012) and confidence and morale (Steven, Oxley and Fleming, 2008; Kalen, Ponzer and Silen, 2012; Drolet et al., 2014). There also appear to be benefits from being a mentor, with trained mentors reporting that they use skills and frameworks in a variety of clinical and personal situations (Connor and Pokora, 2007; Steven, Oxley and Fleming, 2008; Overeem et al., 2010), as well as in mentoring.

This chapter is timely, given the growing appreciation of the importance of staff wellbeing across health care. Furthermore, there is a need for more multifaceted studies which employ mixed methods to enhance our understandings of the impact of support mechanisms such as mentoring on health and wellbeing. In the following sections, we will explore some of the studies we have undertaken and highlight some of the issues we have faced – so that other researchers and students may benefit from our insights in future research.

The studies

The chapter draws on a series of studies undertaken between 2002 and 2018 into mentoring in medicine, later culminating in research specifically on mentoring, and health and wellbeing. All the studies shared the following:

- A common view of mentoring as being a set of complex social processes, individual, socially negotiated and context bound which do not lend themselves to purely quantitative (positivistic/post-positivistic) research. This is akin to many notions of wellbeing and in line with the conceptualisation of wellbeing held by the study team (Wilson et al., 2017).
- A 'world view' in their methodologies which accept complexity and draw on social constructionism and/or critical realism and/or elements of pragmatism.
- Ontologies that assume either no one 'true', 'real' or fixed manifestation of mentoring that can be accessed, observed or measured. Or that the reality of mentoring is multi-layered and complex. This leans towards relativistic positioning, although not completely, as later studies kept some elements of critical realism and a hint of pragmatism.
- Epistemological stances were a mix of critical realism and social constructionism; therefore, mixed methods were used to give diverse viewpoints from slightly different epistemological positions – to be multifaceted in order to try to illuminate from diverse positions.

The studies began back in 2002 with the involvement of AS in a national project specifically aiming to explore the benefits of mentoring (Oxley et al., 2003), followed by a secondary analysis of data from that same study which began to highlight links to wellbeing (Steven, Oxley and Fleming, 2008). This was followed by three further projects: one an evaluation of a mentoring scheme for psychiatrists (Steven, 2008), an exploration and evaluation of mentor training and engagement in mentoring activity (Steven, 2015) and, finally, research exploring the relationships between mentoring and doctors' wellbeing. Table 4.1 sets out the main details of the studies.

Accessing diverse viewpoints – building a jigsaw

Adopting a mixed-methods approach across these sequential studies allowed the research team to access diverse retrospective and contemporary viewpoints from a range of professional groups. Indications of links between mentoring and wellbeing began to emerge as the studies progressed, and these formed pieces of a jigsaw which slowly accumulated, making us more and more curious about the relationships between trained mentor activity and wellbeing. This eventually led to our most recent study, as we will now explain.

Study 1: Hints of wellbeing

Study 1a (Oxley et al., 2003) aimed to investigate perceived benefits of involvement in mentoring. This study combined analysis of interviews, a limited literature review and two workshops that resulted in findings clustered in three broad headings: (1) general benefits to individuals, (2) help with specific problems and (3) benefits to organisations. Although the detail of the data and findings hinted at wellbeing, this remained largely implicit and descriptive, with wellbeing only mentioned briefly in a supplementary document (Fleming et al., 2003).

> In the experiences of mentoring these doctors reported increased confidence was accompanied by increased feelings of personal wellbeing.
>
> (p. 33)

The somewhat condensed, descriptive nature of the analysis and final study report was perhaps a consequence of funders' requirements. The project was funded by the then UK Department of Health as part of the work of a doctors' forum and as such required the production of a 'working paper' with practical, easy-to-digest suggestions and conclusions. Indeed, this is sometimes another thorny issue for researchers who wish to undertake mixed-methods research – they need to find sponsorship and funding for such research, but this can also bring certain requirements which may feel constraining. As a result, the desire to explore the findings in a more nuanced, conceptual manner led the research team to undertake a secondary analysis of the data (Steven, Oxley and Fleming, 2008) forming Study 1b.

While some might question the secondary analysis of data using a set of research aims or questions which differ from those which steered the initial data collection, it can also be argued that it may actually be seen as being ethical to make best use of existing data (Irwin, 2013; Mitchell, 2015; Sligo, Nairn and McGee, 2017).

TABLE 4.1 Overview of studies

Study number	Year	Aim	Design	Methods, participants and sample type	Theoretical underpinning	Reference
1a	2002–3	Investigate perceived benefits of involvement in mentoring	Qualitative design mixed-methods design	Interviews (x1) 49 participants (range of specialties) Literature review Workshops x2	Interpretivist	Oxley J., Fleming B., Golding L., Pask H. and Steven A. (2003). Improving working lives for doctors. Mentoring for doctors: enhancing the benefit. A working paper. Available at: https://www.academia.edu/1402110/Mentoring_for_doctors_enhancing_the_benefit.
1b	2008	Explore overlaps and relationships between areas of benefit	Qualitative design	Secondary analysis of interviews (range of specialties) Conceptual model	Interpretivist/ social constructivist	Steven A., Oxley, J. and Fleming, W. G. (2008). Mentoring for NHS doctors: perceived benefits across the personal-professional interface. *Journal of the Royal Society of Medicine*, 101, 552–557.
2	2008	Develop an understanding of how psychiatrists perceive and evaluate experiences of a mentoring scheme	Explanatory sequential mixed-methods design	Questionnaire 22 Interviews 14 Feedback session/ workshop x1 (single medical specialty)	Interpretivist	Steven, A. (2008.) Mentoring schemes for psychiatrists in the north east: an evaluation and exploration. Report. University of Newcastle upon Tyne. ISBN 13 978-0-9552799-1-1

(Continued)

TABLE 4.1 (Continued)

Study number	Year	Aim	Design	Methods, participants and sample type	Theoretical underpinning	Reference
3	2015	Explore and evaluate impact of learning about mentoring and engaging in mentoring activities	Explanatory sequential mixed-methods design	Questionnaire x2 : 22 (x1), 17 (x2) Interviews 11 Evaluation forms 98 (single medical specialty)	Drew broadly on RE principles Critical realism	Steven, A. (2015.) An evaluation of the implementation and impact of a mentoring programme for anaesthetists in the north east. Northumbria University Newcastle. ISBN 97818613546 55
4	2014–17	Exploring the relationship between engagement in mentoring activities and Drs health and wellbeing	Convergent mixed-methods design	Systematic narrative lit review Questionnaire 57 interview series (over two years), 13 interviewees (total 43 interviews) (range of specialties)	RE principles Critical realism	Wilson, G., Larkin, V. Redfern, N. Stewart, J. and Steven, A. (2017). Exploring the relationship between mentoring and doctors' health and wellbeing: a narrative review. *Journal of the Royal Society of Medicine*, 110, 188–197.

Mixed methods and wellbeing **87**

People have given up their time and given of themselves to allow us researchers to collect their 'data' – be they experiences, opinions or physiological measurements. Thus, doing justice to that data and those participants by 'getting' the most from it, and seeking insights from diverse perspectives, would seem to us to be appropriate and ethically sound. Furthermore, we held the advantage of having already collected much of the data, and, therefore, we had a contextual awareness and authentic understanding of it (Irwin, 2013) that we were able to bring to bear on the secondary analysis.

This analysis began by mapping areas of overlap between the categories of perceived benefits, followed by a more theoretically abstracted exploration – looking beyond the descriptive lists and posing the question, 'What is going on here?' This led to the development of a conceptual model illustrating ways in which the benefits of mentoring seemed to cross the personal-professional interface, with wellbeing emerging more strongly as an aspect of the doctors' lives positively influenced by involvement in mentoring.

> The interlinked categories of professional practice and personal well-being emerged strongly from the secondary analysis and one appeared to enhance the other.
>
> (Steven, Oxley and Fleming, 2008, p. 554)

While the benefits of mentoring were predominantly reported as pertaining to mentees, this secondary analysis also identified subtle indications that mentors may also be benefiting. Thus, the secondary analysis enabled the data to be explored from diverse perspectives using different analytical 'lenses' which surfaced links to wellbeing and possible benefits for both mentors and mentees that may not have been captured using only one method of analysis.

Study 2: Further glimpses

As with the first study, the second was commissioned by funders as an evaluation (Steven, 2008) with an interest in 'if' a mentoring scheme for consultant psychiatrists 'worked' and any improvements that could be made. For this evaluation, we adopted an explanatory sequential design based in interpretivism (Crotty, 1998), with methods moving from quantitative to qualitative to help develop a more in-depth, multifaceted approach. However, the research team remained mindful of the tentative links to wellbeing emerging from the first study and kept this in mind while trying not to let it cloud or skew our approach.

First, a questionnaire comprised mainly of multiple-choice questions and Likert scales was used to collect a range of demographic and experience data. This data offered a picture of the duration and frequency of mentoring meetings and some sense of the spread of perceptions regarding the usefulness of mentoring. This also acted as a sampling frame, enabling a range of participants and experiences to be identified for participation in semi-structured qualitative interviews (each ~ one hour long). The interviews gathered descriptions and perceptions of mentoring experiences. Where appropriate, issues raised by participants were followed up during the interview and incorporated into subsequent interviews to try to ascertain if these were particular to the individual or shared with others and explore them in more depth. The third stage was a feedback session.

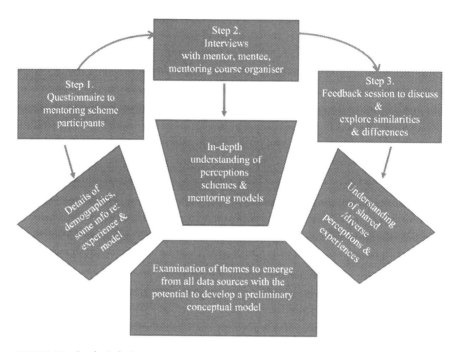

FIGURE 4.1 Study 2 design

Such 'inductive' follow-up of issues emerging from participants is common in qualitative research and encourages exploration of previously unidentified or under-researched areas (Kvale, 1996; Silverman, 2017) – such as links between mentoring and wellbeing. However, care needs to be taken in these circumstances to avoid 'tunnel vision' and following only the interests of the researcher (or commissioner) – making the emerging analysis fit what you want even if unconsciously; (Buetow, 2019). Rigour mechanisms such as reflexivity and using 'sounding boards' can be useful in this setting to regularly help surface and examine the reasons and assumptions behind the decisions being made and in some respects to help maintain a sense of perspective (Koch, 1998; Ramani et al., 2018; Buetow, 2019). This is where the use of several methods can also help – in enabling diverse viewpoints and data types to be brought to bear on these emerging issues or ideas and offering diverse analytical lenses.

Decisions about which emerging perspectives, issues or ideas to follow up in subsequent data collection are in a sense analytical and may happen from day one.

In this case, the research team or groups made up of researchers, participants and other stakeholders can act as useful sounding boards – to whom the researcher can present emerging issues, findings and ideas. In such forums, debate and discussion about emerging issues and findings can take place. Depending on the ontological underpinning of the study, this may not be a way of ascertaining some truth, agreement or consensus but a way of unpicking, exploring, challenging and debating (Buetow, 2019). It may also help understand if the emerging ideas, patterns and findings have resonance with others and ultimately assist team decisions (or student and supervisors discussions) regarding if the findings and ideas merit further follow-up as the study progresses.

Using sounding boards can be helpful at any stage of the research – helping illuminate researcher blind spots. During the early stages while initial data collection is happening, this may remain within the research team. Later in the study when emerging analysis and findings are more formed, a larger stakeholder forum or workshop can be useful for unpicking, discussing, challenging and generally trying out, adding to and refining the analysis. With these rigour and reflexivity considerations in mind, we held research team meetings throughout Study 2. We also included a stakeholder feedback session as part of the planned methods, and this was held at the point where analysis was well underway and findings were beginning to form, thus feeding into the final analytical stages (see Figure 4.1).

Once more, the findings emerging from the study showed glimpses of links and relationships between mentoring activity (learning about mentoring or being mentored) and broader notions of wellbeing. Reflecting on the study – how the mentoring scheme had been experienced and how it had worked for those involved – it became clear yet again that mentoring did indeed seem to have an impact on wellbeing, as illustrated in the following examples of participant quotes (underlining added for emphasis).

> *During the interviews none of the mentees reported using mentoring sessions to cover issues to do with patients or clinical cases, which concurs with the low positive response in Table 6 (questionnaire results). The majority of comments related to dealing with issues involving; clinical practice and professional relationships, <u>and more personal aspects of life, such as work life balance and career decisions</u>.*
>
> (Steven, 2008)

> *I think it allowed me to look at work <u>in a wider context of my whole life</u> … sort of explaining what I wanted from a job, <u>what I wanted from life</u>, thinking about things all much more widely with somebody who was sort of separate and being able to open that up all a lot more.*
>
> (Steven, 2008)

Thus, the thread of evidence suggesting a relationship between mentoring activity and wellbeing impacts seemed to strengthen.

90 Alison Steven and Gemma Wilson

Study 3: A picture appearing

The third study emerged from yet another opportunity to apply for funding to evaluate a range of mentoring initiatives, this time from the viewpoint of UK anaesthetists (Steven, 2015). Mindful of our interests and wishing to enable a broad approach so as not to constrain the study, we were careful to word the aim as *exploring* and evaluating the impact of learning about mentoring (via a training programme) and engaging in a range of mentoring activities (schemes, taster days, networks, etc.).

This study drew on the principles of realistic evaluation (RE) based in critical realism (Pawson, 2013), which suggests that '*outcomes are explained by the action of particular mechanisms in particular contexts*' (Pawson and Tilley, 1997 p. 59). RE proposes that by comparing what works, how and why, and under what circumstances, commonalities and variations across contexts (e.g. environmental factors), mechanisms (e.g. individual agency and actions, systems and processes) and outcomes (perceptions and experiences of health and wellbeing) can be explored. Thus, it is argued causal powers reside not in objects or individuals but in the social relations and organisational structures that they form – so giving a more nuanced approach which acknowledges complexity but is underpinned by realist foundations.

This approach is attractive and understandable to those more familiar with realist/positivist type research – such as some traditional science-orientated funding bodies. Furthermore, this methodology enables an 'evaluation' to be undertaken (so fulfilling funding body aims) while also allowing flexibility to explore and follow up any new or unusual emerging insights.

It is important to have a clear logic model or project theory underpinning any study design. This model or theory embodies the reasoning and assumptions which guide the study and should be able to be clearly expressed. For this study, it is as follows:

- The questionnaires acted as a quasi-baseline and follow-up – the assumption being that any additional activity related to mentoring reported in the second questionnaire would have been a result of attending the initiative.
- Training programme evaluation sheets offered a snapshot of participants' reactions and feelings – the assumption being that these would be 'fresh', before they had time to reflect on the programme and reformulate their reactions.
- Interviews offered more space and spontaneity to participants than other forms of data collection – the assumption being that there may be issues, topics, opinions and experiences that the researcher may not anticipate or ask about. Thus, interviews are less constraining, allowing participants to raise issues of importance to them and giving the interviewer the chance to follow things up in more depth.
- The mentee evaluation sheets presented a different perspective on mentoring activity – that of the mentees who were 'recipients' of the mentoring skills learnt.

This study was again a mixed-methods study which echoed an explanatory sequential design (Creswell, 2018) incorporating four types of data over five collection points:

1. A questionnaire was distributed at the start of the training programme. Designed to gather opinions regarding attendance, a 'baseline' of mentoring activity and initial perceptions of mentoring usefulness. It also served as a sampling frame for the subsequent interviews.
2. Evaluation forms were completed by those attending the training programme.
3. Semi-structured interviews were undertaken two to four months after completion of the training programme to collect opinions, experiences and information regarding any activities that had developed.
4. A second questionnaire was distributed approximately 12 months after the first and approximately 6 months after the interviews. It gathered information about activity and impact, including opinions regarding skills learnt, attendance at the initiatives, subsequent mentoring activities and opinions regarding the usefulness of mentoring.
5. Evaluation sheets were collected from mentees attending taster sessions run by those who had participated in the training programme.

The analysis included descriptive statistics, content and thematic analysis and the framework used in each drew on the aims and objectives of the study and the principles of RE (Pawson and Tilley, 1997; Pawson, 2013) to identify salient contextual factors, mechanisms such as barriers and facilitators and outcomes such as perceived benefits, activity and impact.

Once again issues relating to wellbeing emerged both for the mentors and mentees and beyond to other colleagues and individuals.

> *You know, mentoring,…to help people work through their problems, to enhance, ultimately, I felt well, if I can help people in my work place, you know, it enhances team work, it enhances people's satisfaction, staff satisfaction at work, enhances quality of care…above all else this is something <u>that can be seen as a positive improvement in people's lives</u>.*

(Steven, 2015)

> *And by engaging other people [using mentoring skills], and trying to get them to kind of open up as to their motivations behind things actually makes it easier for me because then actually <u>everyone is happier</u>.*

(Steven, 2015)

Indeed, in the second questionnaire, 77% of respondents felt being involved in mentoring had been useful in personal aspects of their life. Eighty-four percent said it was useful for managing personal dilemmas and opportunities, and nearly all mentees reported finding the mentoring session useful or very useful. This is suggestive of broader reach and impact and indicates the usefulness of diverse methods of data collection. Thus, we became more convinced of the need to follow this up with a specific research study.

92 Alison Steven and Gemma Wilson

Study 4: The finishing pieces

An opportunity then arose to seek funding from the British Medical Association, and we were fortunate to be funded for a three-year study. This enabled us to undertake a focused mixed-methods design using several methods, which incorporated a more longitudinal element and was specifically aimed at exploring the relationship between engagement in mentoring activities by trained mentors and doctors' health and wellbeing (Steven et al., 2018).

Therefore, once again the methodological approach drew on the principles of RE (Pawson and Tilley, 1997; Pawson, 2013) but also incorporated the Business in the Community (BITC) Workwell model (Business in the Community; Adshead, 2020) as a heuristic device – offering a broad conceptualisation of wellbeing and acting as a lose analytical framework. The BITC Workwell model incorporates physical, psychological and social components of health and wellbeing and suggests that to create a healthy environment, and to support the health and wellbeing of employees, these components need to act together.

Building on the previous studies, this project was based on the following underlying assumptions:

- That both education (e.g. mentor training and development programmes) and professional support activities (e.g. mentoring activities) are complex social processes which take place in complex settings and are context bound, thus requiring in-depth exploration
- That mentoring models and skills learnt on training courses may be used in a variety of formal and informal activities, not all labelled or badged as mentoring and that these may be related to wellbeing impacts
- Doctors with more than two years' experience as trained mentors may have accumulated a range of mentoring experiences, but their use of skills and models may have become somewhat 'tacit' or embedded (Eraut, 2000)
- Doctors who are within two years of their training as mentors may have less accumulated experience but may be more aware or conscious of the skills and models, or approaches they use in mentoring (Eraut, 2000; Eraut, 2004)

The study was structured in two linked parts (see Figure 4.3) designed to look retrospectively for indications of any relationships (Wilson et al., 2017) and prospectively to track and understand any emergent relationships as far as possible in 'real time'. This study utilised mixed methods and accessed diverse viewpoints from experienced mentors, as well as those who were new to mentoring. This diversity was an advantage of the research and allowed us to gather data from multiple experiential perspectives, but it also meant that we could not fully integrate the mix of methods due to differences in sampling. The two parts of the study also overlapped slightly and were not completely sequential. Therefore, while this study does not fall neatly into any particular mixed-methods design description (Creswell, 2018), it could be described as a mainly convergent parallel design but with elements of an explanatory sequential approach (Creswell, 2018) given tentative initial findings from the survey marginally informed the interviews in the contemporary tracking of 'live cases' (Figure 4.2).

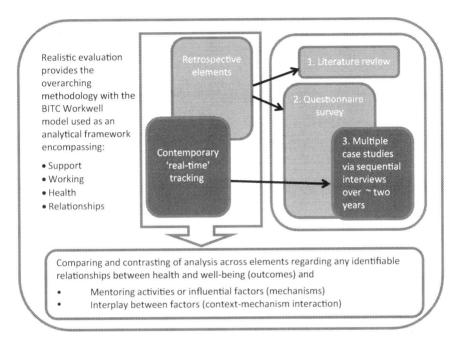

FIGURE 4.2 BMA study design

While analysis of each separate dataset can be straightforward, the work that needs to be done alongside this to compare, contrast, extrapolate, abstract and theorise from those sets of findings should not be underestimated. Looking at, and beyond, the separate parts to make an analytical 'sense' of them and then synthesising this as findings takes time and, we would argue, requires that multiple perspectives be used.

Therefore, in this, and all of the studies, we built-in team meetings throughout – both to enhance rigour (as noted previously) but also to facilitate discussion, allow different views on combined data to be presented, explored and discussed and to enable combined critical and analytical thinking to inform the findings throughout the course of the analysis process.

While conclusions were drawn across both phases of this study, data could not be fully integrated, as the sample of participants was different, which restricted the merging of data. However, the use of the BITC Workwell model facilitated interpretation across the datasets through its use as a lens to aid the analysis process and loosely position the data findings. The research team was, however, very mindful throughout not to constrain or force the data to 'fit' the BITC Workwell model, and team meetings helped to maintain an awareness and vigilance of this risk.

Findings were configured as four themes with related subcategories:

1. Mentorship as a vehicle for better specialist support
2. Mentorship supporting better personal and professional relationship building
3. Mentorship supporting better professional and personal wellbeing
4. Mentorship supporting better working communities and cultures

However, we did not stop at the level of themes but simultaneously interrogated the datasets, themes and subcategories in line with RE principles. This enabled the mixed-methods findings to be expressed as

- context, mechanism and outcome configurations;
- a conceptual diagram of the linkages and relationships between mentoring activities and wellbeing outcomes (see Figure 4.3); and
- composite vignettes for each theme illustrating a C,M,O trajectory and relationship between mentoring activity and wellbeing (see Table 4.2)

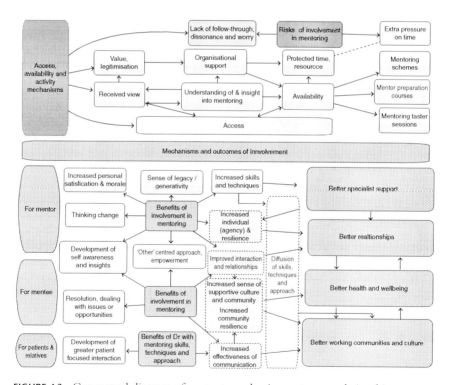

FIGURE 4.3 Conceptual diagram of context, mechanism outcome relationships

Mixed methods and wellbeing   **95**

TABLE 4.2 Composite vignette

Composite vignette of mentoring as supporting better professional and personal wellbeing

Context:

Some people in particular can find it very difficult to seek support formally and do not like the idea of anybody thinking they are failing or weak, or anything else. This colleague is like that and would have found it very difficult at the start to come to me formally in my mentoring capacity, but me just chatting about stuff in the corridor and using my mentoring framework and skills in the conversations enabled that person to actually make a decision to come for mentoring.

This mentee's issue seemed career related but ended up being very much about dealing with far too much, plus a family and feeling overwhelmed by trying to juggle career and family life. It was soon clear they had experienced a couple of bad cases and come to a point where work-life issues were overwhelming, and they were really struggling with the stress it was inducing; tiredness was also a factor. This person expressed feeling burnt out – it can affect most of us really, and I think we're all very bad at seeing that.

What the mentoring process did:

It was around a year's worth of mentoring, so about every six to eight weeks or so we had a mentoring session. Using mentoring skills and the framework and through those conversations, the person seemed enabled to actually unpick things, make a plan and some decisions, to tackle their workload in terms of the wider team they worked with, have time away and a holiday – and more, importantly, it was the decision that made them happy and resolved the problems at the time.

People such as this mentee like something quite concrete from mentoring such as a timeline with a set list of things to do that feel very achievable. Because a lot of the time they are dealing with that overwhelming feeling of not really knowing where to go next.

They like a relatively short session, 45 to 60 minutes; you can get away from a feeling that you can't even see what the problem is and end up with a very concrete plan that you can hopefully do some of. That's what a lot of people have found useful.

Outcome:

So now that person is fully back and confident again. I think the mentoring took this mentee through quite a challenging time and gave quite a lot of opportunities to try and reflect. They got a lot out of it. So as far as what the person approached me about, that seems to have resolved now. So, I think mentoring helped them probably come to terms with what they needed to do at the time.

In this study, we were specifically interested in the relationships between mentoring and wellbeing, and the findings clearly evidenced such links as exemplified by the following quotes.

> *Was really struggling my way through. And actually some of the [mentoring] sessions I've had, some of the time I've spent, has been incredibly valuable in terms of psychological wellbeing.*

(participant PB 1)

96 Alison Steven and Gemma Wilson

> *I've created a real safe zone for her. A trusted friend, and a person who is listening and believes in her, because a thing not being believed is a major issue in parts of the… spiral, that got her to where she got.*

(participant PF 1)

From the analysis, we were able to conclude that mentoring can act as a vehicle for better specialist support, which may

> *emerge as signposting and referral to specialist services, or, when the mentoring relationship becomes in and of itself the targeted specialist support.*

(Steven et al., 2018 p. 78)

We are currently seeking to publish these findings and move forward with more mixed-methods research in this area.

Looking back over the studies

Using mixed methods across this series of studies has undoubtedly assisted in building a clearer picture of the relationships between mentoring activities and wellbeing. For these studies, using a sequence of methods facilitated the emergence of an unanticipated area for research (i.e. relationships between mentoring and wellbeing). The initial studies were undertaken during a period when the notion of wellbeing was not often the focus of research, and although the satisfaction or career development of mentees was given some emphasis, prior to the inception of our work, the wellbeing of mentors themselves was not considered. If exploratory, open-ended research approaches were not used in the research we carried out with mentors, this would not have allowed us to bring this issue to light. Furthermore, the use of several different methods not only enabled us to see more and more emerging glimpses of this relationship but also offered a multifaceted approach which appealed to many research funders and sponsors and ultimately assisted in securing funding for the most recent study. Indeed, to secure funding for the development of a body of work over several years requires researchers to carefully consider not only the area of investigation but also the funders' requirements and preferences in terms of methods – with a careful balance needing to be struck between the two. However, looking back across the studies, there are cross-cutting issues which we feel are important in any research around wellbeing – be it mixed methods or otherwise – dealing with assumptions, attending to sensitive issues and anonymity and the participant-researcher relationship. The following sections cover these three topics.

Beware of shared unspoken and spoken assumptions

At the outset of designing any study, there are a number of issues taken into consideration, some of these will be consciously discussed (as highlighted in previous sections where the studies are described), while others may remain in the background as shared unspoken assumptions.

One such issue that we have become more conscious of over the years is thinking about participant 'availability' and how that may influence the methods used. Through our work in the NHS, and subsequent work as researchers in this environment, it is easy (and we are certain we have done so in the past) to work on the basis of some shared simplistic assumptions regarding groups of research participants. This can impact the data collection methods chosen, having an impact on the research outcomes. For example, choosing to use pen and paper for older participants over digital devices, or in the case of our research, it may be easy to make the assumption that doctors are very important, and are very busy people, which in turn can prompt a sense of not wanting to overburden them. This can lead us to make assumptions about which methods of data collection are most suitable for this sample, such as a less intrusive, less time-consuming online questionnaire, and otherwise overlook other more suitable research methods, such as longitudinal interviews.

We may make assumptions about the routinely collected data that we may/may not have access to or the time in which it would take to access. Again, this can impact the research questions we seek to answer or the way we look to answer them. This has the potential to stunt the research that we undertake and the insights that we gain into phenomena, and there is a need to be reflexive in our practice, bringing both our spoken and unspoken assumptions to the fore. Participants, including 'busy' professionals, may want to engage in research. They may want to be heard, have the opportunity, space, place to engage more deeply and in ways which are less stifling or imposing of certain research areas, topics or questions (i.e. a questionnaire like much realist research are top-down and impose researcher/academic notions of the issue, they constrain answers – even where there are free-text boxes, these are often limited).

Thus, well-meaning intentions can actually have the result of either 'cutting out' and marginalising the group by not affording them higher levels of participation or engagement, not offering alternatives and constraining data collection and answer types, restricting broader thinking. Or condescending upon them in a patronising manner underpinned by notions of power and self-righteousness (albeit possibly unconscious and with the best of intentions) and of it being in 'our gift' as researchers to offer potential participants these opportunities to be involved. In relation to some groups, such as older people or those unemployed, it may manifest in a sense of 'ah that's nice it will give them an interest and something to do with all that time they have' – something to be guarded against by researchers. However, there are other assumptions that can impact data collection, which come not from the researchers but from the participants.

In carrying out this research, GW had expertise in psychosocial wellbeing and staff wellbeing, but mentoring was a relatively new area of research. Despite being open about the role as a researcher, and GW not being a mentor, there were various assumptions made during the qualitative data collection during interviews or upon qualitative data analysis of interviews or open-ended survey questions. Participants assumed expertise in this area of mentoring and frequently assumed GW was a trained mentor herself. This often led to participants not airing their own thoughts, assumptions or experiences and instead saying things like 'you know what I mean', or 'well you will know better than me' – implying expertise and shared understanding. For AS, these participants' assumptions led to a different set of issues, as some participants believed her to be a mentor and confused the interview with a mentoring session. Despite receiving written and verbal information at the start of each interview regarding qualifications and the nature of the meeting, in several of the interviews, participants had to be reminded that we were collecting data and not engaging in mentoring. Thus, like the assumptions made by the researcher, those made by participants can impact both data collection and subsequent analysis.

Therefore, we suggest that researchers brainstorm potential assumptions at the very beginning of research – when ideas are being discussed for a project and when the plan, proposal or design of the study is being drafted. Furthermore, the subject of assumptions needs to be revisited regularly throughout the entire course of the research and here again, it is useful to do this in a group where diverse perspectives are present. While it is impossible to surface or recognise all assumptions around a researcher's perceptions of mentoring, methodological assumptions of using specific mixed-methods strategies or assumptions from participants regarding the study's aim or the researcher's role, being reflexive in this way is important for the quality and rigour of the study.

Attending to anonymity and confidentiality

Attention to sensitivities, anonymity and confidentiality (Creswell and Creswell, 2018; Goodwin, Mays and Pope, 2019) has been key throughout all the mentoring studies described and may be particularly pertinent in studies related to wellbeing. While some may assume that confidentiality and anonymity are synonymous and therefore by attending to one (e.g. confidentiality) the other is automatically taken care of (i.e. anonymity). This is not always the case. While the two concepts are linked, they require separate consideration and sensitive handling throughout a study.

Confidentiality relates mainly to a 'promise' given to the participant to not disclose their identity beyond the research team without permission (Goodwin, Mays and Pope, 2019). Thus, confidentiality is about pledging to maintain privacy or keeping secret certain information – such as personal identification details. A participant may also ask the researcher to keep some information only between the researcher and participant – to be kept 'secret', 'private' and 'confidential'. Therefore, confidentiality often comprises a set of rules or procedures for keeping participant information restricted to a small number of the research team members – thus attempting to ensure they are safe/hidden. Procedures often involve assigning ID numbers, code names or pseudonyms to participants and holding a 'key' to the real identification of the participants in a secure list or database. Such 'keys' should only be accessible by those in the research team who need this information to carry out the study or hold overall responsibility for the study. This may be the researchers or students who need to contact participants to arrange or undertake consent procedures and/or data collection. A study lead, principal investigator or main supervisor may also have access to this information as part of their overall responsibility for the project.

However, it is necessary that the 'promise' or statement of confidentiality agreed by the participant and researcher at the outset include some form of clause that will let the researcher break that confidence if the participant reveals something that the researcher feels may indicate imminent harm to the participant or others. This consideration may be particularly pertinent in research related to wellbeing and may necessitate not only a statement to be agreed between researcher and participant, but also a process and procedure to follow should such an occasion occur.

Anonymity relates to keeping the identity of a participant hidden in any research reports, publications or presentations. Thus the data (words from an interview or responses to a questionnaire) can be used by the research team but must not be assigned to or linked to an identifiable participant – they must remain anonymous.

Several of the studies we describe involved specific groups of doctors from particular geographical areas or medical specialties, which can make participants easier for others to identify. Furthermore, while mentoring may be useful and beneficial, doctors can be reluctant to seek out and use a mentor due to the stigma often attached to accessing such support, and mentoring is sometimes misinterpreted as being for the 'needy', those who have problems, or underachievers. Thus, some individuals may be reluctant to participate in this type of research through fear of breaking their own anonymity or that of others if they are a mentor discussing a mentee. Although, this is an assumption made by the research team and should not impact the choices of methods utilised. This is where mixed-methods designs are potentially valuable, allowing data to be collected in multiple ways and increasing the options for participation.

Furthermore, data collection methods may also have implications for anonymity. Mentoring relationships are often focused on sensitive issues, are usually personal, individualised, context bound and somewhat 'intimate' in nature. While mentoring can be done in a group (Connor and Pokora, 2007), it is much more common on a one-to-one basis. This means certain types of research and data collection methods may not be suited or easily adapted to mentoring situations and may be felt to impinge on the relationship between mentor and mentee. For example, ethnographic approaches using observation may feel obtrusive. The sense of intrusion may be heightened if a researcher is present at a mentoring session but would perhaps also be felt even if video recordings were used. Similarly, focus groups may reduce the sense of anonymity and may go some way to explaining the predominance of survey-based approaches, which are often assumed to be less intrusive and more anonymous. Once again, this suggests assumptions we may make about individuals being more willing to speak more about issues of health and wellbeing through an anonymous online survey than via other methods. However, this is not always true. Often, open-ended sections of surveys are left empty, whereas interviews can often be rich detailed personal discussions. Perhaps having the relationship with the interviewer, seeing a face and developing an understanding of who is going to be analysing this data (as well as knowing where it is going) is important to some participants. Indeed, this certainly seemed to be the case in the most recent study where we tracked participants through sequential interviews. This is only brought to light by using several research methods and both qualitative and quantitative designs. Again, the use of mixed methods can be a strength in building this evidence base and allowing data to be collected using several methods, without restricting data collection based on our own assumptions as researchers. This again highlights the importance of surfacing as far as possible the assumptions underpinning a study and trying not to make such assumptions based on an individual's consideration of anonymity.

Anonymity and confidentiality are often dealt with at the start of a study and while data collecting but is often overlooked in the latter stages – i.e. when writing a final report. However, attending to anonymity in the later stages of a project is important, perhaps especially so when related to research with small populations such as the doctors in some of our studies. An issue in final reports or publications is the potential for readers to identify participants through tracking quotes or other data across the document. To try to mitigate this risk, great care was taken in our study reports (Studies 2–4). To avoid the use of any data (direct quotes or comments etc.) that might be especially specific and easily linked to someone in the study population – such as extreme views or other identifying features such as details of personal situation or disabilities etc., and to change the identifying codes for participants from chapter to chapter. It was hoped that this would make it more difficult for readers to track participants and identify them.

For example, in Study 2, we became aware of the potential for participants to be identified because of the opinions or experiences included in the quotes used, so we took the following stance regarding ID codes in the final report.

> *The use of ID codes: Given the small population involved in this study different identity codes have been used in each chapter of this report in an attempt to safeguard the anonymity of respondents. Where a code such as ID7 Q15 is used the first part denotes a specific questionnaire respondent and the second part the question number. Interview respondents are identified as mentors or mentees and given a number or letter code.*

(Steven, 2008 p. 14)

However, there is a tension here and balance to be struck between giving sufficient information about participants (if important for the interpretation of results/findings – e.g. grade of doctor, ethnicity, gender) and showing sufficient data adequacy and spread (depending on the methodology and underpinning paradigm – e.g. illustrating you are not just picking quotes from a small number of participants or to suit a certain conclusion). With the use of mixed-methods designs, these challenges should not be underestimated.

The participant-researcher relationship: Not so cut and dry

A mixed-methods design can bring complexity to the participant-researcher relationship, as using several methods from multiple paradigms increases the likelihood of differing researcher-participant relationships in one study. Typically, within positivist enquiry, elements of objectivity, measurement, replicability and predictability are the expected outcomes (Eide and Kahn, 2008), whereas, contrastingly, qualitative research involves conversation and dialogue, often concerning very personal experiences (Eide and Kahn, 2008). To create the space for such conversations, and to gather meaningful qualitative research data, it is important to gain a sense of trust and rapport in the researcher-participant relationship, and this is often encouraged through the use of qualitative interviewing strategies, including prompting, active listening and empathetic cues (Rossetto, 2014). Conversely, a one-off online survey does not provide this relationship. The participant remains entirely anonymous and so does the research team. While eliminating potential boundary blurring, a non-existent relationship between the researcher and participant is not always beneficial. Evidence suggests that using online dissemination strategies may result in lower response rates, partly due to the lack of relationship between researcher and respondents (Sills and Song, 2002). Unless they directly contact the research team, the participant cannot gather an understanding of who is doing this research and their motivations for doing so; their affiliation with other institutions, including governing bodies; or gain a real sense of anonymity and confidentiality. Of course, it is imperative that all of this is set out in the documentation for participant information and consent, but a lack of relationship and rapport *may* impact the participants' motivations and ease of opening up fully.

However, a more complex participant-researcher relationship is evident in mixed-methods research where both qualitative and quantitative work may be involved and interlinked, and in our studies, particularly the BMA mentoring research (Study 3), we employed two forms of data collection (as described elsewhere in this chapter): online surveys and longitudinal semi-structured interviews. One consideration for the qualitative data collection in this study was the nature of longitudinal interviews, which were carried out at approximately six-monthly intervals over a two-year period. This repeated interaction allowed the researcher and participant to get to know each other and establish a relationship of familiarity and trust. Participants were aware that the researchers were bringing with them an interest in mentoring and thus felt that we understood mentoring and often assumed we were mentors ourselves. They considered us confidants and shared some personal and harrowing experiences related to mentoring. As the research progressed, we became increasingly conscious of the potential issues and sensitivities arising from the bonds formed and blurring of boundaries that might occur and of our ethical obligations as researchers.

There were several other aspects of the research which further compounded this blurring of boundaries from participants' perspective. Firstly, participants were mentors and perhaps considered the research interview as being akin to a mentoring relationship. On the surface, this research interview was set up in a similar manner with a similar environment and similar skills were being used across both; however, its aim was very different. Secondly, mentoring is confidential, and as mentors could be open with us about their experiences of mentoring within the interviews, they may also have felt the situation was akin to a mentoring relationship. Finally, with relatively few mentors available, individuals do not necessarily have opportunities to discuss their role of mentor with peers. As the research team studying mentoring, the participants knew that we understood their experiences and the difficulties they encountered and perhaps, unconsciously, relied on this relationship more so because of this.

There is an inherently therapeutic element of qualitative research in which the participant contributes to a deeply personal dialogue and sense making (Rossetto, 2014). It is important to have an awareness of, and to attend to, both this 'psychotherapeutic' dimension of qualitative interviews and associated issues such as role parameters, emotional investment and ending or closing the relationship (Lee-Treweek and Linkogle, 2000). These issues must be recognised, negotiated and re-negotiated throughout the research relationship (Gilbert, 2001; Rossetto, 2014) and are perhaps especially important where long-term contact is combined with sensitive and personal topics – such as those featured in research into mentoring and wellbeing. Such blurring of boundaries not only pose potential ethical issues for participants such as the creation of emotional dependence or a sense of abandonment on conclusion of the relationships but can also have consequences for the researcher (Lee-Treweek and Linkogle, 2000; Dickson-Swift et al., 2006; Andersen and Ivarsson, 2015; Batty, 2020).

In the BMA mentoring research (Study 3) to try to ensure that professional boundaries remained visible, and the participant recognised clarity between this as a research interview as opposed to being a therapeutic relationship (or mentoring session), at the beginning of each interview, we repeated the study aims, reminded participants of the nature of the meeting and highlighted the number of remaining interviews. All types of research are to a greater or lesser extent exploitative and reliant on the participants' goodwill but should not cause harm (Andersen and Ivarsson, 2015). We were aware of our ethical obligations and did not want participants to feel any detriment from the research experience, so these reminders were designed to give a clear timeframe with an ending and prepare participants for emotional closure to the relationship (Lee-Treweek and Linkogle, 2000; Batty, 2020). In addition, we offered information on national mentoring groups in case participants felt they wanted to seek support or mentoring after the research had concluded.

However, such intense research relationships can also have issues for the researchers involved, including emotional difficulties in leaving research relationships, feeling physically overwhelmed, experiencing physical symptoms and, if prolonged, suffering burnout (Dickson-Swift et al., 2006; Batty, 2020). Indeed, qualitative interviewing is not one-way, as the researcher also brings their own emotions and previous experience to the situation. Furthermore, if, as may happen in mixed-methods research, the researcher also has knowledge regarding the participant gathered through prior

Mixed methods and wellbeing **103**

data collection (e.g. questionnaires), they come to the interview in a position of greater power. To build the research relationship and engender rapport and openness, researchers often give of themselves, offering some personal information and exchanging stories (Batty, 2020). Furthermore, over the course of multiple interviews, familiarity can grow and bonds develop, resulting in the researcher thinking about the participant and their predicament or experiences long after the study has finished (Dickson-Swift et al., 2006; Sikic Micanovic, Stelko and Sakic, 2019; Batty, 2020). However, there is a fine balance to be struck, and maintaining an awareness of boundary blurring is important, as researchers can feel emotional anguish when data collection ends or be left with feelings of concern or regret (Batty, 2020). To acknowledge and deal with these issues in Study 3, we met frequently with the members of the wider research team (one of whom is an extremely experienced mentor) to discuss in a reflective and supportive manner not only data collection progress and emerging findings but also our experiences and feelings regarding the research relationships. We would suggest that attention to both the wellbeing of the participants and the research team is a core ethical obligation for any research, and there may be additional complexities when undertaking mixed-methods studies, which should be carefully considered by the research team at the outset.

Conclusions

Given the increasing understanding of the importance of staff wellbeing across health care, research in mentoring in medicine is imperative. However, most research into mentoring in medicine has either concentrated on schemes and processes or focused on mentee benefits and outcomes. Thus, the mentor was overlooked, assumed to act simply as a facilitator, with any benefits or impacts of that role being overlooked. With limited research in this area, multifaceted studies employing mixed-methods design are beneficial to enhance our understandings of the impact of mentoring on the health and wellbeing of those involved – including mentors themselves.

In this chapter, we have described our use of mixed methods in relation to a body of work around mentoring for doctors which has been undertaken over nearly two decades. The studies were often commissioned predominantly as evaluations of mentoring schemes, not as investigations of wellbeing benefits. However, through the first three consecutive studies and facilitated by mixed-methods designs, unanticipated findings relating to mentoring activity and links to mentor's wellbeing slowly emerged and accumulated. These findings were generated via the sequential use of methods which facilitated the emergence of an area that was not often the focus of this particular area of research and, initially, was not the focus of our research. Not only was this beneficial for the research subject, but this multifaceted approach also appealed to research funders and sponsors, resulting in successful funding applications, culminating in a study specifically focused on the relationship between mentoring activity and wellbeing.

However, the use of mixed methods, and multiple methods, can be fraught with wider issues. One such issue described in this chapter is the shared and unspoken assumptions which had the potential to change the way data was collected, the relationship between the researcher and participant and the study's focus. While these assumptions are not always conscious, it is important to reflect on these assumptions throughout the research process. Attending to sensitive issues and anonymity was also of great importance, especially in the field of mentoring and wellbeing where highly personal sensitive issues and experiences may be shared with the research team. There is a balance to be struck when using mixed methods between giving sufficient information about participants and showing sufficient data adequacy and spread. Finally, a mixed-methods design can bring complexity to the participant-researcher relationship, as using several methods from multiple paradigms increases the likelihood of differing researcher-participant relationships in one study. While quantitative designs may foster a limited relationship between research and participant, qualitative designs can be more therapeutic and intense, especially if data collection occurs at multiple points. Furthermore, we feel strongly that if we are researching wellbeing, we should consider it in our own research practice. Thus, attending to the participant-researcher relationship is of importance for the wellbeing of both the participant and the researchers involved.

Mixed-methods research has been critical to this body of work, resulting in the importance of mentoring and wellbeing emerging from studies with another, more evaluative, focus. While the use of a mixed-methods design has been critical to our work, it is not without its shortcomings, and using several methods from multiple paradigms must be carefully considered within any body of work.

Questions for discussion and further reflection

What points do the authors make about the constraints (as well as obvious benefits) that may result from research funding and sponsorship?

How did the use of mixed methods, in particular secondary analysis of their data, allow the authors to access richer understandings in Study 1?

Could you apply this technique in your own research?

How do the authors suggest unspoken assumptions may affect inclusivity in research – and how do they suggest such assumptions could be acknowledged/mitigated?

What complexities do the authors highlight with regard to the participant/researcher relationship?

References

Adshead, F. (Producer). (2020). About BITC's Workwell model. Business in the Community 2020 [Fact sheet]. Available at: https://www.bitc.org.uk/wp-content/uploads/2020/03/bitc-wellbeingfactsheet-workwellmodelreferencedoc-March20.pdf.

Andersen, M. B. and Ivarsson, A. (2015). A methodology of loving kindness: how interpersonal neurobiology, compassion and transference can inform researcher–participant encounters and storytelling. *Qualitative Research in Sport, Exercise and Health*, 8(1), 1–20.

Batty, E. (2020). Sorry to say goodbye: the dilemmas of letting go in longitudinal research. *Qualitative Research*, 20(6), 784–799.

Blanco, M. A. and Qualters, D. M. (2020). Mutual mentoring: effect on faculty career achievements and experiences. *Medical Teacher*, 42(7), 799–805.

Buddeberg-Fischer, B. and Herta, K. D. (2006). Formal mentoring programmes for medical students and doctors – a review of the Medline literature. *Medical Teacher*, 28(3), 248–257.

Buetow, S. (2019). Apophenia, unconscious bias and reflexivity in nursing qualitative research. *The International Journal of Nursing Studies*, 89, 8–13.

Business in the Community. (2019). The wellbeing Workwell model. Available at: https://www.bitc.org.uk/the-wellbeing-workwell-model/.

Cheong, C. W. S., Chia, E. W. Y., Tay, K. T., Chua, W. J., Lee, F. Q. H., Koh, E. Y. H., … Krishna, L. K. R. (2020). A systematic scoping review of ethical issues in mentoring in internal medicine, family medicine and academic medicine. *Advances in Health Sciences Education*, 25(2), 415–439.

Cheong, K. X. (2014). The mentor-protege relationship in medicine. *The Clinical Teacher*, 11(3), 225–226.

Connor, M. and Pokora, J. (2007). *Coaching and mentoring at work: developing effective practice* Maidenhead: Open University Press.

Creswell, J. (2018). Mixed methods procedures. In J. W. Creswell and J. D. Creswell (Eds.), *Research design: qualitative, quantitative, and mixed methods approaches* (5th ed., pp. 215–239). Los Angeles: SAGE Publications.

Creswell, J. W. and Creswell, J. D. (2018). *Research design: qualitative, quantitative, and mixed methods approaches.* Los Angeles: SAGE Publications.

Crisp, G. and Cruz, I. (2009). Mentoring college students: a critical review of the literature between 1990 and 2007. *Research in Higher Education*, 50(6), 525–545.

Cross, M., Lee, S., Bridgman, H., Thapa, D. K., Cleary, M. and Kornhaber, R. (2019). Benefits, barriers and enablers of mentoring female health academics: an integrative review. *PLoS One*, 14(4), e0215319.

Crotty, M. J. (1998). *The Foundations of Social Research: Meaning and Perspective in the Research Process.* London: SAGE Publications.

Cruz-Correa, M. (2014). Personal perspective on mentoring. *Gastroenterology*, 146(2), 331–333.

Department of Health. (2010). *Invisible patients: report of the working group on the health of health professionals* (13688). Available at: http://www.champspublichealth.com/writedir/4344Invisible%20patients%20%20The%20Working%0Group%20on%20the%20Health%20of%20Health%20Professionals%20%20Report.pdf.

Dickson-Swift, V., James, E. L., Kippen, S. and Liamputtong, P. (2006). Blurring boundaries in qualitative health research on sensitive topics. *Qualitative Health Research*, 16(6), 853–871.

Driessen, E. W., Overeem, K. and van der Vleuten, C. P. (2011). Get yourself a mentor. *Medical Education*, 45(5), 438–439.

Drolet, B. C., Sangisetty, S., Mulvaney, P. M., Ryder, B. A. and Cioffi, W. G. (2014). A mentorship based preclinical elective increases exposure, confidence, and interest in surgery. *The American Journal of Surgery*, 207(2), 179–186.

Dutta, R., Hawkes, S. L., Kuipers, E., Guest, D., Fear, N. T. and Iversen, A. C. (2011). One year outcomes of a mentoring scheme for female academics: a pilot study at the Institute of Psychiatry, King's College London. *BMC Medical Education*, 11(13). https://bmcmededuc.biomedcentral.com/articles/10.1186/1472-6920-11-13.

Efstathiou, J. A., Drumm, M. R., Paly, J. P., Lawton, D. M., O'Neill, R. M., Niemierko, A., … Shih, H. A. (2018). Long-term impact of a faculty mentoring program in academic medicine. *PLoS One*, 13(11), e0207634.

Eide, P. and Kahn, D. (2008). Ethical issues in the qualitative researcher–participant relationship. *Nursing Ethics*, 15, 199–207.

Eisen, S., Sukhani, S., Brightwell, A., Stoneham, S. and Long, A. (2014). Peer mentoring: evaluation of a novel programme in paediatrics. *Archives of Disease in Childhood*, 99(2), 142–146.

Eraut, M. (2000). Non-formal learning and tacit knowledge in professional work. *British Journal of Educational Psychology*, 70, 113–136.

Eraut, M. (2004). *Developing professional knowledge and competence* London: Falmer Press.

Farkas, A. H., Allenbaugh, J., Bonifacino, E., Turner, R. and Corbelli, J. A. (2019a). Mentorship of US medical students: a systematic review. *Journal of General Internal Medicine*, 34(11), 2602–2609.

Farkas, A. H., Bonifacino, E., Turner, R., Tilstra, S. A. and Corbelli, J. A. (2019b). Mentorship of women in academic medicine: a systematic review. *Journal of General Internal Medicine*, 34(7), 1322–1329.

Feldman, M. D., Huang, L., Guglielmo, B. J., Jordan, R., Kahn, J., Creasman, J. M., … Brown, J. S. (2009). Training the next generation of research mentors: the University of California, San Francisco, Clinical and Translational Science Institute Mentor Development Program. *Clinical and Translational Science*, 2(3), 216–221.

Fleming, B., Golding, L., Oxley, J., Steven, A., Pask, H., Warrington, C. and Gay, J. (2003). *Mentoring for doctors: talking about the experience.*

Frei, E., Stamm, M. and Buddeberg-Fischer, B. (2010). Mentoring programs for medical students—a review of the PubMed literature 2000–2008. *BMC Medical Education*, 10, 32.

Garr, R. O. and Dewe, P. (2013). A qualitative study of mentoring and career progression among junior medical doctors. *International Journal of Medical Education*, 4, 247–252.

Geraci, S. A. and Thigpen, S. C. (2017). A review of mentoring in academic medicine. *The American Journal of the Medical Sciences*, 353(2), 151–157.

Gilbert, K. R. (2001). Why are we interested in emotions? In Gilbert, K. R. (ed.), *The emotional nature of qualitative research* (pp. 3–15). London: CRC.

Gong, Z. X., Van Swol, L. M., Hou, W. L. and Zhang, N. (2020) Relationship between proteges' self concordance and life purpose: The moderating role of mentor feedback environment. *Nursing Open*, 7(2), 1–7.

Goodwin, D., Mays, N., and Pope, C. (2019). Ethical issues in qualitative research. In Pope, C. and Mays, N. (eds.), *Qualitative research in health care.* (4th ed.). Hoboken, NJ: Wiley.

Greene, J. C. (2015). Preserving distinctions within the multimethod and mixed methods research merger. In S. N. HesseBiber and R. B. Johnson (eds.), *The Oxford handbook of multimethod and mixed methods research inquiry* (pp. 606–615). Oxford: Oxford University Press.

Harrington, S. (2011). Mentoring new nurse practitioners to accelerate their development as primary care providers: a literature review. *Journal of the American Academy of Nurse Practitioners*, 23(4), 168–174.

Heeneman, S. and de Grave, W. (2019). Development and initial validation of a dual-purpose questionnaire capturing mentors' and mentees' perceptions and expectations of the mentoring process. *BMC Medical Education*, 19(1), 133.

Huggett, K. N., Borges, N. J., Blanco, M. A., Wulf, K. and Hurtubise, L. (2020). A perfect match? A scoping review of the influence of personality matching on adult mentoring relationships implications for academic medicine. *The Journal of Continuing Education in the Health Professions*, 40(2), 89–99.

Irwin, S. (2013). Qualitative secondary data analysis: ethics, epistemology and context. *Progress in Development Studies*, 13(4), 295–306.

Johnson, W. B. (2002). The intentional mentor: strategies and guidelines for the practice of mentoring. *Professional Psychology-Research and Practice*, 33(1), 88–96.

Kalén, S., Ponzer, S., Seeberger, A., Kiessling, A. and Silén, C. (2012). Continuous mentoring of medical students provides space for reflection and awareness of their own development. *International Journal of Medical Education*, 3, 236–244.

Kalen, S., Ponzer, S. and Silen, C. (2012). The core of mentorship: medical students' experiences of one-to-one mentoring in a clinical environment. *Advances in Health Sciences Education*, 17(3), 389–401.

Kashiwagi, D. T., Varkey, P. and Cook, D. A. (2013). Mentoring programs for physicians in academic medicine: a systematic review. *Academic Medicine*, 88(7), 1029–1037.

Kirsch, J. D., Duran, A., Kaizer, A. M., Buum, H. T., Robiner, W. N. and Weber-Main, A. M. (2018). Career-focused mentoring for early-career clinician educators in academic general internal medicine. *The American Journal of Medicine*, 131(11), 1387–1394.

Koch, T. (1998). Reconceptualizing rigour: the case for reˉexivity. *Journal of Advanced Nursing*, 2, 882–890.

Kow, C. S., Teo, Y. H., Teo, Y. N., Chua, K. Z. Y., Quah, E. L. Y., Kamal, N., … Krishna, L. K. R. (2020). A systematic scoping review of ethical issues in mentoring in medical schools. *BMC Medical Education*, 20(1), 246.

Kram, K. (1988). *Mentoring at work: developmental relationships in organizational life*. Lanham: University Press of America.

Kurré, J., Bullinger, M., Petersen-Ewert, C. and Guse, A. H. (2012). Differential mentorship for medical students: development, implementation and initial evaluation. *International Journal of Medical Education*, 3, 216–224.

Kvale, S. (1996). *Interviews: an introduction to qualitative research interviewing*. London: SAGE Publications.

Lee-Treweek, G. and Linkogle, S. (2000). *Danger in the field: risk and ethics in social research*. London: Routledge.

Lee, F. Q. H., Chua, W. J., Cheong, C. W. S., Tay, K. T., Hian, E. K. Y., Chin, A. M. C., … Krishna, L. K. R. (2019). A systematic scoping review of ethical issues in mentoring in surgery. 6, 2382120519888915.

Liao, L., Xiao, L. D., Chen, H., Wu, X. Y., Zhao, Y., Hu, M., … Feng, H. (2020). Nursing home staff experiences of implementing mentorship programmes: a systematic review and qualitative meta synthesis. *The Journal of Nursing Management*, 28(2), 188–198.

Loosveld, L. M., Van Gerven, P. W. M., Vanassche, E. and Driessen, E. W. (2020). Mentors' beliefs about their roles in health care education: a qualitative study of mentors' personal interpretative framework. *Academic Medicine*, 95(10), 1600–1606.

Mann, M. P. (1992). Faculty mentors for medical students: a critical review. *Medical Teacher*, 14(4), 311–319

Mann, R., Ball, K. and Watson, G. (2011). Mentoring for NHS general practitioners: a prospective pilot study of an action learning approach. *Education for Primary Care*, 22(4), 235–240.

Mitchell, F. (2015). Reflections on the process of conducting secondary analysis of qualitative data concerning informed choice for young people with a disability in transition. *Forum Qualitative Sozialforschung/Forum: Qualitative Social Research*, 16, Art. 10.

Ng, K. Y. B., Lynch, S., Kelly, J. and Mba, O. (2020a). Medical students' experiences of the benefits and influences regarding a placement mentoring programme preparing them for future practice as junior doctors: a qualitative study. *BMJ Open*, 10: e032643.

Ng, Y. X., Koh, Z. Y. K., Yap, H. W., Tay, K. T., Tan, X. H., Ong, Y. T., … Krishna, L. (2020b). Assessing mentoring: a scoping review of mentoring assessment tools in internal medicine between 1990 and 2019. *PLoS One*, 15(5), e0232511.

Nowell, L., White, D. E., Mrklas, K. and Norris, J. M. (2015). Mentorship in nursing academia: a systematic review protocol. *Systematic Reviews*, 4, 16.

Ong, J., Swift, C., Magill, N., Ong, S., Day, A., Al-Naeeb, Y. and Shankar, A. (2018). The association between mentoring and training outcomes in junior doctors in medicine: an observational study. *BMJ Open*, 8(9), e020721.

Ortega, G., Smith, C., Pichardo, M. S., Ramirez, A., Soto-Greene, M. and Sanchez, J. P. (2018). Preparing for an academic career: the significance of mentoring. *MedEdPORTAL*, 14, 10690.

Overeem, K., Driessen, E. W., Arah, O. A., Lombarts, K., Wollersheim, H. C. and Grol, R. (2010). Peer mentoring in doctor performance assessment: strategies, obstacles and benefits. *Medical Education*, 44(2), 140–147.

Oxley, J. (1998). *Supporting doctors and dentists at work: an enquiry into mentoring.* London: SCOPME. https://www.worldcat.org/title/supporting-doctors-and-dentists-at-work-an-enquiry-into-mentoring/oclc/43181836.

Oxley J., Fleming B., Golding L., Pask H. and A. Steven. (2003). Improving working lives for doctors. Mentoring for doctors: enhancing the benefit. A working paper produced for the Department of Health on behalf of the Doctors Forum. Retrieved from London.

Pawson, R. (2013). *The science of evaluation: a realist manifesto.* London: SAGE Publications.

Pawson, R. and Tilley, N. (1997). *Realistic evaluation.* London: SAGE Publications.

Pethrick, H., Nowell, L., Oddone Paolucci, E., Lorenzetti, L., Jacobsen, M., Clancy, T. and Lorenzetti, D. L. (2017). Psychosocial and career outcomes of peer mentorship in medical resident education: a systematic review protocol. *Systematic Reviews*, 6(1), 178.

Pfund, C., House, S., Spencer, K., Asquith, P., Carney, P., Masters, K. S., … Fleming, M. (2013). A research mentor training curriculum for clinical and translational researchers. *Clinical and Translational Science*, 6(1), 26–33.

Polley, C., Cisternino, A. and Gray, A. (2021). A novel approach to medical mentoring. *Clinical Teacher*, 18(1), 37–42.

Prendergast, H. M., Heinert, S. W., Erickson, T. B., Thompson, T. M. and Vanden Hoek, T. L. (2019). Evaluation of an enhanced peer mentoring program on scholarly productivity and promotion in academic emergency medicine: a five-year review. *Journal of the National Medical Association*, 111(6), 600–605.

Ramani, S., Könings, K. D., Mann, K. and van der Vleuten, C. P. M. (2018). A guide to reflexivity for qualitative researchers in education. *Academic Medicine*, 93(8), 1257.

Rossetto, K. R. (2014). Qualitative research interviews. *Journal of Social and Personal Relationships*, 31(4), 482–489.

Sambunjak, D., Straus, S. E. and Marusic, A. (2006). Mentoring in academic medicine: a systematic review. *JAMA*, 296(9), 1103–1115.

Sambunjak, D., Straus, S. E. and Marusic, A. (2010). A systematic review of qualitative research on the meaning and characteristics of mentoring in academic medicine. *The Journal of General Internal Medicine*, 25(1), 72–78.

Sayan, M., Ohri, N., Lee, A., Abou Yehia, Z., Gupta, A., Byun, J., … Kim, S. (2019). The impact of formal mentorship programs on mentorship experience among radiation oncology residents from the Northeast. *Frontiers in Oncology*, 4(9), 1369.

Sheri, K., Too, J. Y. J., Chuah, S. E. L., Toh, Y. P., Mason, S. and Radha Krishna, L. K. (2019). A scoping review of mentor training programs in medicine between 1990 and 2017. *Medical Education Online*, 24(1), 1555435.

Sikic Micanovic, L., Stelko, S. and Sakic, S. (2019). Who else needs protection? Reflecting on researcher vulnerability in sensitive research. *Societies*, 10(1), 1–12.

Sills, S. and Song, C. (2002). Innovations in survey research: an application of web-based surveys. *Science Computer Review*, 20, 22–30.

Silverman, D. (2017). *Doing qualitative research* (5th ed.). London: SAGE Publications.

Skjevik, E. P., Boudreau, J. D., Ringberg, U., Schei, E., Stenfors, T., Kvernenes, M. and Ofstad, E. H. (2020). Group mentorship for undergraduate medical students – a systematic review. *Perspectives on Medical Education*, 9, (5), 272–280.

Sligo, J. L., Nairn, K. M. and McGee, R. O. (2017). Rethinking integration in mixed methods research using data from different eras: lessons from a project about teenage vocational behaviour. *International Journal of Social Research Methodology*, 21(1), 63–75.

Sng, J. H., Pei, Y., Toh, Y. P., Peh, T. Y., Neo, S. H. and Krishna, L. K. R. (2017). Mentoring relationships between senior physicians and junior doctors and/or medical students: a thematic review. *Medical Teacher*, 39(8), 866–875.

Stamm, M. and Buddeberg-Fischer, B. (2011). The impact of mentoring during postgraduate training on doctors' career success. *Medical Education*, 45(5), 488–496.

Standing Committee on Postgraduate Medical and Dental Education. (1998). *Supporting doctors and dentists at work: an inquiry into mentoring*. Retrieved from London: SCOPME.

Steele, M. M., Fisman, S. and Davidson, B. (2013). Mentoring and role models in recruitment and retention: a study of junior medical faculty perceptions. *Medical Teacher*, 35(5), e1130–e1138.

Steiner J. F., Curtis, P., …Lanphear B. P. (2004). Assessing the role of influential mentors in the research development of primary care fellows. *Academic Mediciine*, 79, 865–872.

Steven, A. (2008). *Mentoring schemes for psychiatrists in the north east: an evaluation and exploration. Report for Northumberland Tyne and Wear NHS Trust, NIMHE and The Northern Deanery*. University of Newcastle upon Tyne.

Steven, A. (2015). *An evaluation of the implementation and impact of a mentoring programme for anaesthetists in the north east*. Northumbria University Newcastle.

Steven, A., Larkin, V., Wilson, G., Stewart, J., Wilcockson, J. and Redfern, N. (2018). *Exploring the relationship between engagement in mentoring activities and doctors' health and well-being: Final report*. Newcastle: Northumbria University.

Steven, A., Oxley, J. and Fleming, W. G. (2008). Mentoring for NHS doctors: perceived benefits across the personal-professional interface. *Journal of the Royal Society of Medicine*, 101(11), 552–557.

Swann, A., Ramsay, R. and Bijlani, N. (2008). *Mentoring and coaching*. (OP66 RCP). London: RCP.

Welch, J. L., Jimenez, H. L., Walthall, J. and Allen, S. E. (2012). The women in emergency medicine mentoring program: an innovative approach to mentoring. *The Journal of Graduate Medical Education*, 4(3), 362–366.

Wilson, G., Larkin, V., Redfern, N., Stewart, J. and Steven, A. (2017). Exploring the relationship between mentoring and doctors' health and wellbeing: a narrative review. *The Journal of the Royal Society of Medicine*, 110(5), 188–197.

Yoon, L., Campbell, T., Bellemore, W., Ghawi, N., Lai, P., Desveaux, L., … Brooks, D. (2017). Exploring mentorship from the perspective of physiotherapy mentors in Canada. *Physiotherapy Canada*, 69(1), 38–46.

5

MIXING METHODS AND DATA

Exploring health and wellbeing on a social scale

David Harrison, Asta Medisauskaite and Eliot L. Rees

Introduction to mixed-methods research

Johnson et al. (2007) reviewed and analysed 19 definitions of mixed-methods research in published literature and constructed a synthesised definition:

> Mixed methods research is the type of research in which a researcher, or team of researchers combine qualitative and quantitative research approaches (e.g., use of qualitative and quantitative viewpoints, data collection, analysis, inference techniques) for the broad purposes of breadth and depth of understanding and corroboration.

> (p. 123)

Is mixed methods a distinct methodology set alongside qualitative and quantitative, or should mixed methods be considered more broadly as the use of multiple methods within one study or one programme of work? A key feature in the preceding definition is the use of both quantitative and qualitative data, and this will resonate with many mixed-methods researchers. As will the idea that mixing of methods can occur within a single study (mixed-methods study) or between different studies addressing the same research question (mixed-methods programme of research). Some argue that mixing methods within a single study is essential for mixed-methods research (Curry and Nunez-Smith, 2017). While this is true in order for the research to count as a mixed-methods project, one should consider why one intends to use mixed methods and whether using a programme of studies around the same research question, but using different methodological approaches, would be appropriate to meet its aims. In this chapter, attention is paid not only to mixing of methods but also using a mix of data, or as Wisdom and Creswell (2013) define

DOI: 10.4324/9780429263484-6

mixed methods as (p. 1) the systematic integration, or 'mixing', of quantitative and qualitative data within a single investigation or sustained program of inquiry.

Thus, just as the mixed-methods methodology moves beyond the simple dichotomy of qualitative versus quantitative research methods to produce a different methodology, in this chapter, the idea that the categorisation of data types can go beyond qualitative or quantitative will be explored by looking at two case studies in which researchers used a mix of primary and secondary data.

Why mix methods?

There are a number of reasons to mix different methods in pursuit of answering a research question. A review by Bryman (2011) found the five most frequently cited reasons for conducting mixed-methods research were as follows:

1. *Enhancement* – using a second research method (quantitative or qualitative) to build on the findings of the first
2. *Sampling* – using one research method to identify cases to sample from for the second (e.g. using responses to a questionnaire to facilitate purposive sampling for interviews)
3. *Completeness* – to generate more comprehensive findings by using both approaches
4. *Triangulation* – defined by Denzin (1978, 291) as 'the combination of methodologies in the study of the same phenomenon' describes the uses of multiple different sources, researchers, theories or methods to approach a topic from different angles to fully illuminate a topic. It is also considered to demonstrate greater validity if similar findings are generated from different approaches
5. *Diversity of views* – combining the perspectives of participants (through qualitative) and researchers (through their interpretation of quantitative deductions) and combining an understanding of the relationship between quantitative variables with their qualitative meanings

These are the most common reasons why one might want to undertake mixed-methods research, and it is important to have a clear justification for adopting a mixed-methods approach. There are, however, challenges in combining different methods in a single project. The most significant of which is that these methods arise from different paradigms and are aligned with different understandings of ontology and epistemology. When mixing methods within a single project, therefore, some of these assumptions may conflict. While we as researchers are aware of such, discussion of such conflicts can be found elsewhere (e.g. Fàbregues and Molina-Azorín, 2017). Furthermore, synthesising the findings of different types of data can be difficult to achieve in a meaningful way (i.e. beyond simply reporting qualitative findings and quantitative findings in different sections of the results and having separate analyses discussed without any attempts to draw them together). Synthesising and

112 David Harrison et al.

integrating findings from different methods to enhance the discussion is one of the key benefits of undertaking programmes of research around the same research question using different methodological approaches between individual studies.

Mixing data types

Beyond considering mixed-methods research as combining quantitative and qualitative methods, we see advantages in using multiple methods and making use of different types of data. While there are a number of distinct data types, in this chapter, we focus on using both primary and secondary data, defined by Hox and Boeije (2005, 593) as follows:

> *Primary data*: 'Data that are collected for the specific research problem at hand, using procedures that fit the research problem best'.
> *Secondary data*: 'Data originally collected for a different purpose and reused for another research question'.

These definitions look straightforward; primary data is data collected specifically to address a research problem or answer a particular research question, while secondary data is data collected for a different (often non-research) purpose and then reused. The shift between specific research problem, specific research question and specific purpose introduces some ambiguity. If data is collected for a particular project and then another research project is an update seeking to answer the same research question using the same data, does this make it primary data? Is it important that the data be collected using procedures for the specific research problem? If so, then with a change of research problem during the project, does the collected data become secondary data?

Such philosophical considerations may not impact directly on practice, but it is important to be clear on definitions in order for those reading your research to be able to interpret it accurately and appropriately.

There are a number of different types of primary data (see Table 5.1). These can be categorised into qualitative or quantitative and either explicitly 'solicited' (asked

TABLE 5.1 Types of primary data

	Solicited	*Spontaneous*
Quantitative	Questionnaire	Administrative data
	Experimental data	Monitoring
	Assessment data	
Qualitative	Individual interviews	Participant observation
	Focus groups	Written records
	Audio diaries	
	Written diaries	
	Reflective statements	

for by researchers) or data that is 'spontaneous' (not a response to specific research instruments; Hox and Boeije, 2005).

Secondary data will be in the same format but will not have been explicitly collected for the purposes of an individual project. For most purposes, the effective definition can be that secondary data is data collected by one project and then reused by another project, though it often includes data collected for a specific (often administrative) purpose and then repurposed by researchers. Secondary data accessible to those who have not commissioned or collected it is predominantly quantitative in much health-care research, although existing documents such as interview transcripts or video recordings may be available for qualitative analysis. Thanks to the growth of open access research and databases, archives of both quantitative and qualitative data are becoming more common and widely available to researchers. Many universities now hold archives of data collected by researchers at that institution for previous research studies, with consent that it is available for future research.

There is a range of sources of accessible secondary data in health and medical education in the UK, including, for example, the following:

- UK Medical Education Database (UKMED) – a platform for collating data on the performance of UK medical students and trainee doctors across their education and future career
- National Health Service (NHS) Digital – standardising, collecting and publishing data and information from across the health and social care system in England
- Longitudinal Educational Outcomes – Department of Education database of employment and earnings outcomes of higher education graduates
- Clinical Practice Research Datalink – collects de-identified patient data from general practitioner practices and links to a range of other health-related data to provide a longitudinal, representative UK population health dataset
- Timescapes – a qualitative longitudinal study exploring how personal and family relationships develop and change over time.

Both primary and secondary data have their advantages and disadvantages. These are summarised in Table 5.2.

Much like how one might combine qualitative and quantitative data in a mixed-methods study to overcome the limitations of each of the methods individually, one can combine primary and secondary data in order to benefit from the advantages of both (this can include both qualitative and quantitative as well, if available). Combining primary and secondary data enables researchers to benefit from having data that was specifically designed to answer their research questions (primary) with a large dataset that enjoys a completeness and a lack of response bias (secondary). Yet it can also be challenging, time-consuming and require expertise in all of the individual data types and methods, as well as in data linkage.

114 David Harrison et al.

TABLE 5.2 Advantages and disadvantages of primary and secondary data (adapted from K. Woolf and E. Rees ASME workshop 2018)

	Advantages	*Disadvantages*
Primary data	Designed to answer your research question	Can be expensive to collect
	Often relatively easy to access (you collect them)	Often small or single institution/ location samples
	Easy to understand (because they are yours)	Typically suffer from response/ self-report bias
	Often don't require linking to other data	Limited scope (e.g. variables limited due to expensive data collection)
Secondary data	Can be free to access	Not designed to answer your research question (e.g. missing appropriate variables, collected from a different participant population)
	Easier to get larger sample sizes so higher statistical power	
	Can provide many variables and be longitudinal (especially if linked to other data sources)	
	Can encompass whole populations	Can be hard to access (e.g., data protection, commercial interests, slow reply organisations)
	Administrative data can bypass self-report bias and problems due to low response	Can be difficult to understand
		Can require linkage* (which requires expertise and time)

* Data linkage enables the mixing of different data types from different sources to allow for enhancement, triangulation and other elaborations of the analysis (see the 'Data Protection and Ethics' section).

In addition to distinguishing between primary and secondary data, a distinction can be drawn between primary and secondary analysis:

> Primary analysis is the original analysis of data in a research study.... Secondary analysis is the re-analysis of data for the purpose of answering the original research question with better statistical techniques, or answering new questions with old data.
>
> (Glass, 1976, 3)

Mixed-methods research in action

This section will discuss how researchers can mix data using two research projects as examples. We start by explaining how health and wellbeing was understood in our research projects. Then the key considerations regarding the use of various methods and data sources to answer research questions and challenges of the two projects will be discussed in the main text and examples will be provided in the boxes. Boxes 5.1 and 5.2 describe the two research projects used throughout this chapter:

1. Case Study 1: A mixed-methods investigation into the impact of social background on choice of medical school (UK Medical Applicant Cohort Study [UKMACS]).
2. Case Study 2: A mixed-methods approach to understanding career choices in psychiatry (UCCiP).

Health and wellbeing on a social scale

The focus of this book is on issues in mixed-methods wellbeing and health research. In our research projects, we have defined wellbeing at the society level (Marmot, 2020) as a measure of social progress. That is, wellbeing is a requirement for a better society over and above improving individual health and wellbeing. Clearly, national wellbeing is not just individual wellbeing.

> Put simply, if health has stopped improving, then society has stopped improving. Evidence, assembled globally, shows that health is a good measure of social and economic progress. When a society is flourishing, health tends to flourish. When a society has large social and economic inequalities, it also has large inequalities in health.
>
> (Marmot, 2020, 1)

This definition thus holds that true national wellbeing encompasses equality distributed across all of society and part of that is having fair, diverse, and equitable systems. That requires that any growth be sustainable, inclusive and encourage the participation of all parts of our society. This underlying concept of health and wellbeing on a social, rather than individual, level is what unites the two projects used as case studies (as detailed in Boxes 5.1 and 5.2).

The NHS is not seen as being in the best of health – it currently requires transfusions of doctors from other countries to help sustain it. There are issues with both recruitment into the health-care sector, in particular recruitment into so-called shortage specialties, and with the retention of trained health-care specialists.

While for some time there has been a political intent to have enough UK doctors in the NHS, in 2016, the UK government explicitly announced their intention that 'by the end of the next Parliament [2025] we will make the NHS self-sufficient in doctors' (Hunt, 2016). Then in 2017, the secretary of state for health also charged the NHS to deliver a programme of support around improving turnover rates for clinical staff in mental health Trusts in the NHS Long Term Plan (2019a) and the supporting Interim NHS People Plan (2019b). This was against a backdrop of rising turnover rates over the previous five years and an intention to extend the support to all Trusts and into general practice (for example, see the King's Fund, 2019).

The growth in doctors was to be achieved mainly via a policy of increasing medical school places and an additional 1,500 medical school places were created in England in 2018 and 2019. The new medical school places also aimed to increase the number of doctors working in shortage specialties, particularly general practice and mental health, and in parts of the country with relatively few doctors per head of population, and to increase the proportion of doctors from under-represented social groups. The places were therefore allocated to medical schools that could demonstrate a commitment to widening participation and address the lack of people from lower socio-economic backgrounds entering the profession (Medical Schools Council, 2016) and resulted in the creation of five new medical schools located in under-doctored parts of the country.

Despite these laudable aims, there are concerns over where the increased numbers of medical students will be recruited from and concerns as to whether increasing places and lowering entry requirements will result in doctors of a lower standard (McManus, 2016). It is, however, clear that applying to medical school in the UK is complex and highly competitive, with applicants choosing four medical courses from a large number of potential choices and medical schools using an array of selection methods resulting in differing entry rates. During the 2017–2018 application cycle, there were 20,730 applications for 7,767 places (application ratio 2.7:1), and applicants from poorer backgrounds were less likely to be successful (Steven et al., 2016). With 80% of all applicants to medical school in the UK coming from just 20% of schools (Medical Schools Council, 2014), and medical schools having highly demanding and complex entry criteria, concerns have been raised that some students, despite having the necessary aptitude to study medicine, are being excluded from this career pathway to the detriment of the profession. So Case Study 1 focuses on exploring the social factors that impact medical school applicants trying to enter the system.

For doctors already in the system, it is clear that if one is satisfied with their workplace, then one will be much less likely to consider leaving it. On the other hand, overworked and exhausted doctors might well think about alternative career paths and leaving the profession or health-care system altogether. As illustrated next, in Figure 5.1, doctors' choices to stay or leave the profession will depend on individual and environmental level factors – e.g. the (un)healthy environment (work characteristics) might affect individual wellbeing (satisfaction, burnout, etc.) and in turn the systems (retention/attrition; leaving the system understaffed and unhealthy or appropriately staffed and healthy). Considering the number of people

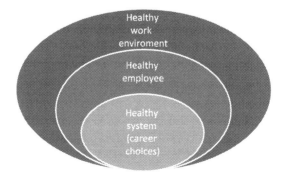

FIGURE 5.1 Health and wellbeing at the individual, environmental, and system levels

with mental health conditions, such as anxiety or depression, increased in recent years (McManus et al., 2016), having a sufficient number of psychiatrists is more important than ever. Therefore, Case Study 2, more specifically, focuses on a healthy workforce in psychiatry – i.e. environmental and individual factors contributing to psychiatry trainees' decision to continue training or not (see Box 5.2). This is a complex task, especially considering limited prior knowledge (few studies in the area), and, therefore, requires mixed-methods as no one method would be able to achieve the study's wide-reaching aims.

In the broadest sense, both projects described in this chapter are dealing with the health system's wellbeing. One addresses issues around bringing individuals into the system (i.e. dealing with symptoms of an unhealthy system that lacks diversity in medical school applicants; Case Study 1). The other focuses on losing individuals who are already in the system (i.e. dealing with symptoms of an unhealthy system that does not retain a higher number of trainees in psychiatry; Case Study 2). Both seek to uncover the variety of impacting factors at the individual and environmental levels.

BOX 5.1 CASE STUDY 1: DESCRIPTION OF THE UKMACS

AIMS AND CONTEXT:

Medical schools attract and produce different types of doctors; however, the reason as to why remains unclear. For example, some medical schools attract and accept more applicants from non-traditional backgrounds than others; some produce more of a certain specialism than others do. To understand why this is, we need to find out what factors affect students' applications to medicine, such as the type of support they receive, what challenges they face, the type of people that they are and what criteria they use to select medical schools.

The medical selection process is challenging for applicants. Admissions tests are used to select the most able medical applicant. Students may choose to sit one or more tests: University Clinical Aptitude Test (UCAT), BioMedical Admissions Tests (BMAT) or Graduate Medical School Admissions Test (GAMSAT), but the universities each have their own way to standardise the results. In order to get a place for an interview, students must meet various entry requirements and produce a successful personal statement to convey their interest and dedication to medicine to their chosen medical schools. Medical interviews come in two forms, Multiple Mini Interviews (MMIs) or traditional interviews. MMIs consist of multiple interview stations whereas traditional interviews involve sitting opposite a panel of interviews. Topics such as teamwork, work experience, medical ethics, and the NHS may be discussed.

The UKMACS is a National Institute for Health Research–funded programme investigating how applicant choice varies by social background running from 2018 to 2020.

The study has two core questions answered through three research elements:

1. How does an applicant's background influence which medical schools they choose to apply to?
   - Qualitative study interviewing applicants and entrants from diverse backgrounds.
   - Questionnaire/survey of all UK medical school applicants in 2019.
2. What is the impact of choices on outcomes?
   - Applications and outcomes study involving statistical modelling of linked administrative data the Universities and Colleges Admissions Service, UCAT, BMAT, the Higher Education Statistics Agency on medical school choice, offers and acceptances by applicant characteristics.

Methods used:
- Semi-structured interviews
- Thematic analysis
- Questionnaire using closed- and open-text questions
- Statistical Imputation of missing data
- Data linkage of 'big data' in databases
- Systematic literature review

Data types:
Primary data: Interview transcripts, main questionnaire and follow-up questionnaire.
Secondary data: UKMED, UCAS, UCAT and BMAT. Other administrative data in secure databases, e.g. National Pupil Database. Previous surveys and cohort studies.

Ethics/data protection:
Ethics: The main ethical issues for UKMACS are (1) obtaining personal and sensitive data from under-18s and (2) obtaining informed consent for data linkage.

Data protection: Data is transferred between organisations and then linked and made accessible for research. UKMED database is essential in allowing this but does not cover everything, as not all potential applicants are in UKMED.

The project received ethical and data protection approvals. Informed consent was obtained from all participants. Researchers anonymised all the data and assigned unique project IDs to all participants. The UKMED data were accessed through Data Safe Haven.

Mixing methods and data **119**

Key issues:

- Mixed-methods design and development of research instruments
- Data protection and ethics around accessing and linking data
- Accessing participants and improving response rates
- Mixing data – particularly using secondary data with missing values

---

BOX 5.2 CASE STUDY 2: DESCRIPTION OF STUDY ON UCCIP

Aims and context:

Attrition is a major concern within psychiatric training. Just 65.8% of psychiatry trainees in the UK planned to stay in psychiatry, as reported in Barras and Harris (2012). Moreover, in 2017, the 'fill rates' for many higher specialty programmes in psychiatry were lower than 60% (NHS, 2017), which may result in staff gaps. Having such gaps poses a threat to effective mental health service delivery. High dropout rates are not easy to explain considering trainees' investment of time and efforts to reach the specialty training level. This might suggest that there are systematic challenges that contribute to trainees considering and eventually leaving their training. Studies identify that there is a particular profile of people who are more likely to drop out from training (e.g., female, Khoushhal et al., 2017), which might uncover issues around fairness and equal opportunities for everyone to complete their training. Studies also reveal that trainees talk about work and learning environment factors (e.g. lack of resources; Choudry & Farooq, 2017) as contributing to the decision to leave. The main aim of this study is to investigate career progression and attrition in psychiatry training. This study has three research objectives:

1. Explore rates of and reasons for trainees' progression through training with and without delays.
2. Identify the factors that contribute to psychiatry trainees leaving (intending to leave) their training and the factors that contribute to trainees staying.
3. Examine in more depth how and why these (and other) factors contribute to attrition or retention.

Methods used:

To achieve the aim of this study, it used a mixed-methods design incorporating quantitative and qualitative analysis of secondary (the UKMED; the List of Registered Medical Practitioners) and primary (survey and interview) data.

Secondary data: The List of Registered Medical Practitioners (LRMP) is a database of all doctors eligible to practice in the UK. The UKMED holds data on the performance of UK undergraduate and postgraduate medical students and trainees. The secondary data was chosen (1) to explore the time required to progress to a consultant post in psychiatry (LRMP – from medical school graduation to consultancy; UKMED – through psychiatry training), (2) to explore the dropout rates and when in the training process the dropout rates are the highest and (3) to investigate if (how) socio-demographic characteristics link to trainees' progression.

Survey: The survey aimed to investigate in more detail the reasons for psychiatry trainees leaving/staying in/considering leaving their training. We used a theoretically grounded model to develop the survey, the results of which aimed to answer if (how) work/learning environment links to individual-level health and wellbeing and in turn affects intentions to leave the profession. To do this, we used a mix of previously used questionnaires (validated/reliable) and exploratory questions (multiple option, open-ended questions), which covered a broad variety of aspects.

Interviews: The purpose of the interviews was to explore in-depth why psychiatry trainees decide to continue with or leave their specialty training. Narrative interviews were chosen to truly explore trainees' experiences. Such interviews encourage individuals to share their stories with others, including their own perceptions about, interpretations of and responses to, their lived experiences. Through narrative interviews, in-depth life stories were collected, as well as information about how these stories are told (e.g. tone, how language is used to construct the story), producing a detailed understanding of what it is like to be a psychiatry trainee.

Data types:

- Primary (questionnaire; interviews)
- Secondary (UKMED; LRMP)

Ethics/data protection:
The project received ethical and data protection approvals. Informed consent was obtained from all participants. Researchers anonymised all the data and assigned unique project IDs to all participants. The UKMED data were accessed through Data Safe Haven.

Key issues:

- Mixing data
- Triangulation
- Handling big datasets

Mixing methods and data **121**

Why mix data?

The data collected by these projects is a mix of qualitative and quantitative, primary and secondary, longitudinal and cross-sectional or one-off data involving large numbers and individual details. The reasons for mixing data can vary as discussed previously, and the two projects choose to mix methods and data types for different reasons. For Case Study 1, UKMACS, mixed methods are important, as findings from one method are used to develop another (*enhancement of methods*; see introduction section). A variety of methods and data types also helps to generate more comprehensive findings (*completeness of methods*; see introduction section). The latter is also relevant for Case Study 2, UCCiP, but this project is also concerned with *triangulation* – i.e. approaching the same topic from different angles to fully understand the phenomenon of interest. More details on what methods/data types were chosen for each project and why are presented in Boxes 5.3 and 5.4.

BOX 5.3 UKMACS: WHY MIX DATA?

To fully explore how potential applicants to medical school go about making their choices, the study required a mix of data. UKMACS has three main components and uses a mix of methods – a qualitative interview study, a questionnaire study and an applications and outcomes study using quantitative, administrative data to collect and analyse secondary data from a variety of sources, such as the UKMED, and data on the education systems of England, Northern Ireland, Scotland and Wales.

Fundamental to the UKMACS project is the belief that widening participation is about ensuring those with the potential to become a doctor are given the opportunity by making the right choices for themselves. This included analysing large-scale information on patterns of choices, information sources used and socio-demographics and qualitative findings on the decision-making processes and the thoughts of medical school applicants. To be able to predict the outcomes of selection, we needed to develop an understanding of the process, strategies and thinking behind applicant choices and the factors impacting those choices.

The secondary, administrative data on individual applicants (e.g. socio-demographics, academic achievement) gathered from UCAS, UCAT, BMAT, HESA and other sources and held in UKMED allows for the primary data collected by UKMACS to be linked to data from previous years and so adds a longitudinal element to the study while also allowing the research to be completed in a short amount of time and thus deliver timely research findings and so have an impact on policy and practice.

Each component and dataset feeds forward to the next phase of the project, which allows findings to inform the design, development and analysis of successive phases. Beginning with the qualitative interview study – a series of semi-structured interviews of current medical students and applicants to medical school – which informed the questionnaire design – particularly in terms of how to analyse applicant choice strategies and in terms of specific questions and response options. This allowed the questionnaire to focus on the actual priorities, concerns, strategies, etc., of applicants. The questionnaire allows for the primary collection of some data and the linking of that to secondary data (specifically in the UKMED), which then informs the applications and outcomes phase, in particular in developing a model of the choice process allowing for the predictive analysis.

Analysis of each phase informs both the questions that need to be asked and the theoretical underpinnings of other phases. For instance, much of the literature refers to traditional medical school applicants, so with the interviews, a clear definition of traditional versus non-traditional applicants was required. Using secondary data on previous cohorts of applicants and medical school definitions of non-traditional or under-represented groups led to the development of a scale based on four factors ((1) school type, (2) parent education level, (3) ethnicity and (4) HE participation level of home address) rather than a binary distinction. From the interviews, UKMACS also developed a choice set analysis of how applicants chose medical schools.

BOX 5.4   UCCIP: WHY MIX DATA?

This project investigates a complex topic consisting of multiple layers and, therefore, to achieve the objectives outlined previously, a mixed-methods design was chosen using secondary (UKMED, LRMP) and primary (survey and interview) data. Each method used explores the same problem from a different perspective and helps to deal with the other method's limitations. Secondary data are usually large datasets that enable researchers to investigate the phenomenon longitudinally. In this project, large datasets are important, as they help to, first, more generally better understand the problem (attrition) and, second, observe differences in patterns of attrition amongst groups of psychiatry trainees. The UKMED and LRMP datasets (secondary data) include data about all psychiatry trainees and consultants in the UK, and these big nationwide datasets are great resources, as they help to make conclusions that are far more generalisable. However, it is very rare that routinely collected administrative data like this will include all variables that might be of interest. Psychological constructs can be especially difficult to find. For example, this project explores individual and environmental factors that might link to trainees leaving or successfully progressing through their training: the UKMED and LRMP holds some data on demographic characteristics of trainees/consultants and some information about learning and working environments (psychological constructs); however, for example, there is limited information about individual-level wellbeing or the reasons for trainees leaving their training. Moreover, the validity and reliability of psychological constructs can be an issue where the data is not collected for research purposes.

Primary data is, therefore, also collected, as the secondary data is collected for administrative purposes and is limited with regards to what research questions it can answer and in how much detail. Survey as a research method was chosen because this is an easier way to reach larger numbers of trainees and the best instrument to explore the research topic in more detail across a wide group. Specifically, surveys can explore various constructs that were not covered in the secondary data via exploratory open-ended questions and validated questionnaires to measure psychological constructs, such as individual-level wellbeing. Even though surveys give more flexibility compared to secondary data, it still has its limitations. In this research, it is challenging to choose which work/learning environment factors to measure (e.g. which factors might be important to explore quantitatively) because this topic has not been widely researched previously. Therefore, the last phase of this project is a qualitative study (interviews), which adds an additional layer of details to the existing data. Interviews help to explain 'how and why' by offering invaluable in-depth insight into the experience of being a psychiatry trainee and the opportunity to hear first-hand why retention is a problem in this medical specialty. Interviews can also reveal other important factors for attrition not identified in the quantitative studies (survey and secondary data). It is impossible to investigate every possible environmental factor in the survey, but interviews allow participants to respond freely, offering information that the research team might not have thought to ask.

The main reason for mixing methods and data types for this project is to triangulate data and thus facilitate a more comprehensive and deeper understanding of the factors that contribute to phenomena of interest (retention in psychiatry). A great variety of data are collected and analysed in this project, and these cover a wide range of aspects related to attrition: training patterns which show attrition/retention rates (secondary data), socio-demographic, personal and environmental factors linked to attrition/retention (secondary data; primary data: survey) and in-depth exploration of reasons for attrition/retention (primary data: interviews). The advantage and challenge of having such a variety of data, however, is to synthesise this together in a meaningful way: each dataset helps add to the understanding of the others – e.g. primary data (survey and interviews) help to explain the patterns observed in the secondary data; interviews can help to better understand and explain the findings from a survey.

124 David Harrison et al.

How to mix data

How to organise, analyse and present data is an ongoing challenge for any research project. How it is done will mainly depend on the purpose of mixing methods and data types. If the main purpose is to use mixed methods for the enhancement of methods (as for the UKMACS project), a researcher will use the findings from one research method to develop another. If the main purpose is to triangulate (as for the UCCiP project), all data may be collected at the same time, and findings will be triangulated and combined. Combining findings from various studies might be challenging and, therefore, ensuring that data collected are compatible, clearly defining objectives for each project stage and considering, in advance, how all findings will link together can really help to meaningfully combine the findings.

Many mixed-methods approaches collect data using multiple instruments/methods, and typically, each instrument collects a particular type of data. What data and how it should be collected requires thought, as previously mentioned, thinking about how data can be organised, analysed and presented. Different data types, however, do not necessarily need to be collected using different data collection tools. For example, with instruments such as complex questionnaires, there is the potential to use a single instrument to collect both quantitative and qualitative data that are already directly linked. This allows for more efficient data collection, as it collects different data from a participant at one time with a single instrument. Therefore, researchers need to consider if one method of collecting data can produce a different type of data and would that be sufficient and plan accordingly. Both case study projects used questionnaires to collect quantitative and qualitative data (see the example from UKMACS in Box 5.5).

BOX 5.5   UKMACS: DEVELOPING INTEGRATED RESEARCH INSTRUMENTS

In designing questions around how and which medical schools potential applicants considered and chose, we were aware that in answering some questions, respondents want to elaborate on their thinking, provide information that is more detailed or even actively engage in the process of choosing medical schools and so be influenced by the questions themselves. The inclusion of an *Other* option with an open text box or an Additional/Further Comments option can go some way to gathering more detail. Thought needs to be given to how a quantitative item, such as stating which information sources are being used or asking which medical schools a respondent is aware of, can also inform the respondent and so change the answer or generate a desire to offer more explanation. In other cases, a question initially conceived as a qualitative data item can be reconfigured into a quantitative item. In the UKMACS interviews, we asked what makes a medical school attractive and unattractive

Mixing methods and data **125**

> to potential medical students. Analysis of the interview responses allowed the generation of a list of features. Analysis also showed that there were generally no more than four attractive features named. Therefore, the questionnaire item was constructed as 'select up to four features' with an *Other* option (which in itself produced mainly re-wordings of already listed features tailored to individual circumstances).

Challenges of mixing methods and data types

There are numerous challenges of mixing methods and data types. If a project is to adopt a fully mixed-methods research methodology, it is imperative that the research instruments (data collection, analysis, etc.) all align. While this can be assumed to be the case, as they are directed at the same research question(s), such alignment and integration can be strengthened by ensuring that the design and development of individual research instruments fit together. While using a mix of primary and secondary data, there is an initial challenge to collect a wide range of data on a suitable number of individuals and then to make sure that the different types of data from different sources are actually compatible (and so capable of being linked together). In using a mix of primary and secondary data, both projects faced the challenges of finding ways to link and integrate data on individuals and cohorts, accessing secure databases and dealing with considerable complexity while still allowing for a coherent analysis that successfully integrates diverse data types and methods. Added to this is the fact that other elements require consideration when thinking about a mixed-methods project: data protection and ethics, accessing participants and handling large datasets. As these challenges tend to be particular to specific projects, the two case studies are used in the following sections to highlight potential issues.

Data protection and ethics

Any project using mixed data types will require an appropriate, accessible description of data (often within the information sheet provided to participants) and an explanation of how data will be used to ensure there is properly informed consent. It is especially important if collecting personal data, linking different datasets together or ensuring that in the future collected data could be used to answer different research questions.

Challenges concerning ethics/data protection encountered by the UKMACS project are in particular related to data linkage (Box 5.6). The data linkage enables the mixing of different data types from different sources to allow for enhancement, triangulation and other elaborations of the analysis. With data linkage, it is important to not only obtain specific informed consent for linkage (by defining what data linkage is and stating the various databases that will be used) but also to future-proof the consent to cover the possibility that there would be future datasets relevant to

126 David Harrison et al.

the research. Explaining data linkage is vital to gaining informed consent from participants, and it can be necessary to state that in some cases, the linkage will be mutual, with researchers both providing data and linking to data.

BOX 5.6 UKMACS: ETHICS AND CONSENT

Collecting personal data (even if not sensitive data) on under 18s, obtaining informed consent (particularly around data linkage) and protecting such data are all challenges UKMACS faced. To guarantee fully informed consent, it was important to state exactly what data would be collected for data linkage, define what data linkage is and state the various databases that we were planning to link with the project data.

Essentially, data linkage here involved identifying individuals by some common data (using such information as full name, date of birth, etc.) within different datasets and linking them to increase the amount of information available on each individual. For UKMACS, this enabled the use of a range of data on school type, socio-economic grouping, disadvantage and deprivation, etc. without the need to collect the data with the questionnaire.

With the questionnaire component of UKMACS, we received responses from nearly 6,500 individuals who were seriously considering applying to UK medical schools in 2019. Once the questionnaire responses were added to UKMED, it was then necessary to link the responses to other data held on the respondents. Some participants were serious enough to start applying for medicine and to respond to the questionnaire but then decided not to continue with their application to study medicine. This group is extremely interesting from the perspective of the research, as they provide a comparison, yet they are difficult to locate within other administrative datasets. With their consent and the mix of data collected by the questionnaire, it was possible for the majority to be linked to other sets of administrative data and so increased the scope of the research and possible analyses.

Accessing participants

Different data collection methods will have their own challenges of accessing the sample of interest. For example, accessing participants is not an issue with secondary datasets (data has been collected already); however, accessing and using such data might be challenging. Organisations might be sensitive about sharing their data with researchers and agreeing on data sharing terms and conditions might take time; organisations might also ask researchers to work from a particular location or through certain online platforms.

Mixing methods and data **127**

Another two popular data collection methods, questionnaires and interviews, can be challenging when trying to collect data from hard-to-reach populations. Even questionnaires that can reach a large number of people typically struggle with low response rates (especially online ones). Both projects are trying to access notoriously difficult to reach populations – whether due to reluctance to respond or no direct contact with a target group. Where initial responses to an invitation to take part in interviews or questionnaire are not as good as expected, it is important to determine why this is so, as this might be due to misperceptions or lack of understanding of the purpose of the research. The challenges of accessing participants/data and solutions from the two projects are described in Boxes 5.7 and 5.8.

BOX 5.7   UCCIP: SAMPLING

The UKMED dataset gives a unique opportunity to longitudinally explore psychiatry trainees' career paths in the UK. However, the UKMED does not hold information explicitly about attrition – e.g. there is no variable showing if a trainee left their training or not. Not having a variable of interest in the dataset makes it harder to identify the sample of interest. In this project, we defined 'attrition' using other available information (e.g. if a trainee progressed to a higher training level). This is an example showing that most likely secondary data will dictate how key constructs will be understood. Primary data collection can help to overcome this limitation and explore attrition in more detail. Nevertheless, considering that trainees who left their training are a difficult group to reach, primary data collection methods also have challenges. To reach an appropriate number of participants (a larger number is necessary for a survey analysis), we invited trainees who left training and those current psychiatry trainees who intended to leave to take part in the survey. Intentions are considered a suitable proxy for the behaviour and, therefore, are valuable to investigate in order to understand attrition. Interviews do not require a large number of participants (compared to a survey, for example), which is an important advantage. To maximise the recruitment, trainees who took part in the survey were invited for interviews, and a snowballing method (Streeton et al., 2004) was used to recruit other relevant study participants.

BOX 5.8   UKMACS: WIDENING COVERAGE

To be successful, UKMACS had to receive questionnaire responses from as many of those seriously considering applying to medicine as possible. This required the use of incentives, reminders and 'publicity' through social media and other forms to raise awareness. It also required two paths to the

128 David Harrison et al.

questionnaire: many potential participants received a personalised invitation to the questionnaire where UKMACS had received their contact information from secondary data. This allowed for some questionnaire items to be pre-populated with basic information to reduce the time taken in completing the questionnaire. However, it was also necessary to create an 'open' questionnaire accessible to anyone via a web link.

This did mean that in increasing access and opportunities to respond, there was the potential for some to respond to the questionnaire more than once. After the questionnaire closed, it was important to begin 'cleaning' the data. Although this also involved correcting typos and handling incomplete questionnaire responses, the majority of the cleaning was in identifying multiple responders and deduplicating responses.

Respondents provided some personal data, including full name, date of birth, email address, mobile and landline telephone numbers. These were all used to identify duplicate responses. However, once they had been identified, the choice had to be made about which response was to be included in the data. The decision was to include the response with the most free text responses (qualitative data) and in cases where the responses were very similar to select the first response (based on date submitted). This solution was only possible because quantitative and qualitative data were being collected.

Handling big datasets

Working with secondary datasets is a complex and time-consuming process rarely planned for when it comes to project design. When collecting primary data, one can plan what data will be collected and how the data will be recorded, plan the data cleaning process and statistical analysis, know exactly what challenges were encountered during the data collection process and understand how these challenges may affect data quality and eventual findings. Using secondary datasets, however, it is not always clear what the data will look like and, hence, the process of cleaning big secondary datasets might be one of the most challenging elements of research and require a significant amount of time and resources. In Box 5.9, we describe what challenges researchers working on the UCCiP project experienced working with big datasets.

BOX 5.9 UCCIP: CHALLENGES WITH USING BIG DATASETS

There are a number of challenges encountered when using the UKMED data because of the complexity of big datasets that have typically been collected for administrative purposes rather than direct research. First, because datasets are big, the challenge is to make the data manageable. For example, while it is possible to scroll through a smaller dataset to investigate available data, when there are thousands of variables and hundreds of thousands of participants, that becomes impossible. Second, it might be difficult to interpret variables (e.g. what it means, how it is coded), as the data is collected by somebody else. The UKMED produces a data dictionary that defines the variables it contains. However, not all explanations are detailed enough, especially if you are less familiar with the topic. Also, when analysing longitudinal data, researchers need to account for changes over time. For example, there might be changes in what variables are collected, in coding or in the system that affects available data (e.g. what exams trainees are taking or how exams are scored). Therefore, one might need to deal with various cases for which different information is available. Related to that, because of the nature of secondary data, there might be a lot of missing data, and the challenge is to investigate the reasons for it and choose an appropriate way to deal with this issue. If data is missing not at random, it will have different implications for the analysis and interpretation compared to dealing with data missing at random.

Conclusions and reflections

Both studies presented here involve a mix of qualitative and quantitative methods to collect and analyse data from a variety of sources. In particular, they both explore large datasets from the UKMED (Dowell et al., 2018) and other datasets held by government and national organisations.

Throughout this chapter, and for much of our research activity, we have put aside the theoretical question of whether these approaches constitute mixed-methods research or research using multiple methods. Our focus is on practical real-world research and making effective use of available data.

So, rather than treating mixed-methods research as one of three 'research paradigms' (qualitative, quantitative and mixed) and accepting the difficulties created by making rigid distinctions, we have focused on a more pragmatic and broad definition of mixed methods. Both projects see mixed methods as being defined by the inclusion of various methods of data collection, as well as research methods, of mixed analyses and, fundamentally, about mixing data types, not just using qualitative and quantitative data but also making use of primary and secondary data that can be linked and mixed.

Therefore, mixed-methods research does not just mean using qualitative and quantitative data in parallel on a research project. It is about integrating a variety of methods and types of data to produce something new and different from the separate project components. Research might be described as mixed methods because it has collected both quantitative and qualitative data, yet if the analysis of the data is conducted separately with no 'mixing' taking place, these are just two separate studies which do not utilise the benefits of combining different methods in a coherent mixed-methods methodology.

The two example projects in this chapter demonstrate that there are both strengths and challenges to combining research methods and types of data. For example, it can be advantageous in enhancing the findings; however, combining data can require a lot of time and expertise in multiple methods and data linkage. This is particularly true when handling big datasets and using secondary data. Moreover, collecting different types of data or conducting an analysis using more than one method can be problematic when the purpose of doing so is not clearly defined beforehand. Researchers need to be clear about what benefits using a mix of methods brings to the research. Often, this can allow for triangulation in order to strengthen the justification for the conclusions drawn – though the researchers must also be ready to deal with any contradictions that the results from different studies might bring! This requires some additional effort.

This is particularly true when it comes to making use of different types of data along the primary/secondary distinction. There are many sources of secondary data available to researchers, which make for a very powerful resource. With ever more data becoming (relatively easily) available in health and medical education (particularly UKMED), there is a growing temptation to make use of it. However, some secondary data is hard to use in practice, as it can require prior knowledge of the nature or even existence of the data, and, without appropriate expertise and familiarity with the data itself, it cannot always be used to answer your research question.

Mixing methods and data is beneficial for enhancing our scientific knowledge of the phenomenon of interest but also has a practical value. Both of the projects sought to have an impact beyond the research environment with reporting potential policy implications – mixed data can enable the production of research that non-researchers can more easily understand and that policy makers will value and be achievable in the time and resources available. This does still require good communication with these groups, however.

With the discussed projects, the initial planning endeavoured to use the strengths of mixing methods to answer the research questions within the time available and the pragmatic constraints of real-world research. What was probably unclear at the start was just how different mixed-methods research is from both quantitative and qualitative research. That difference has an impact on all elements of the research project and requires the development of new expertise. Despite, or perhaps because of, the challenge of mixing methods and combining data sources, we believe that all researchers and the research can employ both primary (designed to answer your question) and secondary (complete data lacking in response bias) data to their advantage. For us, the development of techniques for data linkage and mixing primary and secondary data to produce unique analyses have presented us with the opportunity to confront unexpected challenges and grow as researchers.

Questions for discussion and further reflection

The authors define primary and secondary data and suggest a list of advantages and disadvantages associated with each. Can you think of possible secondary data resources of relevance to your own interests – could their use enhance your research?

What were the practical considerations that limited collecting primary data in these studies?

What are the ethical considerations related to the use of secondary data?

What philosophical underpinnings do the researchers adopt?

References

Barras, C. and Harris, J. (2012). Psychiatry recruited you, but will it retain you? Survey of trainees' opinions. *The Psychiatrist*, 36 (2), 71–77.

Bryman, A. (2011). Why do researchers integrate/combine/mesh/blend/mix/merge/fuse quantitative and qualitative research?. In M. Bergman (ed.), *Advances in mixed methods research*, London: SAGE Publications.

Choudry, A. and Farooq, S. (2017). Systematic review into factors associated with the recruitment crisis in psychiatry in the UK: students', trainees' and consultants' views. *BJPsych bulletin*, 41 (6), 345–352.

Curry, L. and Nunez-Smith, M. (2017). Definition and overview of mixed methods designs. In L. Curry and M. Nunez-Smith (eds.), *Mixed methods in health sciences research: a practical primer*. Thousand Oaks: SAGE Publications.

Denzin, N. (1978). *The research act: a theoretical introduction to sociological methods*. Thousand Oaks: SAGE Publications.

Dowell, J., Cleland, J., Fitzpatrick, S., McManus, C., Nicholson, S., Oppé, T., Petty-Saphon, K., King, OS., Smith, D., Thornton, S. and White, K. (2018). The UK medical education database (UKMED) what is it? Why and how might you use it?. *BMC Medical Education*, 18 (6), 1–8.

Fàbregues, S. and Molina-Azorín, J. F. (2017). Addressing quality in mixed methods research: a review and recommendations for a future agenda. *Quality & Quantity*, 51, 2847–2863.

Glass, G. (1976). Primary, secondary, and meta-analysis of research. *Educational Researcher*, 5 (10), 3–8.

Hox, J. and Boeije, H. (2005). Data collection, primary vs. secondary. In K. Kempf-Leonard (ed.), *Encyclopedia of social measurement (pp. 593–599)*. London: Elsevier.

Hunt, J. (2016). *Speech to Conservative Party conference*, 4 October 2016. Available at: http://press.conservatives.com/post/151337276050/hunt-speech-to-conservative-party-conference-2016.

Johnson, R., Onwuegbuzie, A. and Turner, L. (2007). Toward a definition of mixed methods research. *Journal of Mixed Methods Research*, 1 (2), 112–133.

Khoushhal, Z., Hussain M., …Greco, E. (2017). Prevalence and causes of attrition among surgical residents: a systematic review and meta-analysis. *JAMA Surgery*, 152 (3), 265–272.

Marmot, M. (2020). Health equity in England: the Marmot review 10 years on. *BMJ*, 2020, 368.

McManus, S., Bebbington, P., Jenkins, R. and Brugha, T. (eds.) (2016). *Mental health and wellbeing in England: adult psychiatric morbidity survey 2014*. Leeds: NHS Digital.

132 David Harrison et al.

Medical Schools Council. (2014). *Selecting for excellence: final report*. Available at: www.med-schools.ac.uk/SiteCollectionDocuments/Selecting-for-Excellence-Final-Report.pdf.

Medical Schools Council. (2016). *Implementing selecting for excellence: a progress update*. Available at: www.medschools.ac.uk/SiteCollectionDocuments/Selecting-for-Excellence-2016-update-MSC.pdf.

NHS. (2019a). *NHS long term plan*. Available at: https://www.longtermplan.nhs.uk/publication/nhs-long-term-plan/.

NHS. (2019b). *Interim NHS people plan*. Available at: https://www.longtermplan.nhs.uk/publication/interim-nhs-people-plan/.

NHS. (2017). *National psychiatry recruitment – fill rates & competition ratios*. Available at: https://www.nwpgmd.nhs.uk/national_Psychiatry_Recruitment_Comp_Ratios_Fill_Rates.

Streeton, R., Cooke, M. and Campbell, J. (2004). Researching the researchers: Using a snow-balling technique. *Nurse Researcher*, 12 (1), 35–46.

Steven, K., Dowell, J., Jackson, C. et al. (2016). Fair access to medicine? Retrospective analysis of UK medical schools application data 2009-2012 using three measures of socioeconomic status. *BMC Medical Education*, 16 11, 1–10.

The King's Fund. (2019). *Closing the gap: key areas for action on the health and care workforce*. Available at: https://www.kingsfund.org.uk/publications/closing-gap-health-care-workforce?utm_source=The%20King%27s%20Fund%20newsletters%20%28main%20account%29%20&utm_medium=email&utm_campaign=10393870_NEWSL_The%20Weekly%20Update%202019%C2%AC03-21&utm_content=Closing_the_gap_button&dm_i=21A8,66RYM,FLX9OH,OCYQ7,1.

Wisdom, J. and Creswell, J. (2013). *Mixed methods: integrating quantitative and qualitative data collection and analysis while studying patient-centered medical home models* [AHRQ Publication No. 13-0028-EF]. Rockville, MD: Agency for Healthcare Research and Quality.

6

COMMUNITY-PARTICIPATORY INVESTIGATION OF THE HEALTH-ENVIRONMENT-WELLBEING NEXUS OF WASH IN RURAL ESWATINI

Michelle R. Brear

Background

Water, sanitation and hygiene (WaSH) resources (Table 6.1), including infrastructure, access, behaviours and beliefs, influence human and environmental health and wellbeing in profound and complex ways (Bartram and Cairncross, 2010). Enhancing WaSH resources could avert 1.5% of all deaths and 5.5% of child deaths globally, including over half a million deaths each year associated with inadequate water and over a quarter of a million related to inadequate sanitation (Prüss-Ustün et al., 2014). Access to sanitation infrastructure and behavioural changes that adequately contained and/or treated human excreta would also significantly reduce water and soil pollution, improving ecological integrity and biodiversity in ways that supported human health (Hutton and Chase, 2016). Further, enhancing WaSH has great potential to improve wellbeing, for example, by enabling women in sub-Saharan Africa who use 40 billion hours annually labouring to fetch water (UNDP, 2019) to divert their time and energy to more rewarding and/or productive work. Achieving universal access to WaSH is the focus of United Nations sustainable development goal (SDG) 6, and a prerequisite for achieving other SDGs (e.g. gender equality, health and sustainable community development; Contzen, Pasquale and Mosler, 2015a).

Enhancing WaSH to achieve the SDGs requires understanding its complexity. Accurately measuring WaSH infrastructure is important but inadequate. Research also needs to elicit how individual behaviours and structural factors influence access to and actual use of WaSH infrastructure. Mixed-methods research is ideally suited to understanding this complexity.

DOI: 10.4324/9780429263484-7

134 Michelle R. Brear

TABLE 6.1 WaSH infrastructure and related practices

Term	Definition	Related infrastructure	Related practices
Water	Infrastructure and behaviours that make accessible for individual (domestic) use, a water supply that meets health guidelines for bacterial (e.g. *E. coli*) and toxin (e.g. arsenic) contamination	• Water pipes • Water treatment facilities • Water storage equipment (tanks, drums) • Barriers to protect water sources (e.g. fences around springs)	• Walking to fetch water from a distant source • Head-loading or using draught (animal) or machine power to transport water • Turning on the tap • On-site solar, heat or chlorine treatment • Harvesting rainwater • Building a barrier to protect a water source • Perceptions and beliefs about water safety and treatment practices
Sanitation	Infrastructure and practices that result in the separation of human excreta	• Flushing toilets • Pit latrines • Composting toilets • Separation of sanitary (menstrual hygiene) products from human contact • Sewage storage facilities (e.g. septic tanks) • Sewage treatment facilities	• Open defecation or defecation using a toilet or latrine • Re-use of human waste as fertiliser in food systems • Disposal of nappies and children's stools • Choice of sanitary products • Washing or disposal techniques for sanitary towels • Cultural beliefs about appropriate toileting practices
Hygiene	Infrastructure and practices that reduce the spread of infectious disease	• Running water and soap • Waste disposal sites and infrastructure	• Washing hands with soap, especially after contact with human excreta and before eating • Digging a rubbish pit • Waste removal, including menstrual waste • Food hygiene, including washing food utensils and food storage • Safe on-site water storage • Perceptions regarding hygiene practices

(Hutton and Chase, 2016; McMichael, 2018; Bartram et al., 2014, JMP, 2019)

In this chapter, I describe a community-participatory approach to developing a qualitatively driven mixed-methods study (i.e. a mixed-methods study in which qualitative formed the core and quantitative the supplementary data; Morse and Cheek, 2015), which produced a comprehensive WaSH dataset. I detail the various methods a group of community co-researchers and I designed and implemented to 'find out' about WaSH and how I integrated WaSH data generated using the different qualitative and quantitative methods for abductive analysis (i.e. iterative analysis in which the researcher switches between inductive/empirical and abstract/theoretical reasoning so that insights drawn from data are considered in relation to theory and new theoretical insights checked through further engagement with data). The chapter concludes with a presentation of findings that highlight the 'meta-inferences' (i.e. findings that reveal more than the sum of their qualitative and quantitative parts and that could not have been gleaned by considering either the qualitative or quantitative data alone) that resulted from integrated analysis of the mixed-methods data (Onwuegbuzie and Combs, 2010; Fetters and Freshwater, 2015). The study formed the basis of my PhD thesis and was conducted in the Kingdom of Eswatini (formerly Swaziland), a southern African nation of 1.2 million people, with the highest prevalence (27%) of HIV globally. The majority of the Swazi population (63%) live in poverty, and considerable proportions lack access to improved water (28%) and/or sanitation (43%) facilities (UNICEF, 2013).

Strengths and limitations of quantitative and qualitative approaches to researching WaSH

The primary source of data used to monitor the achievement of SDG6, clean water and sanitation for all, is large-scale household surveys implemented either with nationally representative samples or entire populations (Bartram et al., 2014). These include national censuses, multiple indicator cluster surveys, demographic and health surveys (DHS) and living standards measurement surveys. These quantitative research instruments typically enquire about WaSH in different locations within and between countries using standardised indicators (i.e. the same survey questions or variables; JMP, 2019). Such standardisation enables geographic and temporal comparisons – that is, comparisons within and between countries and over time (Bartram et al., 2014). Standardised data about WaSH infrastructure and behaviours are typically collected alongside and/or linked to infectious disease prevalence data to infer the degree of protection or risk associated with WaSH (Hutton and Chase, 2016).

However, meaningful comparison requires that data derived from asking the same survey questions to different populations and/or at different times are both valid (measure what they intend to) and reliable (consistently return the same answer) (Neumayer, 2002). Both validity and reliability require that the standard terminology used in survey questions has universal meaning – for example, that words like 'household', 'toilet' and/or 'handwashing' mean the same thing to all people, in all places, at all points in time. Conversely, most terms have culturally specific meanings, that differ between, for example, survey designers, analysts and respondents (Neumayer, 2002; Steinert et al., 2018) and change over time, including as a result of research interventions (Contzen, Pasquale and Mosler, 2015a; Uprichard and Dawney, 2019). For example, people may be reluctant to admit to 'open defecation' after being taught that they should use a toilet (Bardosh, 2015; McMichael, 2018). If assumptions regarding the universal meaning of survey terminology are false, as evidence suggests they are (Neumayer, 2002; Steinert et al., 2018), standardised survey questions designed in one context could not be expected to return valid and reliable data in all other (often linguistically and culturally different) contexts.

In addition to potential problems with reliability and validity of data, standard international surveys focus primarily on WaSH infrastructure (Bartram et al., 2014). Access to WaSH infrastructure is often used as a proxy for actual behaviour. For example, having a tap, toilet or handwashing area and soap in one's yard are, respectively, assumed to represent access to safe water, use of the toilet for defecation and implementation of appropriate handwashing practices. These assumptions are problematised by available evidence. Even in high-income countries, the quality of piped water may not consistently meet guidelines for safe levels of bacterial and toxic contaminants (Bartram and Cairncross, 2010). There are numerous reasons why people who own toilets do not always use them, including cultural preferences and seasonal water shortages (McMichael, 2018). Available evidence suggests that people who have access to handwashing facilities do not consistently wash their hands at important moments, such as after using the toilet (Contzen, Meili and Mosler, 2015b).

Quantitative survey data provide an important source of evidence that enables monitoring changes and making comparisons over time and between groups. These can highlight inequalities and priority areas for intervention. However, survey data produce a limited understanding of, and potentially misrepresent, people's access to WaSH infrastructure and their WaSH-related practices (Bartram et al., 2014).

Qualitative studies of WaSH and its health-environment-wellbeing associations can generate insights that standardised, large-scale, quantitative surveys are not designed to produce. This includes, for example, information about people's lived experiences of changing access to WaSH resources and the socially constructed meanings they derive from them (O'reilly and Louis, 2014). Qualitative research can also reveal specificities of validity and reliability problems in quantitative data and/or inform the development of more valid and reliable quantitative research instruments (Bond et al., 2019). For example, although time-consuming and costly, qualitative direct observation methods are widely considered to produce the most reliable data about hygiene behaviours (e.g. handwashing; Contzen, Pasquale and Mosler, 2015a). Qualitative research has also provided insights regarding validity problems of standard sanitation survey protocols.

The potential of mixed-methods approaches to understand the complexity of WaSH

The strengths and limitations of both qualitative and quantitative approaches hint at the potential mixed-methods approaches have to generate accurate and holistic understandings of the complexity of WaSH, which are adequate to inform policy and practice for achieving SDG6 (Bartram et al., 2014). For example, qualitative studies can enhance knowledge of what people think about WaSH and why they do not develop and/or use WaSH infrastructure, as well as the sensitivities which require consideration in data collection procedures (e.g. trusted interviewers or anonymity because of the social stigma that can be attached to behaviours such as open defecation; McMichael, 2018). However, qualitative findings are not generalisable, do not enable comparison over time nor provide an overview of WaSH resources at a given point in time or longitudinally (Bartram et al., 2014). These limitations can and must be overcome with quantitative data if health researchers and practitioners are to adequately understand the complexities of WaSH and its inter-relations with, and the potential and actual effectiveness of, WaSH interventions.

Mixed-methods approaches plausibly generate more robust understandings of the phenomenon and provide more policy- and change- relevant insights. However, mixed-methods research remains an emerging field, still dominated by the assumption that it involves adding a small qualitative enquiry to 'supplement' the 'real' quantitative data (Morse and Cheek, 2015). Although the importance of qualitatively driven approaches to mixed-methods research is receiving increasing attention, practical examples of how to de-centre quantitative methods are limited.

Aims

In this chapter, I describe a participatory approach to designing a qualitatively driven mixed-methods study that generated a comprehensive WaSH dataset. I begin by describing the participatory design of qualitative and quantitative instruments used to collect data about WaSH, before detailing various ways in which data were integrated with the aim of achieving 'meta-inference' (i.e. understandings that could not be gleaned from either the qualitative or quantitative data alone; Onwuegbuzie and Combs, 2010; Fetters and Freshwater, 2015). My aims are to demonstrate the insights that qualitatively driven mixed-methods research enables and provide an example that stimulates creative thinking about the variety of ways in which methods might be mixed to better understand health-related concepts and objects, such as WaSH.

Participatory mixed-methods study design process

I address this aim utilising data from a participatory, qualitatively driven mixed-methods study that I designed and implemented in partnership with ten community co-researchers in rural Eswatini. Primary analysis of the data focused on health capability deprivations (Brear et al., 2018). However, the comprehensive data generated through the study provided considerable scope for understanding the complexities of specific health capabilities through further analysis of focused datasets. In this chapter, I present results of analysing a dataset combining all WaSH-related data from the study, which incorporated participatory mapping and photography, focus group, interview, participant observation and survey methods (Table 6.2).

138 Michelle R. Brear

TABLE 6.2 Data sources from which the WaSH dataset was constructed

Data source	Sampling unit	Responses N (%)	In-text data reference	Description and notes
Participatory mapping and photography	Homesteads and water sources	N/A	N/A	Fieldwork to identify, photograph[1] and plot on a map all water sources and homesteads
Homestead survey	Homestead[2]	125 (99)	HM:NNN (e.g. HM034)	Questions about toilet type, water source and number of households in the homestead[3]
Household survey	Household	151 (99)	HS:NNN (e.g. HS035)	Questions about household membership, transporting water and access to soap and a section for qualitative comments[3]
Health capability focus group discussions	Individual community members	120 (76)	Pseudonym[4]- Age-Sex (e.g. Tipho-45-F)	Focused on the health-related benefits and challenges in the community
Co-researcher focus group discussions and interviews	Individual community members	N/A	Pseudonym[4]- Sex (e.g. Mary-F)	Focused on the participatory research process and the co-researchers' experiences designing and implementing a study about health capability
Participant observation-research process	Research workshop or fieldwork event	N/A	PO:DD-MM-YYYY (e.g. PO:12-12-2013)	Documenting workshops and fieldwork with community-co-researchers

[1] Only publicly accessible water sources were photographed systematically. Selected toilets, located on private land were photographed for illustrative purposes.

[2] A homestead is the key unit of land tenure in rural Swaziland and a domestic grouping, potentially including more than one household (e.g. an extended family unit). Homesteads were identified through the participatory mapping exercise.

[3] Including questions that utilised the water source mapping results and through which toilets were mapped.

[4] Community member pseudonyms are all Siswati-language names and were chosen and allocated by a co-researcher. Co-researcher pseudonyms are all English-language names selected by the co-researchers, as discussed in Brear et al. (2018).

Community-participatory investigation **139**

The participatory research co-design process involved community members as co-researchers in all stages of the research process, including designing the study and interpreting the results. The process is described fully in Brear, Hammarberg and Fisher (2020). The process of co-designing the health capability research involved 21 participatory workshops in which the co-researchers contributed their ideas and knowledge through activities that I modified from an HIV-focused participatory methods toolkit (International HIV/AIDS Alliance, 2009). The co-researchers read introductory materials in preparation for the workshops, each of which involved two to three activities designed to facilitate their exploration of the range of possible research methodologies, methods, instruments, variables and sampling techniques that could be used and deciding which ones to actually use to study health capability in their community. The intention was to make the research optimally sensitive to, and appropriate for, the community context.

The co-researchers decided to employ a mixed-methods study design which incorporated three data collection methods: (1) participatory mapping of all homesteads (extended family units potentially including multiple households) and water collection points in the community, (2) a DHS that combined standard *etic* (foreign) and unique *emic* (local) variables to collect data about a range of health-related behaviours and characteristics at three levels (homestead, household and individual) and (3) focus group discussions about the health-related benefits and challenges community members faced. The following section describes how each of these methods was used to generate data about WaSH. I used participant observation and interview methods to capture the process through which the co-researchers and I co-designed and implemented the study, including for example their deliberations about how best to find out about WaSH infrastructure and behaviours.

Finding out about WaSH

Water

Standard water survey variables (Table 6.3a), although relatively quick and easy to collect data for, have proven invalid. For example, because it is too time-consuming to measure actual distance to water sources, the standard survey question, a proxy indicator for distance, asks respondents to self-report total time taken to collect water (Table 6.3a). The co-researchers for this study reported that women (those responsible for collecting household water according to local gender norms) were unlikely to keep track of the time when they collected water. The five women co-researchers felt unable to accurately estimate the time they took to collect water for their households. Even if accurate estimations of time were possible, the co-researchers perceived time would be a meaningless proxy for distance because walking speeds varied and 'too far' to water was a relative concept that depended on factors like age and physical condition (PO:14-01-2013).

The co-researchers also reported they were unfamiliar with some of the standard water survey terminology (e.g. 'protected spring' and 'surface water'; Table 6.3a).

140 Michelle R. Brear

They suspected these terms would also be foreign to community members. We thus developed unique quantitative survey questions (Table 6.3a) that integrated qualitative data from a participatory water source mapping exercise (described next).

TABLE 6.3A Standardised and corresponding unique water survey variables developed for the participatory health capability study

Standard etic (foreign, external) variables	Unique emic (indigenous, local) variables
What is the main source of drinking water used by members of your household?	*Does this homestead[1] get most of its drinking water…?*
• Piped water	• Piped into your homestead fence
o Piped into dwelling	• From a source away from your homestead
o Piped to yard/plot	• Other
o Piped to neighbour	*How many water tanks do the members of your homestead own?*
o Public tap/standpipe	• Number response
• Tube well/borehole	*How many water drums do the members of your homestead own?*
• Dug well	• Number response
o Protected well	*If the homestead gets water from a source away from the homestead, indicate where (on the map)?*
o Unprotected well	• Water source identification number
• Spring	*How do members of your household[1] usually transport water from the source?*
o Protected spring	• Water is piped to the homestead
o Unprotected spring	• On head
• Rainwater	• In a wheelbarrow
• Tanker truck	• Other
• Cart with small tank	*Do you treat your water before drinking it?*
• Water kiosk	• Yes
• Surface water (river, dam, lake, pond, stream, canal, irrigation channel)	• No
• Packaged water (bottles or sachets)	• Don't know
o Bottled water	*If yes, what is done to treat the water?*
o Sachet water	• Boil
• Other (*specify*)	• Add Jik/bleach
(A separate question with the same response categories is asked for cooking and hand washing)	• Leave it to settle
Where is that water source located?	• Other
• In own dwelling	
• In own yard/plot	
• Elsewhere	
How long does it take for members of your household to go there, get water and come back?	
• Members do not collect	
• Number of minutes	
• Don't know	

[1] *Water survey questions were variously asked at the homestead or household level. For example, water source was asked at the homestead level, as all households in the homestead would use the same source. However, members of each household would collect their own water separately using the transport method of their choice.*

Participatory mapping and photography

The co-researchers worked in pairs to map all 'water sources' (i.e. points at which women collected water, typically using a 20- or 25-litre container). Carrying print-outs of Google Earth satellite maps, they walked around the village, asking their fellow community members where they collected water. They marked each water source on the map and labelled it using a number before walking to, photograph-ing and recording notes about what they observed at each. Photographs and notes were linked to the water source identification number. I plotted the co-researchers' paper-based water source data to an electronic Google Earth map, on which I had already plotted all homesteads (extended family units potentially including mul-tiple households) in the community (using paper-based data produced by the co-researchers in conjunction with community headmen).

Survey

The co-researchers and I utilised the water source maps to develop unique water questions for our homestead and household surveys (Table 6.3a). These were intended to overcome the known limitations of standardised variables (e.g. poor correspondence between self-reported water collection times and distance to water source) and problems we expected to occur in our community context (e.g. respon-dents not understanding terminology such as 'surface water'). The unique variables we developed were intended to be easily understood by the co-researchers who would enumerate, and the community members who would respond to, the survey questions. We also wanted to produce optimally valid and reliable data that could, if necessary, be recoded to match the response categories of standard water variables. For example, we intended to use photographs and observations of each water source to classify it according to standard terminology, as (protected or unprotected) sur-face, well or spring water.

Sanitation

Standard sanitation questions rely on participants' self-reported latrine ownership or access and therefore their understanding, of specific latrine-type terminology (Table 6.3b). Standard survey protocols only ask the enumerator to observe the latrine if it is a flush or pour latrine, and the respondent does not know where it pours to (JMP, 2019). This approach implies a universal understanding of standard sanitation termi-nology. However, socially constructed terms such as 'ventilated improved pit latrine' (VIP latrine) do not always easily or directly translate meaningfully into vernacu-lar. This is acknowledged in the alternative approach to enumerating toilet survey variables recommended by the World Bank Group of using photographs 'to help illustrate the different latrine response options' to survey enumerators, who then prompt respondents for details to help them determine latrine type and/or observe the latrine directly (WBG, 2014). This approach implies that respondents are unable

142 Michelle R. Brear

to accurately report their latrine type but that enumerators can determine toilet type through a subjective questioning process.

Our participatory design experience indicated that in our community, survey respondents would not be able to accurately self-report their toilet type. For example, the co-researchers used the term 'healthy toilet' to refer to any latrine with a cement slab and 'chimney' (i.e. ventilation pipe), whether or not it was a VIP latrine (i.e. a lidless toilet in an unlit, door-less building with an air vent and gauze-covered pipe, features which collectively function to hasten biodegradation and ensure flies that enter the latrine are trapped inside (WHO, 2004)). Although all the co-researchers initially suggested including the standard DHS toilet question (Table 6.3b), none knew what a VIP latrine was (PO:04-01-2013).

TABLE 6.3B Standardised and corresponding unique sanitation survey variables developed for the participatory health capability study

Standard variables	Unique variables
What kind of toilet facility do members of your household usually use?	*What sort of toilet does your homestead have?*
• **Flush/pour flush**	• Flush toilet
o flush to piped sewer system	• Pit latrine
o flush to septic tank	• No toilet/forest
o flush to pit latrine	• Other
o flush to open drain	*If the toilet is a pit latrine, does it*
o flush to don't know where	*have (read options, tick all that*
• **Pit latrine**	*apply)*
o VIP latrine	• Cement floor
o pit latrine with slab	• Chimney covered with gauze
o pit latrine without slab	• Lid
o open pit	• None of the above
• Composting toilet	*If the homestead has a toilet, ask*
• Bucket	*the respondent to indicate on the*
• Hanging toilet/hanging latrine	*homestead map which building*
• No facility/bush/field	*houses the toilet or latrine.*
Other (*specify*)	
IF 'FLUSH' OR 'POUR FLUSH', PROBE:	
• Where does it flush to?	
If not possible to determine, ask permission to observe the facility.	

The co-researchers also reported that in multi-household homesteads, there was usually one shared toilet (PO:04-01-2013). As standard WaSH data is collected at the household level, and one of the requirements for classifying sanitation facilities as 'improved' is that the latrine should not be shared by multiple households (more for dignity and safety than health reasons; WHO, 2016), this insight had important implications for our survey design. Had we collected data at the household level we might inadvertently have over-estimated latrine ownership if each household in the homestead reported having a latrine when they actually shared one. However, sharing a latrine at the homestead level (i.e. with extended family members who live in close proximity) has very different dignity and safety implications compared to sharing distant and/or public toilets. We would also have lost important data about the meaning of sharing a toilet if unable to distinguish between sharing with the general public compared to family members.

Survey

Our unique sanitation survey variables (Table 6.3b) were intended to overcome both the global and context-specific limitations of standardised variables that we identified through the participatory design process. They were further intended to produce data that corresponded with, and could be mapped back to, standard variable response categories. The homestead survey, which was completed by a single respondent (the official head to whom the land was tenured, typically an older man), asked about latrine ownership and characteristics of the latrine, using local terminology (Table 6.3b). As each homestead survey was linked to a separate survey for each of its households, this approach enabled us to determine the number of households within each homestead and calculate variables about household latrine access and homestead-level latrine sharing.

Participatory mapping

The co-researchers embedded a further participatory mapping activity into the homestead-level survey to determine the location of homesteads in the community that had a latrine and the location of the latrine within the homestead in relation to other dwellings (e.g. kitchen, sleeping quarters). Our homestead survey included a printed satellite image of the homestead, which the enumerator annotated to indicate the uses of different dwellings (living, cooking and storage huts and the toilet) and outdoor (animal husbandry, crop production) areas based on the respondents' answers. Latrine location data was plotted to the Google Earth satellite map by a co-researcher.

Hygiene

Although improved hygiene, especially handwashing, could substantially reduce infectious disease and related deaths (Bartram and Cairncross, 2010), it was relatively neglected in our mixed-methods health capability study, compared to water and sanitation. This was primarily because the co-researchers reported that handwashing with soap was so uncommon, and dedicated handwashing facilities so rare, that we could assume washing hands with soap was an exceptional behaviour. The co-researchers and I had initially planned to include survey questions about menstrual waste disposal and handwashing behaviours, as well as handwashing facilities. However, when reducing our survey to a length that we could feasibly implement within our time

144 Michelle R. Brear

and budgetary constraints, we decided to elide most of the hygiene questions and enquire only about the availability of soap (Table 6.3c; PO:09-04-2013).

TABLE 6.3C Standardised and corresponding unique hygiene survey variables developed for the participatory health capability study

Standard variables	Unique variables
Where do you or other members of your household most often wash your hands?	Can your household always afford to buy enough soap?
• Fixed facility (sink/tap)	• Yes
o in dwelling	• No
o in yard/plot	
• Mobile object	
o (bucket/jug/kettle)	
• No handwashing place in dwelling/yard/plot	
• Other (specify)	
Do you have any soap or detergent or ash/mud/sand in your house for washing hands?	
• Yes	
• No	
Thereafter, enumerators are instructed to observe the handwashing facilities and soap and record the type.	

Supplementary techniques for collecting data about all aspects of WaSH

The mixed-method study also incorporated three qualitative data collection techniques for enquiring about health capability broadly. These were participant observation, focus group discussions and a qualitative comments question on the household surveys. All were expected to generate data, not only about the individual components of WaSH but also their inter-relations. Water and toilets were expected to be discussed primarily as challenges. Handwashing was not expected to be a prominent topic of discussion.

I collected participant observation data about the participatory research process. This included data about workshops in which co-researchers discussed how to design the study (including the aspects that investigated WaSH) and/or their experiences implementing the research or analysing the data. Following the participatory research principle of using an asset-based approach, focus group discussions enquired first about the benefits of living in the study community and later the challenges. As they were intended to elicit participants' perspectives about priority health capabilities (or deprivations), no probes about WaSH were included in the schedule. The household-level survey included a 'comments' question at which the enumerator could record information they perceived to be important. Enumerators were specifically asked to record information shared by the respondents or observations made while completing the survey through face-to-face interviews at the respondents' households, which were related to health capability but not captured in the survey and/or might influence our interpretation of survey data.

Techniques for integrating data to better understand WaSH

The qualitative and quantitative techniques and data were integrated during the design, implementation and analysis phases to better understand WaSH.

Mixing methods and data for sampling

Using (qualitative) map data to determine the (quantitative) census survey population

The map data qualitatively visualised the spatial layout of homesteads in the community (Figure 6.1). Homesteads on the map served as the census population and the maps were used to track which homesteads had been invited to and/or actually participated in the census survey. As the co-researchers did not have access to

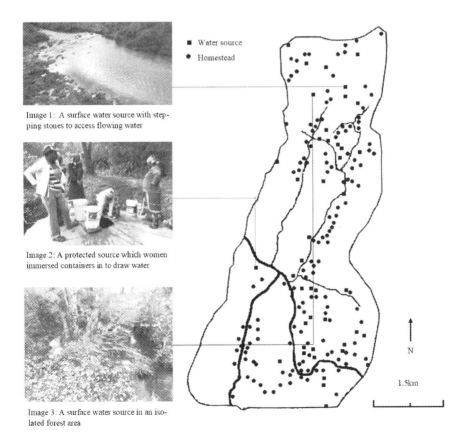

FIGURE 6.1 Community map with images of selected water sources

146 Michelle R. Brear

computers or the internet, this approach involved printing a master satellite map of the entire community and maps of sections of the community, both of which showed all homesteads and water sources and their identification numbers. Section maps were given to survey enumerators each day to carry with them and use to identify the homesteads they would visit and invite to participate in the survey. Each enumerator was also given several survey copies, allocated to specific homesteads or households in the section via the map identification numbers. One co-researcher tracked the comings and goings of surveys and the homesteads that had and had not been invited to and/or completed the survey.

The tracking system was intended to ensure that all homesteads were visited (up to three times) and invited to participate and surveyed (only once if they consented). It was also intended to ensure that, in the unlikely event that one or more surveys were misplaced, we became aware and could follow up with the appropriate enumerator. It achieved this purpose. At the completion of the survey, all homesteads had been visited (and marked on the map with a red sticker), and all paper-based surveys were accounted for.

Sampling focus group discussion participants using and linking their comments to participant demographic survey data

The co-researchers wanted to invite community members of different ages and sexes to participate in their focus group discussions. They decided to use a stratified random sampling technique so that the selection process was perceived to be fair (not with the intention of generalising the results). Demographic data generated through the census survey, which achieved a 99% response rate at both homestead and household levels, were used to define the population from which focus group discussion participants were sampled. We stratified the demographic data by sex (male or female) and age (5–8, 9–12, 13–18, 18–25 and 26 and above) and then printed lists of household members in each stratum and cut them into individual demographic records (i.e. strips of paper each detailing the demographic information and unique identifier of a single household member). The demographic records for each stratum were placed in a 'hat' from which a co-researcher selected ten records. Thereafter, a pair of co-researchers visited the household and invited the person selected (e.g. the 27-year-old female) to participate in a focus group discussion. After conducting the focus group and preparing translations, we linked the narratives of different participants back to their survey data.

Combining data from different qualitative sources for integrated analysis

During the initial exploratory coding of the qualitative data corpus (i.e. all qualitative data from the mixed-method study), I coded to create focused datasets. Some codes related to preidentified (e.g. health capability, power, participation) topics, while others captured issues that my readings of the data indicated were important.

For example, although WaSH was expected to be an important component of health capability, I did not initially intend to conduct any WaSH-specific analysis. The importance and complexities of WaSH and the value of creating a WaSH-specific dataset for further interrogation only became apparent during the primary analysis. Although WaSH was mentioned in passing, I felt unable to adequately detail the complexities in a write-up of my health capability-focused analysis (Brear et al., 2018). I, therefore, combined several codes (water, toilets and handwashing) from the health capability analysis, to form a preliminary qualitative WaSH dataset. I added to the dataset through further manual coding of data sources (e.g. focus group transcripts) and data segments identified through keyword searches (e.g. water, toilet, bathing, washing). The result was a comprehensive set of information that combined the co-researchers' comments on WaSH in the design, implementation and analysis stages of the research and the focus group discussion and survey participants' narratives related to WaSH. This dataset forms the core of the interpretive thematic analysis presented in the ensuing results section. Interpretive analysis approaches aim to go beyond what people say and do by analytically utilising the consistencies and contradictions both explicit and implicit in the data to elucidate meaning.

Interfacing qualitative and quantitative data in the results narrative

Bringing findings from separate analyses together, with the results write-up as the 'point of interface' (Morse, 2016) is a common technique for integrating qualitative and quantitative results in mixed-methods research. I used a qualitatively driven approach. This involved firstly writing a draft narrative based on my qualitative analysis and then selecting relevant quantitative results that provided insights which augmented the qualitative findings.

Results and discussion

Integrating qualitative and quantitative findings provided a comprehensive picture of WaSH and their interactions at the nexus of health-environment-wellbeing.

Water

Although groundwater-fed springs and streams meant that water was available year-round in the community, comments such as, 'There is no water in this area' (Lungelo-57-M) were common. They were references to water being unclean and/or difficult to access. Contamination of surface and 'protected' water sources in the community was fundamentally associated with lack of sanitation infrastructure and, related to that, open defecation (discussed below). However, people also reported that in winter when animals grazed freely, it was common to find, 'cows and goats and pigs [sharing the water sources] and the cows maybe urinate in the water' (Samuel-M) that community members collected for domestic purposes, including drinking. Despite knowing the water was unclean, only 11 survey respondents (7%)

reported treating water (either by boiling or adding chlorine) before drinking it. This was apparently not due to a lack of knowledge of health risks. For example, one participant said, 'We are usually told to cook the water to kill the germs and drink it after it has cooled and put it in a bottle, but we don't do that. When you are thirsty you can't wait to do this' (Sandile-age missing-M). Although the water was unclean, being able to access it for free was important for some participants. For example, one reported, 'We also get water, even though it is not very clean. We don't have to buy it like they do in town' (Thuli-19-F).

Even protected and piped water sources were contaminated. For example, drawing water from one protected source, a 5,000L concrete tank (Figure 6.1, Image 2), required one to stand atop the tank and pass their container through a hole to immerse it. The co-researchers who mapped and photographed the water source observed that the top of the tank was covered in soap residue and explained this was caused by people washing blankets on top of the tank, which also allowed dirty and soapy water to drip into the tank and contaminate the water (PO:07-05-2013). Although a water project had provided 36 homesteads (42 households) in one valley access to piped water, some co-researchers and community members reported the water was drawn from a dam outside the community, which was contaminated by animals and used for baptisms (PO:14-11-2013). Despite being stored in plastic tanks after being drawn from the dam, the water was apparently not treated (PO:14-11-2013).

For the remaining 82 homesteads and 96 households that relied on an off-site source, water was not only dirty but also difficult to access. This was partly because it was relatively far away, although rarely further than the equivalent of 30-minutes-or-less total collection time used to differentiate 'limited' and 'basic' access to water in international classification systems (JMP, 2019). For example, only 31 (20%) households travelled 1 km or further (round trip) to their primary water source (the equivalent of 20 minutes total water collection time assuming an average slow walking speed of 4 km per hour and five minutes to fill the water container). However, women who head-loaded water from source to household, reported water was 'very far, down in the valley. We have to climb mountains to get it back to our homes' (Nomvula-20-F). Several discussed the risk of injury this entailed; for example, young women talked about the possibility of 'injuring our backbones' (Lindiwe-22-F). Older women made comments such as, 'We get water from the springs which are too far. You can't go there twice in a row' (Nomcebo-45-F), 'As old as we are, we are not able to take even a 5 litre and go to the river, we get tired just from carrying that small container' (Phindile-70-F, who was the only adult female in her household and lived 750 m from her primary water source) and 'That forest for the water… the [grandmothers] sometimes they fall down because… there is a lot of mud' (Mary-F). Collecting at some water sources also entailed injury risk, associated, for example, with stepping on stones to access flowing water from rivers (Figure 6.1, Image 1), which the results for sanitation (next) suggest was highly likely to be contaminated with faecal pathogens. Collecting water from isolated sources in the forest (Figure 6.1, Image 3) was also perceived as risky because 'these

Community-participatory investigation **149**

days there are many thieves, you become scared when you go to get water… scared to send your children to fetch water' (Zodwa-45-F).

Sanitation

Co-researcher and community members' narratives indicated that open defecation was common. For example, one said, 'In this community [we] do not have toilets… [we] just go to the nearby forest and when the rain comes it washes [the faeces] away to the river, then we get that water for drinking with my children and cook with that water' (Dumsile-57-F). Survey results concurred, showing that less than half of all homesteads (38%), households (44%) and people living in the community (46%) had any type of toilet. Of the 48 toilets in the community, only 38 were built on a cement slab and only 8 had a ventilation pipe.

Knowledge of the recommended latrine design for reducing fly-borne transmission of faecal pathogens (i.e. a VIP latrine designed to trap flies in the latrine) was apparently limited. Community members only mentioned being taught to prevent flies from entering the latrine by closing the lid. For example, one said, 'We have been taught to cover the toilets. You don't leave the toilet open after using it. There is also this net you have to use [to cover the chimney] so that the flies won't get in' (Lwazi-85-M). The co-researchers indicated that it was common for community members to 'treat' their toilet with chemical disinfectants to reduce flies (PO:18-12-12) a practice that interferes with biodegradation of faeces and faecal pathogens (WHO, 2004).

Most community members (55%) used the forest as a toilet despite having sound knowledge of the health risks associated with open defecation. For example, numerous participants reported, 'Homesteads in this place do not have toilets…we just go to the bushes…[and] that causes sickness because it runs to the water we drink on the other side' (Sandile-age missing-M). Defecating in the forest despite knowing the health risks was explained as being underpinned by a combination of financial poverty, lack of labour power and habit. In a community where two-thirds of all households were headed by widowed women or absent men, and 55% of 18- to 50-year-old men who were listed as household members lived away most of the time (usually as migrant workers), labour power was in short supply. As one community researcher put it, 'They don't have power, the grandmothers, to dig two metres' (Mary-F) down to make a toilet pit. Even if they could dig, many community members could not afford to buy the materials needed to build a toilet. For example, one participant said, 'I dug a toilet but there was no one to continue with it…. My children who could have [bought the building material I needed] have died' (Sbongile-59-F, she lived with only her two grandchildren aged 8 and 13 years). Another, although confident he could dig the toilet pit needed 'help with the material because we don't have the money…[to buy] cement and everything to make it a good toilet so that those from health can say it is well built' (Lungelo-57-M).

A strong, well-built toilet was not just an abstract health department requirement. Expensive building materials were required to make the toilet physically safe.

150 Michelle R. Brear

For example, one survey respondent reported that they were too scared to use their pit latrine because its concrete slab had cracked (HM086). Two told the enumerator that their basic pit latrine (without a concrete slab; HM025 & HM044) had collapsed during heavy rains.

A few participants perceived that some community members could 'afford [to build toilets] but they say, "there is a forest, God provided this forest, so what's wrong with [defecating in] it?"' (Mary-F). This was not only because they wanted to save money. Using a toilet was perceived to be foreign and unpleasant for some people who might 'tell you that they grew up using the forest to release themselves. They say they can't release themselves sitting on the chair, they…wouldn't use [a toilet] even if you can build it' (Makhosonkhe-19-M).

Hygiene

Although few people discussed handwashing practices in focus groups, narratives about soap were prominent, at least partly because the co-researchers gave a bar of laundry soap to each household survey respondent as a token of appreciation. Soap narratives suggested that using it for washing hands was uncommon and that spending money on soap competed with buying food. For example, one participant said, 'If you don't have money you starve, yet if you have that little you can buy mealie meal and eat and get soap for washing. If you don't have money, like the old women, they get dirty because there is no money to buy soap' (Phumaphi-67-F). The majority of survey respondents (75%) indicated that their household did not always have enough money to buy soap. Most of the co-researchers, who received a stipend, reported that soap was amongst the items that they had started purchasing. For example, one reported, 'I'm feeling very happy and proud now [about getting a stipend as a community researcher]…how would I manage to…buy sugar, salt, soap?' (Petunia-F).

Bagcugcuteli, community health workers who provided home-based care to sick people as part of the government's HIV/AIDS-impact mitigation strategy, reported difficulties accessing soap to give and/or bathe their patients (one form of care they provided to bedridden patients). They also reported that other hygiene and sanitation supplies, including adult nappies for patients with diarrhoea and 'Jik' (i.e. bleach, intended for washing towels and bedding) were often unavailable at the government clinics where *bagcugcuteli* were ostensibly able to source these hygiene products free of charge. Although none mentioned it explicitly, their general reports of not having any soap indicated that *bagcugcuteli* may sometimes (perhaps often) have lacked soap with which to wash their own hands while carrying out their community health worker duties (e.g. administering medicine and changing adult nappies).

Comments about the 1-kg bars of laundry soap given to survey respondents as a token of appreciation were prominent. As rumours about the soaps spread around the community, the co-researchers reported neighbours joking with them to hurry up and come to survey their household because they needed soap for washing (PO:05-09-2013) and that survey respondents 'really appreciate the soap and there are some people who you are seeing that this [person] is very, very struggling…no longer having even the soap for washing' (Simon-M). One in ten surveys included a comment that the respondent said thanks for the soap, and several noted the respondent reported they had run out of soap and/or that they would use the soap to wash their own and their children's clothes. Notably, narratives implied soap was used primarily for washing bodies, clothes and food utensils but rarely hands. For example, one woman reported, 'With the bar of soap [we received] we used it for washing, even though we may not have [moisturising] lotion but as long as the clothes are clean, we will send them [our children] to school' (Phumaphi-67-F, a widow who lived with her 13-year-old grandson, who, she commented during the survey, 'does not have parents').

Meta-inferences enabled by integrating data from different sources

Combining qualitative and quantitative data for integrated analysis enabled meta-inferences – that is, synergistic insights that could not have been gleaned from examining the qualitative or quantitative data alone. The qualitatively driven approach to mixed-methods analysis we adopted highlighted important aspects of WaSH and its intersections with health-environment-wellbeing that are typically neglected in research, policies and practices that are informed primarily by the results of linear approaches to analysing quantitative data. These included the profound barriers to WaSH access associated with poverty, the additional importance of WaSH in settings with a high burden of ill-health underpinned by infectious diseases and the ways in which standardised surveys might produce invalid and/or unreliable data.

The assumption that standard WaSH variables produce valid data (i.e. measure what they intend to) was shown to be (at least sometimes) unfounded through this analysis. For example, even if total collection time was a valid proxy for distance to water source (and previous research has shown it is not), these results suggest that time or distance alone are invalid proxies for access to water. For example, an elderly woman who struggles to carry a 5 L container of water would need to travel the distance to the water source four times to access the minimum 20 L per day required for drinking, food preparation and personal hygiene (WHO, 2010). The caregiver of a person living with HIV and experiencing chronic diarrhoea would need to travel to the water source four times per day to access the water needed to maintain their patient's hygiene (including laundering) and go back again for another 20 L of water needed for their own personal requirements (assuming she could carry 20 or 25 L on her head as most women in the study community could). These examples demonstrate the potential invalidity of quantitative data.

The qualitatively driven analysis also highlighted problems with the reliability of standard survey variables. For example, the VIP latrine terminology was foreign in this community. If survey respondents had been asked if they had a VIP latrine, answers would likely have been inconsistent.

The comprehensive mixed-methods WaSH dataset, produced and analysed through a community-participatory approach, suggests that knowledge and feasibly modifiable behaviours played only a minor role in determining unsatisfactory WaSH practices. Despite the indications that some WaSH knowledge was inaccurate and a perception that some people might resist changing their toileting practices, culture was portrayed in this study as having a negligible influence on WaSH-related behaviours. For example, many people that didn't have a toilet indicated they wanted one and were only constrained by finances or availability of labour power. There was no indication that culture might present a barrier to the use of improved water infrastructure. Conversely, women who had no choice but to perform the arduous labour of head-loading 20–25 L containers (of typically contaminated) water via steeply sloping terrain, from sources to households, indicated they would prefer to fetch (clean, treated) water from a tap in their yards, if only they had a choice. It is entirely plausible to think that universal access to clean water could be easily achieved in the community if the necessary infrastructure to treat and transport water were made available free of charge. However, the results suggest that due to poverty some women would probably continue to risk injuries and infections by fetching water from unimproved sources if they needed to pay for clean water. Although evidence internationally indicates that hygienic handwashing practices are difficult to put into practice, access to soap is a prerequisite for enabling handwashing. Not having soap was strongly indicated to be the primary barrier to hygienic practices, including washing clothes, bedding, bodies and hands in this community.

Collectively these results suggest that the primary determinant of WaSH enhancement is material resource access. People in this community, which was highly affected by HIV, poverty and other health capability deprivations (Brear et al., 2018), needed money to support the development of WaSH infrastructure and the enactment of hygienic WaSH practices. That even government-organised community health workers were not able to access soap to use in their home-based care work hints at the considerable lack of attention that had been given to the financial aspects of enabling WaSH in Eswatini, a country in which health is severely undermined by the very high prevalence of infectious disease, especially HIV and tuberculosis (UNICEF, 2013).

The finding that material resources are needed to improve WaSH also highlights the ethical value of using mixed-methods approaches to understand complex health-related behaviours that might otherwise be reduced to (and approached through public health campaigns as) problems with individuals. For example, community-led total sanitation, a prominent approach to improving WaSH in underdeveloped communities, relies heavily on public shaming and fining individuals who do not use toilets (McMichael, 2018). Blaming poor individuals for health problems related to their structural marginalisation, including through deficit narratives presented in research articles, undermines the ethical principle of beneficence (Smith, 2013). It potentially causes direct psychological harm if individuals are exposed to narratives that imply that they are to blame for health-related problems. It also indirectly causes physical harm via increased risk of infectious disease because placing the onus on individuals to change factors beyond their control is ineffective. It distracts attention from developing sustainable solutions that address the underlying

Community-participatory investigation   **153**

material resource deprivations that cause poor WaSH infrastructure and practices (McMichael, 2018).

The qualitatively driven results paint a complex picture of the ways in which WaSH influences and is influenced by the health-environment-wellbeing nexus. They hint at the additional importance of promoting WaSH in order to effectively mitigate the impacts of HIV and related infectious diseases and/or achieve a range of SDGs, including those for gender equality and environmental health. For example, the human and environmental health effects of poor sanitation and hygiene are exacerbated in contexts where there is a high burden of infectious diseases, such as diarrhoea-causing pathogens that enter soils and water via open defecation and respiratory infections that spread via unclean hands. Women expressed their concerns about injuries from head-loading water, the physically arduous nature of the work and their safety while collecting water from isolated sources in the forest. Many participants hinted at the negative emotions invoked by having no choice but to enact practices that undermined their dignity, such as defecating in the open and drinking water they knew to be contaminated. The results suggest that inadequate WaSH affects environmental health and people's physical and psychological wellbeing, particularly for women due to the gendered nature of water collection and care-related labour.

Conclusion

WaSH is a complex foundation for promoting human health and wellbeing, as well as enhancing environmental health. Although culture and knowledge play a role in determining WaSH access and practices, the results of this study indicate they must not be over-emphasised. These results suggest that people from cultures where open defecation, drinking dirty water and running out of soap is the norm, are willing (indeed often want) to change but face insurmountable structural barriers, especially poverty. Emphasising the cultural determinants of unhealthy WaSH practices, which are relatively minor in terms of overall influence, shifts the focus away from structural factors, especially poverty, which leave people with little choice but to enact practices that they rarely have explicit cultural attachments to and often would prefer to avoid. It masks the inequalities and limited power of the people who are so poor they cannot even afford to buy soap, let alone construct the large-scale infrastructure required for adequate water and sanitation access. Neglecting the structural factors that determine WaSH access and behaviours as standard quantitative approaches do, creates an individualistic understanding of WaSH that is ultimately inadequate to inform interventions for achieving SDG6, universal access to clean water and sanitation (to which, based on these results, I would add soap). Mixed-methods research has great potential to develop more rigorous evidence of how structures oppress and leave people with limited choices regarding, and ultimately no way of implementing, the behaviours that they know are needed to support optimal WaSH practices.

154 Michelle R. Brear

Questions for discussion and further reflection

What are the limitations of large-scale household surveys, and quantitative approaches, to identify WaSH resources, and how has Michelle's mixed-methods research design addressed these?

How does Michelle's participatory/qualitatively driven approach fit with her specific research focus?

How has Michelle integrated the findings of the different elements of data collection, and what additional insights did this provide?

In what ways has this research design surfaced issues of social justice and health inequalities?

References

Bardosh, K. (2015). Achieving "total sanitation" in rural African geographies: poverty, participation and pit latrines in Eastern Zambia. *Geoforum*, 66, 53–63.

Bartram, J., Brocklehurst, C., Fisher, M., Luyendijk, R., Hossain, R., Wardlaw, T. and Gordon, B. (2014). Global monitoring of water supply and sanitation: history, methods and future challenges. *International Journal of Environmental Research and Public Health*, 11, 8137–8165.

Bartram, J. and Cairncross, S. (2010). Hygiene, sanitation, and water: forgotten foundations of health. *PLoS Medicine*, 7, e1000367.

Bond, V., Ngwenya, F., Murray, E., Ngwenya, N., Viljoen, L., Gumede, D., Bwalya, C., Mantantana, J., Hoddinott, G. and Dodd, P. J. (2019). Value and limitations of broad brush surveys used in community-randomized trials in Southern Africa. *Qualitative Health Research*, 29, 700–718.

Brear, M. R., Hammarberg, K. and Fisher, J. (2020). Community participation in health research: an ethnography from rural Swaziland. *Health Promotion International*, 35 (1), e59–e69.

Brear, M. R., Shabangu, P. N., Fisher, J. R., Hammarberg, K., Keleher, H. M. and Livingstone, C. (2018). Health capability deprivations in a rural Swazi community: understanding complexity with theoretically informed, qualitatively driven, mixed-method design, participatory action research. *Qualitative Health Research*, 28, 1897–1909.

Contzen, N., Pasquale, S. D. and Mosler, H-J. (2015a). Over-reporting in handwashing self-reports: potential explanatory factors and alternative measurements. *PLoS One*, 10, e0136445.

Contzen, N., Meili, I. H. and Mosler, H-J. (2015b). Changing handwashing behaviour in southern Ethiopia: A longitudinal study on infrastructural and commitment interventions. *Social Science & Medicine*, 124, 103–114.

Fetters, M. D. and Freshwater, D. (2015). The 1+ 1= 3 integration challenge. *Journal of Mixed Methods Research*, 9 (2), 115–117.

Hutton, G. and Chase, C. (2016). The knowledge base for achieving the sustainable development goal targets on water supply, sanitation and hygiene. *International Journal of Environmental Research and Public Health*, 13, 536.

International HIV/AIDS Alliance. (2009). *Tools together now! 100 Participatory tools to mobilise communities for HIV/AIDS*. Available at: https://www.participatorymethods.org/resource/tools-together-now-100-participatory toolsmobilise-communities-hivaids. (Accessed 4 April 2019).

JMP, Joint Monitoring Program. (2019). *Core questions.* WHO and UNICEF. Available at: https://washdata.org/monitoring/methods/core-questions. (Accessed 4 April 2019).

McMichael, C. (2018). Toilet talk: eliminating open defecation and improved sanitation in Nepal. *Medical Anthropology*, 37, 294–310.

Morse, J. M. (2016). *Mixed method design: principles and procedures.* London; New York: Routledge.

Morse, J. M. and Cheek, J. (2015). Introducing qualitatively-driven mixed-method designs. *Qualitative Health Research*, 25, 731–733.

Neumayer, E. (2002). Do we trust the data? On the validity and reliability of cross-national environmental surveys. *Social Science Quarterly*, 83, 332–340.

O'Reilly, K. and Louis, E. (2014). The toilet tripod: understanding successful sanitation in rural India. *Health Place*, 29, 43–51.

Onwuegbuzie, A. J. and Combs, J. P. (2010). Emergent data analysis techniques in mixed methods research: a synthesis. In A. Tashakkori and C. Teddlie (eds.), *Sage hand-book of mixed methods in social and behavioral research*, 2nd ed. Thousand Oaks, CA: SAGE Publications.

Prüss-Ustün, A., Bartram, J., Clasen, T., Colford Jr, J. M., Cumming, O., Curtis, V., Bonjour, S., Dangour, A. D., France, J. D. and Fewtrell, L. (2014). Burden of disease from inadequate water, sanitation and hygiene in low-and middle-income settings: a retrospective analysis of data from 145 countries. *Tropical Medicine & International Health*, 19, 894–905.

Smith, L. T. (2013). *Decolonizing methodologies: Research and indigenous peoples.* London: Zed Books Ltd.

Steinert, J. I., Cluver, L. D., Melendez-Torres, G. J. and Vollmer, S. (2018). One size fits all? The validity of a composite poverty index across urban and rural households in South Africa. *Social Indicators Research*, 136, 51–72.

UNDP, United Nations Development Program. (2019). *Sustainable development goals – goal 6: clean water and sanitation.* Available at: https://www.undp.org/content/undp/en/home/sustainabledevelopment-goals/goal-6-clean-water-and-sanitation.html. (29 March 2019).

UNICEF, United Nations International Children's Fund. (2013). *Swaziland-statistics* Available at: http://www.unicef.org/infobycountry/swaziland_statistics.html.

Uprichard, E. and Dawney, L. (2019). Data diffraction: challenging data integration in mixed methods research. *Journal of Mixed Methods Research*, 13, 19–32.

WBG, World Bank Group. (2014). *Study design and questionnaire tips: things to consider when designing quantitative surveys and questionnaires to better measure, define and understand sanitation behaviors.* Available at: https://www.wsp.org/sites/wsp.org/files/publications/Study-Design-and-Questionnaire-Tips-forSanitation-Research.pdf.

WHO, World Health Organisation. (2004). Sanitation. In *Water, Sanitation and Hygiene* (pp. 103–128). Available at: https://who.int/water_sanitation_health/hygiene/om/linkingchap8.pdf.

WHO, World Health Organisation. (2016). *GEMI-integrated monitoring of water and sanitation related SDG targets.* Available at: https://www.who.int/water_sanitation_health/monitoring/coverage/step-by-step-with-definitions-62120161021.pdf.

WHO, World Health Organisation. (2010). *How to integrate water, sanitation and hygiene into HIV programmes.* Available at: https://apps.who.int/iris/bitstream/handle/10665/44393/9789241548014_eng.pdf;jsessionid=4E4E72F47B0F02958601765C88804C28?sequence=1.

7

USING MIXED AND MULTI-MODAL METHODS IN PSYCHOLOGICAL RESEARCH WITH YOUNG PEOPLE

Debra Gray, Rachel Manning and Shokraneh Oftadeh-Moghadam

Introduction

The use of mixed methods in psychological research has a long history. The formalisation of mixed methods in the discipline is largely credited to an article by Campbell and Fiske (1959) who advocated the use of *multi-methods* by psychological researchers to overcome issues relating to the validation of psychological traits (see Tashakkori and Teddlie, 1998, 2003 for a historical overview). Since this time – and particularly within the last decade – there has been a substantial growth in the use of mixed-methods research across the discipline, particularly in applied and practitioner areas such as counselling psychology (Hanson et al., 2005), the psychology of sport and exercise (e.g. Sparkes, 2015) and health psychology (e.g. Dures, Rumsey, Morris and Gleeson, 2011). There is also increasing trans- and interdisciplinary dialogue between fields that have different traditions of using mixed methodologies (O'Cathain, 2009). For many, mixed methods are conceptualised as a powerful 'third paradigm', one that provides the most 'informative, complete, balanced and useful research results' (Burke Johnson and Onwuegbuzie, 2004, 129).

This is not to say, however, that this 'third paradigm' is unproblematic or, indeed, unchallenged in the discipline. Psychology relies heavily on quantitative research designs, and often, there is little dialogue between quantitative and qualitative researchers, although there is certainly more acceptance for the value of both. For some, quantitative and qualitative approaches are 'incompatible paradigms', underpinned by fundamentally different assumptions about the nature of the world (ontology) and the nature of knowledge (epistemology; Denzin, 2010). This essential differentiation of methods makes it difficult to conceptualise how such methods might be integrated. This extends to the classroom, where these methods are often taught separately and by different people. In response, contemporary mixed-methods researchers have presented alternative frameworks for mixed-methods

DOI: 10.4324/9780429263484-8

research (Greene, 2008). For example, many mixed-methods researchers situate their work within pragmatism (Burke Johnson and Onwuegbuzie, 2004; Tashakkori and Teddlie, 2003), advocating that researchers choose the methods that provide the best understanding of the research problem (Creswell, 2003). However, such approaches are challenged by those who argue that we should be wary of any approach that seeks to dissolve theoretical concerns from methodology, in the sense that it could lead to claims of methods being somehow 'theory free' (e.g. see Lincoln, 2010). Instead, it is argued that any mixing of methods should give due consideration to the core assumptions of those doing the mixing. Such theoretical debates are not straightforwardly resolvable, but we present them here to provide an important historical backdrop from which to understand the use – and status – of mixed-methods research in psychology.

Alongside these long-standing theoretical and methodological debates, there have been calls for more methodological 'pluralism' in psychological research. This debate is not solely about the use of mixed methods, in the traditional sense of combining qualitative and qualitative approaches, but also the need to consider a mix of methods within quantitative and qualitative designs. Researchers working in this tradition point out that human experience is vastly multi-modal – including also the visual, the spatial, the temporal and 'the body' (Reavey, 2012). Therefore, we require methods that enable us to work with participants in different ways, in different places, at different times to understand their perspectives and practices (Chamberlain et al., 2011). Many researchers have sought ways to bring these different 'modalities' to their research studies, including projective techniques (e.g. vignettes), visual methods (e.g. photography, art and drawing) and/or spatial methods (e.g. the use of maps or mobile methodologies). Such multi-modal studies can combine methods in ways that offer innovative insights into topics that are of interest to psychologists and health scientists – e.g. emotion (Silver and Reavey, 2010), social memories (Brookfield, Brown and Reavey, 2008), identities and belonging (e.g. Dixon and Durrheim, 2003; Gray and Manning, 2014) and embodiment (e.g. Brown et al., 2011). These methods also do not always fit into the qualitative–quantitative binary that dominates many conceptualisations of mixed-methods research; indeed, some of these researchers would not identify their studies as mixed methods for that reason. However, such studies do provide critical spaces for dialogue about multiple methods beyond this quantitative/qualitative divide in ways that meet the need for complex and practice-oriented forms of research (cf. Yanchar, Gantt and Clay, 2005).

In this chapter, we provide an overview of the ways in which we have navigated (some of) these debates about the benefits and challenges of using mixed and multi-modal methods in our own research. In doing so, we draw on our experiences of using such methods across different studies (Gray and Manning, 2014; Manning and Gray, forthcoming; Bowe et al., 2020), with a specific focus on two studies that we have conducted with young people. We have chosen these two studies primarily because they illustrate different aspects of the contribution that we believe mixed and multi-modal methods can offer researchers interested in the psychological

158 Debra Gray et al.

aspects of health and wellbeing, while also highlighting some of the key challenges and debates described earlier. They additionally identify some issues that are fundamental to working with young people – and other groups whose voices are not always heard in research – and therefore illustrate the capacity of mixed methods to address critical transformative and social justice agendas.

The studies

The two studies we draw on in this chapter represent different ways of 'mixing' methods and also take different approaches to the study of health and wellbeing. Study 1, conducted by Debra Gray and Rachel Manning, is focused on young people's experiences in 'public' outdoor spaces in their local communities. In this study, we were concerned with the ways in which young people understood their identities (as 'emplaced') within their local communities and neighbourhoods given that their presence and participation within these communities was often problematised by others. Our understanding of health and wellbeing in this study is fundamentally social and relational, focused not just on health and wellbeing as the property of individuals but also related to (and produced by) particular social, material and affective conditions (Atkinson, 2013). Identities are central to this idea of health and wellbeing in the sense that a meaningful sense of belonging to social groups has been shown to be important for a range of physical and mental health outcomes (Haslam et al., 2018; Jetten, Haslam and Haslam, 2012). Likewise, 'place' is important in the sense that places can be 'enabling', providing the necessary resources to facilitate good health and wellbeing (Duff, 2016; Morrow, 2001) or 'disabling', producing stigmatised identities that work against a good sense of health and wellbeing (Gray and Manning, 2014; McNamara, Stevenson and Muldoon, 2013; Popay et al., 1998).

We conducted a multi-method study, mixing quantitative, qualitative and 'multimodal' data at different points. Our data did not always fall neatly into a clear qualitative/quantitative divide – e.g. some of our data was analysed both qualitatively and quantitatively. However, our approach to mixed methods was qualitatively driven (Creswell, 2003; Denscombe, 2008) in the sense that the qualitative methods were used to provide depth and insight into the experiences of young people in public, and then the quantitative methods were either used to examine these experiences in different ways (e.g. using Geographic Information Systems [GIS]) or to determine the applicability to a wider group. Our starting point was focus group workshops with young people (aged 11–16) about their experiences in outdoor community spaces. We developed a collaborative spatial mapping (CSM) method in which young people were asked to hand draw maps of their local area that represented the places that they went to and those that they thought were important. This could be done individually; however, because the young people were in friendship groups and used these places most often together, this often quickly became a collective task. These maps then formed a basis for further discussion, as participants were asked to talk through their maps as a way of examining identity and belonging (Futch and Fine, 2014). Two examples of the maps can be seen in Figure 7.1 (see also Gray and Manning, 2014; Manning and Gray, forthcoming, for further map

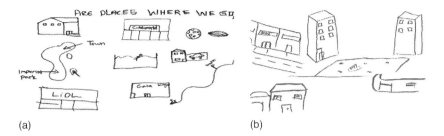

FIGURE 7.1 Young peoples' collaborative spatial maps of their local areas

examples and analyses). Finally, we also conducted a mixed quantitative and qualitative survey in schools, asking young people about their 'favourite' places and about their activities in those spaces. This also involved them drawing maps of their communities, which were then analysed in multiple ways, including qualitatively using discourse analysis and quantitatively using GIS.

Study 2 is a PhD project undertaken by Shokraneh Oftadeh-Moghadam, supervised by Debra Gray. This study focused on developing and evaluating a digital sleep intervention for adolescents, using the person-based approach (PBA) to intervention development (Yardley et al., 2015). This study took a biopsychosocial approach to health and wellbeing, which is the conceptual basis for much of health psychology (Suls and Rothman, 2004). This approach advocates that biological, psychological and social processes are integrally and interactively involved in physical health and illness (Suls and Rothman, 2004). Situated within this broader theoretical perspective is the PBA to intervention development, which is a method of developing health interventions (in this case to tackle sleep behaviour) that are grounded in a profound understanding of the subjective experiences and psychosocial context of the people who will use them. This is key to developing targeted interventions for improved health outcomes, ensuring that the intervention is as acceptable and engaging as possible and improving adherence to the intervention (Yardley et al., 2015).

The PBA involves collecting extensive feedback from target users and modifying the intervention based on this feedback. In practice, this meant a series of project phases, with a mix of qualitative and quantitative methods being used at different points across these phases. Phase 1 involved the design of a prototype version of the intervention on a digital platform based on a scoping review of the barriers and facilitators to sleep behaviour change amongst adolescents and sleep intervention ingredients that had proved effective in improving sleep outcomes for this age group. In Phase 2, this prototype was tested with adolescents using qualitative think-aloud interviews, which is a method for eliciting insight into participants' thoughts of a task by asking them to 'think out loud' while performing that task (Eccles and Arsal, 2017). This phase resulted in an optimised version of the intervention: an interactive digital intervention called SleepWise. In the final phase, this intervention was tested through a feasibility trial, which collected a complex set of quantitative data on intervention usage and the outcomes of the intervention self-reported sleep behaviour, as well as qualitative data on perceptions of user experiences of the

160 Debra Gray et al.

intervention. These different data were analysed using a composite analysis technique (Yardley and Bishop, 2015). This meant that data were collected and analysed separately, and then findings of these studies were then integrated to provide in-depth understanding of the acceptability, feasibility and outcomes of the SleepWise intervention.

Representing complexity

For many researchers, the main value of mixing qualitative and quantitative methods is that it allows researchers to examine a topic and/or an experience in a way that represents more of the inherent complexity of human experience(s) (Ponterotto, Mathew and Raughley, 2013). Mixed methods can answer more complex research questions and can provide more complex – and some argue more robust – explanations of findings. While some conceptualise this as a process of 'triangulation', using different methods to build up a picture of a specific phenomenon under investigation from a range of perspectives (Doyle, Brady and Byrne, 2016), others have pointed to the variety of possible outcomes (e.g. contradiction) in combining methods that can help to engage with the complexity of an area of interest (see Brannen, 2005, who usefully highlights the phasing of different methods). Using divergent methods thereby provides different opportunities for a more complex (and some might argue more complete) understanding than single methods would alone.

This ability to represent the complex experiences of young people was a key reason for us choosing to use mixed and multi-modal methods in our research and was one of the main advantages of this approach, as it helped us to represent (and sometimes resolve) complex realities around health and wellbeing that would be hard to access using single methods on their own. In Study 1, for example, we could have chosen to only interview our participants, or survey them, but we felt that this would not have helped us to explore the range of different experiences of young people within, or as they move through, specific (physical) contexts. For us, this was only possible using a range of methods: collective spatial mapping tasks helped us to understand which contexts were important, focus groups provided access to experiences within those contexts and surveys helped us to understand how these contexts were important (or not) for a broad range of young people. This meant we could explore a range of different practices, including embodied practices (e.g. 'being in place'), social practices (e.g. the construction of group categories and processes) and ideological practices (e.g. moral arguments about 'who belongs where').

In Study 2, the findings from the quantitative and qualitative parts of the study helped to triangulate insights about adolescent sleep behaviour in important ways. For example, as part of the feasibility trial of SleepWise, data was collected about intervention usage – e.g. how long participants spent on each page, the number and order of pages viewed and the total number of sleep logs and goals completed as part of the intervention. Analysis of this usage data indicated that adolescents engaged highly with the first session of the intervention, which was focused on the importance of sleep and eating behaviours. Participants viewed more pages and spent more time on Session 1 when compared to the other weekly sessions. However, it was not clear why this session was seen as more relevant and/or liked more by users. Qualitative follow-up interviews confirmed this usage data and broadened understanding of the context behind the usage findings. For example, these interviews highlighted that adolescents were not typically aware of why sleep was important for their health and so found the information in Session 1 to be novel and engaging. This allowed participants to go beyond simply providing feedback about the intervention but also to discuss the barriers to adequate sleep and what they thought would be useful to help them sleep better. These different methods were, therefore, complementary to one another, providing important insights into the complex realities of how and why users engaged with the intervention in practice.

This complementarity of different methods is an often-cited benefit of mixed methods, the argument being that all research methods have inherent limitations. By systematically combining different methodologies in a single study, these limitations can be 'offset' and overcome through the complementary strengths of the methods used (e.g. see Hanson et al., 2005; Lonner, 2009). Classically, this is described as a 'breadth vs depth trade-off' (Ponterotto, Mathew and Raughley, 2013), where the quantitative element of the study provides breadth (and precision and control) and the qualitative depth (and context and meaning). We do not, however, advocate this position in relation to our own work. We have not always found it to be the case that qualitative methods provide depth while quantitative methods provide breadth. Indeed, in Study 1, it was some of our quantitative analyses (e.g. GIS analyses) that provided us with further depth of understanding in relation to our focus group discussions because they enabled us to compare the actuality of 'place' with talk about that 'place'. Instead, we argue that researchers should consider the complementarity of their methods in relation to the researchers' position and the research question asked, as these will inform what the 'strengths' or 'limitations' of a particular method might be. This will enable critical reflection on how the combination of different methods might provide better, different and/or more complete insight into the complexity of the phenomena of interest than single methods alone. As in Study 2, it may be that depth and breadth of understanding are what is important. Or, as in Study 1, it may be that mixing methods allows researchers to connect to a range of contexts, perspectives or modalities of experience in more complex ways. Finally, it may be that – on reflection – the decision is made not to combine particular methods at all, as their incompatibility is found to be greater than their complementarity. In any event, such reflection can only strengthen the research, making the purpose of mixing methods clearer. A point we will return to later when we discuss some of the challenges of mixing methods.

Disrupting 'reality'

Many would argue that this ability to represent the complexity of human experience is important, as it moves us closer to the 'reality' – or at least the 'true to life' – of an experience. However, we would argue that it is additionally important

162 Debra Gray et al.

because it is able to disrupt our understanding of the 'reality' of an experience. We have found mixed methods to be a critically important tool for exploring contest and contention and for disrupting taken-for-granted narratives about a topic, making room for the unexpected. In Study 1, for example, we (as researchers) had started out from the position that young people would be highly critical of their own regulation in public outdoor spaces (e.g. from the police and members of the public) and that they would feel a sense of community disengagement as a result, as is so often pointed out by commentators (e.g. Crawford and Lister, 2007). However, this was not the case. Instead, we found that young people described a strong, connected identity to their local neighbourhoods based on lifelong, regular and sustained engagement with these places. Moreover, they often supported the regulation of their behaviour within these spaces, seeing this as important to their own and others' safety. Ultimately, we found that young people are often navigating a complex (and irresolvable) set of processes within their communities, where they are often positioned as 'out of place' and 'troublesome' simply due to their age while at the same time actively constructing their own identities and activities within such spaces as entirely ordinary and legitimate (Manning and Gray, forthcoming).

These findings highlight the capacity of mixed and multi-modal methods to make the familiar surprising (see also Brown et al., 2011; Silver and Reavey, 2010). Indeed, without the mapping methods in Study 1, we do not think that we could have accessed the degree to which young people feel such a strong sense of 'autobiographical insideness' (Rowles, 1983) within their communities. These maps (see Figures 7.1a and 7.1b for examples) prompted stories that were full of social memories, social connections and social engagements with places, revealing aspects of young people's lives in public that we would not have been able to otherwise understand, including the degree to which these young people live in, and navigate, environments of contest and contention. This disrupted our own understanding of what these experiences would look and feel like and undermines broader discourses about how young people are not as involved in the community as they should be – which are often related to them not being involved in adult-determined ways. This was echoed in Study 2, which highlighted the ways in which young people were interested in information and behaviour change techniques to improve sleep and health, which contradicts society's misconceptions of 'lazy' adolescents (Kelley et al., 2015). We argue that this moves us beyond psychological models of childhood as simply a period of development (towards adulthood) and instead emphasises that children are active social agents who shape the structures and processes around them (at least at the micro-level) and whose social relationships are worthy of study in their own right (Greig, Taylor and MacKay, 2012; James, Jenks and Prout, 1998; Morrow, 2001). Methods that can access the complexity of these experiences and perspectives are essential, as without them, our understanding of children's worlds and experiences is incomplete.

Psychological research with young people **163**

Engagement and engaging

For us, another important advantage of mixed and multi-modal methods is their capacity to produce and sustain engagement with research participants (see also Morrow, 2001). We found that the young people in our studies responded well to methods which sustained their attention over the data collection period, telling us that taking part in the research was 'fun'. In part, this is because these methods can be flexible, and so participants can move between different forms of data collection rather than being asked to take part in more rigid, structured and (at times) repetitive tasks. For example, in Study 1, participants moved between the different forms of data collection flexibly rather than sticking to a more rigid schedule. This meant that participants could have some group discussion, some mapping, some further group discussion, etc. Overall, this kind of 'workshop' format (as we ended up calling it) meant that more than 1.5 hours of discussion data were generated in each of our groups, along with the maps and the discussion of those maps.

Of course, this format was only possible in Study 1 because we collected data concurrently, rather than collecting qualitative and quantitative data sequentially. Study 2, where data were collected sequentially (at times from different participants), is perhaps a more 'usual' model for mixed methods. However, even in this study, the use of mixed methods allowed for the introduction of flexible and creative methods across the different phases of the study. For example, when optimising the prototype digital intervention, young people engaged with the intervention while 'thinking out loud'. This method of data collection (think-aloud interviews) encouraged users to take their time when working through and talking about different elements of the intervention. As the study progressed, these insights were then integrated with data from other stages in order to clarify how young people engaged with the intervention and what modifications were needed to make the intervention as acceptable and engaging as possible in order to improve the likelihood of behaviour change and thus improved sleep quality.

The main advantage of engaging participants in this way is the quality of the data that we have collected. Indeed, we would argue that such methods – because they are engaging – were instrumental in building rapport in the research situation. Some have argued that building rapport in research with children and young people can be harder, as children are more uncomfortable with adult researchers (Irwin and Johnson, 2005). For many, this is a key advantage of methods that involve young people as researchers (Morrow, 2001; Morrow and Richards, 1996). However, we found that the mixing of different methods seemed to make participants feel at ease and encouraged engagement with the researchers and the research questions. Indeed, we noted that the data collection could become more participant driven, and the conversation was more often between participants rather than between the researcher and the participants. Therefore, these methods can be useful for building engagement with other research participants.

164 Debra Gray et al.

To be clear, we are not suggesting here that young people required specifically 'child-friendly' methods nor that children and young people are somehow less competent or less capable of ordinary conversation than adults (Harden et al., 2000). Rather, these methods did produce and sustain engagement in ways that we felt were important to our research questions, and so we felt that they were successful in these ways. We additionally used these same methods from Study 1 with adult participants and found similarly good levels of engagement – though for this group, there were additional concerns about looking 'silly', which we did not have in any of our young people data collection workshops. Our key take home message here, therefore, is not that these methods are necessarily 'good for young people' but that they are good for promoting participant engagement and enjoyment in research, which many of our participants told us about and which produced good quality data as a result. However, as with all methods, it is likely that the success of these methods may be context – and participant – dependent or at the very least may not move so easily between different groups in a study. This need for care when utilising 'less-familiar' or novel methods is also a useful reminder of the way some more 'taken-for-granted' methods may equally be experienced as strange by participants.

Voice and visibility

We have found that mixed and multi-modal methods can often provide opportunities for multiple voices to emerge – some of which may have been historically silenced – in ways that single methods cannot (see also Ponterotto, Mathew and Raughley, 2013). In part, and as discussed earlier, this is because mixed methods are more flexible than single methods and are capable of representing – and disrupting – complex realities in important ways. By using multiple methods, we get multiple windows into this world, and this enables us to better understand this world and to realise the ways in which it is different to/from our own (e.g. adult-conceived) interpretation of that world. This multiplicity is additionally useful for overcoming the tendency for us to consider groups as homogeneous; in our research, this was helpful in avoiding treating children and childhood as one homogeneous group, with similar concerns and experiences of the world. Instead, we begin to see how there are different childhoods comprising different relationships, interactions and perceptions. In Study 1, we found this important, as we began to see the ways in which young people's engagement in their communities and neighbourhoods was shaped by factors such as gender, age and their economic capacity to 'choose' to be somewhere else (e.g. by using public transport). One note of caution here though: there is a need to ensure that the methods used do not introduce these inequalities, for example, because they require participants to do something that they feel ill equipped to do (e.g. draw), which may therefore limit what those participants can 'say' (Kirk, 2007).

We argue that these questions about voice and visibility are particularly important to consider in research with children and young people, who are often positioned (by adults) not as full members of society but as 'citizens in becoming' (Sharkey

Psychological research with young people **165**

and Shields, 2008, 40), with important implications for their rights to participate, and be visible, in society. This conceptualisation of childhood also shapes the ways in which they are researched and/or their role in the research process (Harden et al., 2000), which is often from an adult perspective and/or is adult controlled. However, creating the potential for children to have their own ideas, contexts and worlds heard and understood is key to creating health policies and interventions that work for them and that address the broader socio-environmental factors that structure the outcomes of efforts to improve the health of young people. Study 2 is a good example of how to use different methods to centre research about health interventions on participants' own perceptions, understandings and experiences of a particular phenomenon. The multiplicity of methods used enabled young people's voices to be incorporated at every stage of the intervention development process. This helped us understand how and to what extent young people implemented the sleep behaviour techniques in practice, both during the optimisation and evaluation phases. This ensured that, as an intervention, SleepWise was motivating, acceptable and informative for users and, most importantly, empowered users to change behaviour and/or improve health outcomes in practice (Yardley et al., 2015).

Within these research contexts, multiple methods were also very useful for readdressing some of the power imbalances of the research process, which otherwise would have been entirely adult directed and controlled. Multiple methods enable us to include methods that are under greater participant control, in comparison to single, more traditional methods. The think-aloud interview technique from Study 2, is a good example of this, as it provided participants with more autonomy over their engagement with the intervention, as well as how they described their own sleep and health behaviours. Participants chose how (and at what pace) to work through the intervention, what parts to focus on and what aspects they found interesting or wanted to discuss rather than these being chosen for them by a researcher using a predetermined set of questions. Likewise, adding a mapping task to Study 1, both in the focus groups and the survey, helped to give more control to participants – enabling them to set the agenda for what they considered to be important through choosing what types of places they put (or chose not to) on their maps (Croghan et al., 2008). In our experience, this helped participants to become more involved in telling their own stories from their own perspectives, and this helped us to engage with what young people themselves saw as being important within this context.

Challenges and advice for other researchers

While we have found mixed and multi-modal methods to be useful and valuable in addressing our research questions of interest, it is also true to say that these methods have not been without their challenges. As articulated within the broader literature on mixed methods, a key challenge is how to integrate the data you have collected, from the different methods you have used, into a coherent set of findings. We have, at various points, found this difficult to do. On one level, this challenge is theoretical, particularly if the different methods you are integrating come from very different

166 Debra Gray et al.

theoretical orientations or perspectives. In Study 1, for example, we had adopted a social constructionist approach to the data, but then it was hard for us to see exactly how we should bring the maps, surveys and GIS analyses into this social constructionist account. From this theoretical perspective, our mapping data could not be straightforwardly treated as 'windows' into participants' concerns but rather as co-constructed and produced as part of the research process. However, it was then difficult to conceptualise the status of these data in a way that would enable its relation to the rest of the data we had collected. It would have been easier – and certainly, we did do this at times in our analyses – to simply use the verbal focus groups' data as the sole focus of the analysis because it is easier to account for such data and because ways of analysing such data already exist. However, we knew that this would mean that the important relationship between the identity work done visually and the identity work done verbally would be lost (see Croghan et al., 2008).

Other mixed-method researchers have outlined various models and processes for integrating data, with some advocating integration at the point of analysis and others after separate analyses have taken place in the interpretation of findings (e.g. see Barnes, 2012; Moran–Ellis et al., 2006). Whichever is chosen, it is clear that the end result should be more than different findings from different methods presented side by side. However, there are no easy solutions to how to achieve this. In our experience, this requires a lot of time spent going back and forth between data and interpretation to ensure a deep engagement with the dataset. It also requires clarity of purpose, which we talked about earlier, in terms of being aware of what different methods bring to the research question and what the different strengths/limitations of different methods are. If you are clear on this from the start, this stage does become much easier.

We also found we needed to have a continual and reflexive engagement with questions of epistemology and ontology, as different types of data are brought together and analysed. We, therefore, suggest that such processes can help you to see the utility of the different elements of the data and to make sure you do not stretch beyond what your data can legitimately tell you. When analysing our mapping data, for example, we did have a broad sense of the kinds of places and spaces that a range of young people used on a day-to-day basis, and we could have reported these, relatively straightforwardly, as being young people's 'favourite places'. However, we knew that the places chosen were produced and constructed within a specific research context and we did not want to impose an adult interpretation that was outside of how the young people themselves discussed their maps. Therefore, one strategy we took was to find the overlaps between the maps and the focus groups' accounts and to see what this told us about young peoples' communities of place. In the main, this meant that the maps were not analysed in their own right, but rather we integrated these analyses together. This was quite hard to do, as it meant that some meaning from the data was necessarily lost, which didn't always feel 'right'. Moreover, we had to accept quite early on that a complete synthesis was not possible – or desirable – and that tensions between the data could actually be quite useful in creating meaning (Dellinger and Leech, 2007).

Psychological research with young people **167**

These concerns about integration are not just theoretical but also practical. Mixed-methods research, in our experience, tends to generate a lot of data – far more than we usually generate using single methods alone. While this is useful and valuable for all of the reasons we have described, it can also be hard to know how to manage and integrate this volume (and variety) of data in a meaningful way. Underlying all of this complexity is the assumption that researchers are multi-skilled and have the ability to design, collect, analyse and integrate a variety of different kinds of data. For example, in Study 2, the researcher did not have any prior experience in collecting or analysing usage data from a website and so had to learn how to download this data, clean and organise it and then analyse and report the findings (including additional methods of visual representation). This data then had to be combined with data from follow-up interviews in order to determine key aspects of the feasibility of the intervention. This was, therefore, a complex task that required considerable additional skill development beyond the specifics of the research questions themselves.

In our experience, it is rarely the case that researchers are sufficiently trained or experienced in all methodologies or in the additional practical requirements of multi-modal data. While this can be learned, in practice, it means that such research is often conducted by teams of researchers who bring different skills to the project. However, where this is the case, this means that analysis is often not just done in different stages but by different people, making the integration even harder. There is very little guidance for researchers on how to navigate these practical concerns and, for less experienced researchers in particular, this can be a profoundly daunting experience. We would therefore caution against trying to do too much in one study. Good data management processes (and training) are key, as well as robust communication practices, and we have found that visual representations can work well to help to maintain shared understandings and manage the complexities of the research processes and describe them to others. We have also found that this is usually where research questions come into their own. While there are few prescriptions on what makes a 'good' mixed-methods research question, there is a view that they should, at the very least, speak to the integration of the data (Collins and O'Cathain, 2009; Tashakkori and Creswell, 2007). At a practical level, this means that you should already have determined before you collect your data what the underlying logic of your integration is going to be – and again reflected on the strengths and limitations of different methods in relation to your research question. When faced with the volume and variety of data you have collected, this is the time to revisit this logic, as it often provides a good road map for how this complexity can and should be managed.

Using mixed and multi-modal methods can sometimes mean that you are in new territory – e.g. because your particular mix of methods has not been tried before or not with your topic or population of interest. This can be exciting, but it can also mean that the justification and procedural aspects of your data collection are not always immediately clear and that you have to navigate these as you conduct the research. So, in Study 1, for example, while individual maps have been used as

168 Debra Gray et al.

projective techniques in psychological research before, CSM has not. However, we wanted our maps to be group-based and inherently social – reflecting young people's use of place in their already existing friendship groups. There were no existing protocols for what this should look like, and we had to find our way through the data collection, altering as we went along based on participant and researcher feedback. In some respects, we only really felt we had this right at the end. In addition, giving over control to your participants can be hard to do, and it can sometimes mean that your data is not always as useable as you might like it to be. Of course, this does raise further questions about who decides on the usefulness of data, and it could be that the concerns raised by participants were more important to them than your research topic. However, it is the case that this does present challenges to researchers in terms of what to do with this data once it has been collected.

We have found mixed methods to raise specific challenges around ethics. This can be because your study takes you into new territory and so the ethical issues are not always entirely clear or because the different methods that you are using have very different ethical considerations, particularly when brought together, which makes thinking through ethics more complex. This was certainly the case in Study 1, where the different data we collected had very different ethical considerations, which were magnified when they were brought together. For example, we needed to maintain participant anonymity across visual data, group discussions and quantitative survey/mapping data, all of which contained different identifying information. Moreover, we needed to ensure that participants were appropriately informed and had appropriately consented to these different but related elements of the project – e.g. that their hand-drawn maps might appear in publications and that this might appear alongside data from their group discussions. Of course, this was all magnified by the fact that participants were under the age of 16, and so this needed to be clear to parents/caregivers as well. Both studies that we have focused on here followed the British Psychological Society Code of Ethics and Conduct (2018), which sets out key principles for the ethical conduct of psychological research. However, we found we needed to carefully consider these principles in terms of how these might be magnified by and/or mitigated in our mixed-methods design. Both studies also went through institutional approval processes successfully. However, we have generally found this process to be more complex with mixed-methods research, particularly where reviewers may need methodological expertise that they do not have. To help with this complexity, we have sometimes found it useful to apply for ethical approval in stages, separating out the different methods and components of the research (where these take place in series) and seeking ethical approval for these individually. However, this is not a perfect solution as it can miss ethical issues that result from the integration of methods, and it can be confusing for reviewers, who did not always understand what had gone before. Moreover, such separation is, of course, not possible in the contemporaneous use of multi-modal data collection. Clarity in the development and specification of procedure are, again, crucial.

These challenges feed directly into questions about how to evaluate the quality of mixed-method and multi-modal research. This is not an easy challenge to address, as there are (often fierce) debates in the literature about what constitutes 'good quality' research within mixed methods – or indeed within qualitative or quantitative – traditions (see Bryman, Becker and Sempik, 2008; Creswell, 2011). While we will not reproduce this debate in full here (for an overview see Creswell, 2011; Heyvaert et al., 2013), we do want to point out that the lack of agreement about the quality of mixed-methods research does present unique challenges for researchers. There is often little practical advice about how to assess research quality in mixed-methods studies and even less so within multi-modal studies. Moreover, it is sometimes the case that researchers working on the same project can have very different understandings of what constitutes good quality research, with little guidance about how to resolve these issues.

In our own work, we have adopted the approach that transparency is of paramount importance when thinking about research quality. We advocate that the judgement criteria to be used are fully discussed and agreed upon from the start of the project, and these are made explicit to other researchers who come into contact with the research. We have at times found appraisal tools useful – e.g. the Mixed Methods Appraisal Tool (MMAT; Hong et al., 2018), as these can provide a consistent approach to the assessment of research quality across different researchers working on the same project. The MMAT, for example, provides a checklist for appraising research studies in systematic reviews. This checklist highlights the importance of an adequate rationale for mixing methods, the effective integration of the different elements of a study in relation to the research question, the overall interpretation of the results as key aspects of quality and the necessity of acknowledging inconsistencies between results from the different components of a study. In addition, this tool also emphasises the need to evaluate the component methods in their own right in relation to the quality criteria of each research tradition. However, while we have found these to be useful ways to approach these issues of research quality in our own work, we also do advocate that researchers remain mindful of the fact that research quality remains a critical and contentious issue within mixed-methods research and that more needs to be done by the wider community of researchers to share their (best) practices in this area in an attempt to resolve some of these debates.

Conclusions

In this chapter, we have provided an overview of some of the advantages and challenges that we have found using mixed and multi-modal methods in our own research with young people. Across our research, we have found mixed methods to be useful in representing the complexity of young people's experiences of health and wellbeing while at the same time disrupting taken-for-granted narratives about young people's lives. We have found these methods to engage our research participants in important ways while also providing spaces and contexts in which to give voice and visibility to young peoples' concerns. However, while we think that mixed methods have a vital place in research on health and wellbeing, it is also must be acknowledged that there are key challenges with this approach. We have

170 Debra Gray et al.

found that mixed methods are good for representing complexity but that this also means that they add greater complexity to the research process. This means that it is not always the case that a mixed-methods approach will be better than single methods on their own. Instead, it is important to use mixed methods thoughtfully, taking care to justify and explain how and why your approach requires a mixing of methods and/or modalities, what the different components bring to the research question and how their findings will be integrated both practically and theoretically. Where these questions can be answered positively, however, then we would argue that mixed modalities and/or methods provide a uniquely flexible and responsive approach to research that can allow different perspectives to emerge and therefore can be an important tool for researchers who want to address critical transformative and social justice agendas.

Questions for discussion and further reflection

What theoretical debates concerning the 'third paradigm' of mixed methods do the authors present – and where would you say that you stand on these?

What do you understand by the term 'multi-modal', and how is this approach implemented in the described studies?

How does this develop your understanding about mixed-methods research?

In what ways have these mixed-methods approaches addressed transformative and social justice agendas?

References

Atkinson, S. (2013). Beyond components of wellbeing: the effects of relational and situated assemblage. *Topoi*, 32 (2), 137–144.

Barnes, B. R. (2012). Using mixed methods in South African psychological research. *South African Journal of Psychology*, 42 (4), 463–475.

Brannen, J. (2005). Mixing methods: the entry of qualitative and quantitative approaches into the research process. *International Journal of Social Research Methodology*, 8 (3), 173–184.

Brookfield, H., Brown, S. D. and Reavey, P. (2008). Vicarious and post-memory practices in adopting families: the re-production of the past through photography and narrative. *Journal of Community and Applied Social Psychology*, 18 (5), 474–491.

Brown, S. D., Cromby, J., Harper, D. J., Johnson, K. and Reavey, P. (2011). Researching "experience": embodiment, methodology, process. *Theory and Psychology*, 21 (4), 493–515.

Bryman, A., Becker, S. and Sempik, J. (2008). Quality criteria for quantitative, qualitative and mixed methods research: a view from social policy. *International Journal of Social Research Methodology*, 11 (4), 261–276.

Bowe, M., Gray, D., Stevenson, C., Cleveland, M., McNamara, N, Wakefield, J., Kellezi, B. and Wilson, I. (2020). A social cure in the community: a mixed-method exploration of the role of social identity in the experiences and well-being of community volunteers. *European Journal of Social Psychology*, 50, (7) 1523–1539.

Burke Johnson, R. and Onwuegbuzie, A. J. (2004). Mixed methods research: a research paradigm whose time has come. *Educational Researcher*, 33 (7), 14–26.

Campbell, D. T. and Fiske, D. W. (1959). Convergent and discriminant validation by the multitrait multimethod matrix. *Psychological Bulletin*, 56 (2), 81.

Chamberlain, K., Cain, T., Sheridan, J. and Dupuis, A. (2011). Pluralisms in qualitative research: from multiple methods to integrated methods. *Qualitative Research in Psychology*, 8 (2), 151–169.

Crawford, A. and Lister, S. (2007). *The use and impact of dispersal orders*. Bristol, UK: Joseph Rowntree Foundation.

Collins, K. M., and O'Cathain, A. (2009). Introduction: ten points about mixed methods research to be considered by the novice researcher. *International Journal of Multiple Research Approaches*, 3 (1), 2–7.

Creswell, J. W. (2003). *Research design: qualitative. Quantitative, and mixed method approaches* (2nd ed.). Thousand Oaks, CA: SAGE Publications.

Creswell, J. W. (2011). Controversies in mixed methods research. *The Sage Handbook of Qualitative Research*, 4, 269–284.

Denscombe, M. (2008). Communities of practice: a research paradigm for the mixed methods approach. *Journal of Mixed Methods Research*, 2 (3), 270–283.

Croghan, R., Griffin, C., Hunter, J. and Phoenix, A. (2008). Young people's construction of self: notes of the use and analysis of the photo-elicitation methods. *International Journal of Social Research Methodology*, 1 (4), 345–356.

Dellinger, A. B. and Leech, N. L. (2007). Toward a unified validation framework in mixed methods research. *Journal of Mixed Methods Research*, 1 (4), 309–332.

Denzin, N. K. (2010). Moments, mixed methods, and paradigm dialogs. *Qualitative Inquiry*, 16 (6), 419–427.

Dixon, J. and Durrheim, K. (2003). Contact and the ecology of racial division: some varieties of informal segregation. *British Journal of Social Psychology*, 42 (1), 1–23.

Doyle, L., Brady, A. M. and Byrne, G. (2016). An overview of mixed methods research–revisited. *Journal of Research in Nursing*, 21 (8), 623–635.

Duff, C. (2016). Atmospheres of recovery: assemblages of health. *Environment and Planning A*, 48 (1), 58–74.

Dures, E., Rumsey, N., Morris, M. and Gleeson, K. (2011). Mixed methods in health psychology: theoretical and practical considerations of the third paradigm. *Journal of Health Psychology*, 16 (2), 332–341.

Eccles, D. W. and Arsal, G. (2017). The think aloud method: what is it and how do I use it? *Qualitative Research in Sport, Exercise and Health*, 9 (4), 514–531.

Futch, V. A. and Fine, M. (2014). Mapping as a method: history and theoretical commitments. *Qualitative Research in Psychology*, 11 (1), 42–59.

Greig, A. D., Taylor, J. and MacKay, T. (2012). *Doing research with children: a practical guide*. Thousand Oaks, CA: SAGE Publications.

Gray, D. and Manning, R. (2014). 'Oh my god, we're not doing nothing': young people's experiences of spatial regulation. *British Journal of Social Psychology*, 53 (4), 640–655.

Greene, J. C. (2008). Is mixed methods social inquiry a distinctive methodology? *Journal of Mixed Methods Research*, 2 (1), 7–22.

Harden, J., Scott, S., Backett-Milburn, K. and Jackson, S. (2000). Can't talk, won't talk? Methodological issues in researching children. *Sociological Research Online*, 5 (2), 104–115.

Haslam, C., Jetten, J., Cruwys, T., Dingle, G. and Haslam, S. A. (2018). *The new psychology of health: unlocking the social cure*. Routledge

Hanson, W. E., Creswell, J. W., Clark, V. L. P., Petska, K. S. and Creswell, J. D. (2005). Mixed methods research designs in counseling psychology. *Journal of Counseling Psychology*, 52 (2), 224.

Heyvaert, M., Maes, B. and Onghena, P. (2013). Mixed methods research synthesis: definition, framework, and potential. *Quality and Quantity*, 47 (2), 659–676.

Hong, Q. N., Pluye, P., Fàbregues, S., Bartlett, G., Boardman, F., Cargo, M., … and O'Cathain, A. (2018). Mixed methods appraisal tool (MMAT), version 2018. *Registration of Copyright, 1148552*.

Irwin, L. G. and Johnson, J. (2005). Interviewing young children: explicating our practices and dilemmas. *Qualitative Health Research*, 15 (6), 821–831.

James, A., Jenks, C. and Prout, A. (1998). *Theorizing childhood*. New York: Polity.

Jetten, J., Haslam, S. A. and Haslam, C. (2012). The case for a social identity analysis of health and well being. *The social cure: identity, health and well-being*, 3–19.

Kelley, P., Lockley, S. W., Foster, R. G. and Kelley, J. (2015). Synchronizing education to adolescent biology: 'let teens sleep, start school later'. *Learning, Media and Technology*, 40 (2), 210–226.

Kirk, S. (2007). Methodological and ethical issues in conducting qualitative research with children and young people: a literature review. *International Journal of Nursing Studies*, 44 (7), 1250–1260.

Lincoln, Y. S. (2010). "What a long, strange trip it's been …": twenty-five years of qualitative and new paradigm research. *Qualitative Inquiry*, 16 (1), 3–9.

Lonner, W. J. (2009). Senior editor's introduction to the special issue: qualitative and mixed methods research in cross-cultural psychology. *Journal of Cross-Cultural Psychology*, 40, 907–908.

Manning, R. and Gray, D. (forthcoming). Constructing the place of young people in public space: conflict, belonging and identity. *Journal of Environmental Psychology*.

McNamara, N., Stevenson, C. and Muldoon, O. T. (2013). Community identity as resource and context: a mixed method investigation of coping and collective action in a disadvantaged community. *European Journal of Social Psychology*, 43 (5), 393–403.

Moran-Ellis, J., Alexander, V. D., Cronin, A., Dickinson, M., Fielding, J., Sleney, J. and Thomas, H. (2006). Triangulation and integration: processes, claims and implications. *Qualitative Research*, 6 (1), 45–59.

Morrow, V. (2001). Using qualitative methods to elicit young people's perspectives on their environments: some ideas for community health initiatives. *Health Education Research*, 16 (3), 255–268.

Morrow, V. and Richards, M. (1996). The ethics of social research with children: an overview. *Children and Society*, 10 (2), 90–105.

O'Cathain, A. (2009). Mixed methods research in the health sciences: a quiet revolution. *Journal of Mixed Methods Research*, 3 (1), 3–6.

Ponterotto, J. G., Mathew, J. T. and Raughley, B. (2013). The value of mixed methods designs to social justice research in counseling and psychology. *Journal for Social Action in Counseling and Psychology*, 5 (2), 42–68.

Popay, J., Williams, G., Thomas, C. and Gatrell, T. (1998). Theorising inequalities in health: the place of lay knowledge. *Sociology of Health and Illness*, 20 (5), 619–644.

Reavey, P. (2012). The return to experience: psychology and the visual. In P. Reavey (ed.), *Visual methods in psychology*. London: Routledge. pp. 40–52.

Rowles, G. D. (1983). Place and personal identity in old age: observations from Appalachia. *Journal of Environmental Psychology*, 3 (4), 299–313.

Sharkey, A. and Shields, R. (2008). Abject citizenship–rethinking exclusion and inclusion: participation, criminality and community at a small town youth centre. *Children's Geographies*, 6 (3), 239–256.

Silver, J. and Reavey, P. (2010). "He's a good-looking chap aint he?": narrative and visualisations of self in body dysmorphic disorder. *Social Science and Medicine*, 70 (10), 1641–1647.

Sparkes, A. C. (2015). Developing mixed methods research in sport and exercise psychology: critical reflections on five points of controversy. *Psychology of Sport and Exercise*, 16, 49–59.

Suls, J., and Rothman, A. (2004). Evolution of the biopsychosocial model: prospects and challenges for health psychology. *Health Psychology*, 23 (2), 119–125.

Tashakkori, A. and Creswell, J. W. (2007). *The new era of mixed methods*. Thousand Oaks, CA: SAGE Publications.

Tashakkori, A. and Teddlie, C. (1998). *Mixed methodology: Combining qualitative and quantitative approaches*. Thousand Oaks, CA: SAGE Publications.

Tashakkori, A. and Teddlie, C. (2003). Issues and dilemmas in teaching research methods courses in social and behavioural sciences: US perspective. *International Journal of Social Research Methodology*, 6 (1), 61–77.

Yanchar, S. C., Gantt, E. E. and Clay, S. L. (2005). On the nature of a critical methodology. *Theory and Psychology*, 15 (1), 27–50.

Yardley, L., Morrison, L., Bradbury, K. and Muller, I. (2015). The person-based approach to intervention development: application to digital health-related behavior change interventions. *Journal of Medical Internet Research*, 17 (1), e30.

Yardley, L. and Bishop, F. L. (2015). Using mixed methods in health research: benefits and challenges. *British Journal of Health Psychology*, 20 (1), 1–4.

8

A MULTIMETHODS APPROACH FOR DEFINING A STRATEGY TO ENGAGE VULNERABLE FAMILIES IN RESEARCH

Amanda Lees and Kit Tapson

Introduction

Before we begin this chapter, a note of explanation and definition is included for the sake of clarity. In this chapter, we use the term 'main study' to describe a substantial piece of planned research for which external funding has been awarded from our local National Institute for Health Research (NIHR) Applied Research Collaboration. The planned main study is an intervention development study which will seek the views of parents/carers living in socially disadvantaged areas about their health literacy support needs. It commenced in January 2021. We use the term 'formative research' to describe the preparatory work we undertook to assist us in determining an appropriate and feasible design for the main study. The formative research we undertook used multimethods and is the main focus of this chapter.

'Socially disadvantaged groups' may be defined as those who are 'socially, culturally or financially disadvantaged compared to the majority of society, implying individual, environmental or social restrictions to their opportunities to participate in health research' (Bonevski et al., 2014). Health and wellbeing researchers have frequently struggled to access, engage and retain respondents from socially disadvantaged groups, leading to the use of terms such as 'hard to reach' or 'hidden' (Bonevski et al., 2014). Not only are these groups underrepresented in health research, but they are more susceptible to adverse health outcomes (e.g. Marmot et al., 2020), and barriers that prevent engagement in research also deter from engagement with health and care services. Such issues may include anxiety, distrust, stigma, fear of disclosure, language/literacy difficulties and practical issues of lack of transport, childcare difficulties, inability to take time away from paid work and so on (Lees et al., 2018; Sutton et al., 2003; Woods et al., 2002). Overcoming these barriers in order to give voice to traditionally disenfranchised groups and to enhance engagement with health-care services is a pressing issue given the exacerbation of health inequalities

DOI: 10.4324/9780429263484-9

Strategy for engaging vulnerable families in research **175**

in the UK in recent years (Marmot et al., 2020) not least with regards to the recent COVID-19 pandemic.

Research that aims to engage harder-to-reach participants must be sensitively designed. Aldridge (2014) points out that power-laden and unequal methods will only reinforce vulnerable participants' position as marginalised and highlights the need for *participant-led* encounters. Increased policy focus in the UK has also stressed the need for participants to be seen as equal contributors (Graham, Grewal and Lewis, 2007) and for the incorporation of recipients' views into the services that affect them. Achieving a sensitive research design necessitates thought as to appropriate sampling, recruitment, data collection and measurement techniques, including factors such as language and literacy barriers.

Getting research designs right can be time-consuming and is likely to require a period of formative research and engagement with relevant stakeholders to determine the best approach (Bonevski et al., 2014). In health research, patient and public involvement (PPI) is recognised to play a crucial role in achieving appropriate research designs. PPI relates to the involvement of patients and the public in conducting and designing research, for example by helping to define research priorities, sitting as project steering group members, commenting on proposed research design and materials and/or undertaking data collection. However, carrying out PPI with 'harder-to-reach groups' is beset with the same types of challenges outlined earlier. Locally, in Wessex, it is acknowledged that PPI networks are not yet well established with underrepresented communities including amongst black, Asian, mixed and non-British white people and amongst people with average or low educational attainment. In other words, a 'typical' PPI representative is likely to be well educated, middle class and white! Work is therefore required to establish PPI contacts and networks within underrepresented communities before any formative engagement about appropriate research design can begin.

Furthermore, formative research often requires additional activities in tandem with PPI. For example, if you plan to carry out an intervention or intervention development study, formative work will be required to determine a baseline understanding of population need, which will require reference to statistics and datasets. An understanding of the types of interventions that have worked previously in similar contexts will also be required, necessitating some literature/systematic review work.

The amount of work required in a formative piece of research is easy to underestimate, especially as, in our experience, bids to 'big funders' such as NIHR require the inclusion of the information derived from the formative work as justification for the proposed main study design. Thus, there is a risk that this 'pre-work' happens with little or no funding, is not seen as a piece of work in its own right and that the process itself is little reflected on or learnt from. In some instances, this may not be too problematic – for example, if you are a medical practitioner with easy access to data on local health needs and treatment data, or if you are a member of a well-established university research group with a long-standing focus/access to data concerning your subject of interest. For others, though, who are keen to 'break new ground' within a research area, the task of formative research is not to

176 Amanda Lees and Kit Tapson

be underestimated. This is all the more true if you wish to engage with underrepresented, harder-to-reach communities.

This chapter goes on to describe a formative research project which used multimethods to establish a feasible design for a subsequent main study aiming to develop health literacy interventions for socially disadvantaged parents and carers. The main study will require qualitative research with socially disadvantaged parents and carers at risk of low health literacy to inform the development of a needs-led health literacy intervention. We describe the process we undertook in our formative research and the learning that we took away. We hope that this chapter will lift the lid on the importance of formative multimethods research and encourage fellow researchers to think about, plan and recognise the importance of this often-underestimated element of the research endeavour.

The remainder of the chapter is structured as follows. We begin by distinguishing between mixed and multimethods research and explain why we classify our formative approach as 'multi' rather than mixed methods. We go on to describe the context and rationale for us wishing to carry out our main study then dedicate the rest of the chapter to describing and reflecting on the multimethods formative research that preceded a successful funding bid for the main study.

Multimethods versus mixed methods

There are many different definitions of mixed-methods research available in the literature, and these tend to focus on key issues such as the types of approaches that can be mixed, when and why methods can be mixed and issues relating to theoretical standpoint and paradigms. These issues are drawn out in the introductory section to this reader. One point in particular helped us to categorise our approach as 'multi' rather than mixed method. This concerned the degree of integration or mixing of methods.

Morse (2017) suggests that mixed-methods research can be thought of as one and a half methods, where there is one core component and one (or more) supplemental component(s). The supplemental component(s) (whether qualitative or quantitative) allows the answering of an extra element of the research question but would not stand in its own right. This suggests that there is a strong integration of methods right from the design phase and focus on one single question. Indeed, the general view is that mixed methods should be employed to examine *the same question* from different perspectives, either for the purposes of validation (triangulation) or broader exploration, thus overcoming any methodological weakness inherent in any one approach.

In the words of Patton (cited in Johnson, Onwuegbuzie and Turner, 2007):

> I consider mixed methods to be inquiring into a question using different data sources and design elements in such a way as to bring different perspectives to bear in the inquiry and therefore to support triangulation of findings. In this regard, using different methods to examine different questions in the same overall study is not mixed methods.

In our formative study, on the other hand, we used different methods to answer different questions, all of which contributed to the understanding that we needed to meet the aim of the formative study. This 'set of investigations' was carried out in parallel and integrated at the end to define the research approach for the main study. This is akin to Bazeley's (cited in Johnson, Onwuegbuzie and Turner, 2007) description:

> Multimethod research is when different approaches or methods are used in parallel or sequence but are not integrated until inferences are being made.

Multimethods approaches are strongly linked with practical pragmatism, in which a research approach is determined predominantly by choosing the best methods for answering a question rather than by guiding epistemological or philosophical principles (Hesse-Biber, 2016) in the words of Hunter and Brewer (2006: 5):

> Which and how many methods are to be employed in a multimethod study depends upon the information required to shed light on the problem being investigated.

We now go on to describe the drivers for our main study. Following this, we will go on to explain the multimethods formative approach we took to investigate a feasible design for this.

Background and context for main study

In recent years, before the COVID-19 pandemic, the number of Accident & Emergency (A&E) Department presentations and emergency admissions had risen for children under 5 (NHS Digital, 2018). Heightened demand increases pressure on overstretched services, and A&E attendance/emergency admission is likely to be stressful for children and families. Demand for general practitioner (GP) services has also risen (NHS Digital, 2009). Frequently, children present to the GP or A&E with minor illnesses or injuries that could be managed at home or by other services (Baird et al., 2016; Holden et al., 2017; Rowe et al., 2017). On the other hand, many admissions to hospital could be avoided with better management of existing health conditions, such as asthma or epilepsy (Kossarova et al., 2017). The main reasons parents take children to A&E non-urgently have been identified by research as parental worry, perception that other health-care services are unsuitable, lack of confidence and low health literacy and perceived advantages of Paediatric Emergency Departments (e.g. access to experts with paediatric expertise). Other factors are the erosion of traditional support networks and a changing landscape of health-care services (e.g. Holden et al., 2017; Rowe et al., 2017). These factors can also act as barriers to the self-management of existing health conditions.

In response, information-based interventions for parents to encourage self-management of minor childhood illness and enhance navigation of the health-care system have been developed. In Hampshire, as part of the *Healthier Together* project, health information resources were launched for parents of children aged

0–5, available via the internet, in paper form and signposted by the range of health professionals with whom families come into contact. These resources are designed to empower parents to manage their young children's health by providing information on how to care for common childhood illnesses. Centred on six childhood conditions ((1) abdominal pain, (2) asthma/wheeze, (3) bronchiolitis, (4) diarrhoea/vomiting, (5) fever and (6) head injury), information is available via a website and paper-based resources to provide guidance on what to do when certain symptoms appear. Guidance is given on caring for children at home when appropriate, as well as signposting parents as to when (and from where) professional help may be needed. The resources were designed in recognition that parents can find it hard to navigate services and that empowering them to care for children at home, and to make appropriate treatment-seeking choices, may reduce unnecessary presentations at primary and secondary care locations.

Our research team conducted a qualitative evaluation of the Healthier Together information resources which were initially piloted in one city in Hampshire (Lees, Tapson and Patel, 2018). The evaluation sought to understand parents' views of the resources and any resultant behaviour change. The evaluation showed that parents valued the resources and appreciated the reassurance and guidance they provided. This was particularly important as parents reported experiencing considerable anxiety about childhood illness and making treatment decisions, some of which could be alleviated by the advice offered. A small number of parents gave examples of things they had done differently because of reading the resources, and several anticipated future behaviour change and a reduction of unnecessary GP visits.

However, one particular finding of the evaluation stemmed from the area within which it was conducted. The evaluation recruited participants from three children's centres and one GP surgery located within areas of socio-economic deprivation (according to Index of Multiple Deprivation), with a diverse population for many of whom English was not the first language. We found that a subsection of parents struggled to engage with the resources. A small number of parents recruited to the study explained their difficulties in understanding and navigating the information and expressed a need for additional support. Other participants suggested that simplification would be needed for those with poorer English skills. A further subsection of parents struggled to engage with the evaluation at all, either agreeing to take part and then withdrawing or refusing due to self-perceived lack of knowledge/language skills. These parents faced several barriers, including anxiety, a lack of confidence to use IT and language difficulties which hampered them in entering search terms, understanding information but also in being interviewed in the first place. In other words, they exhibited characteristics of *low health literacy* linked to social deprivation.

The World Health Organization (WHO; 2009) describes health literacy (HL) as 'the cognitive and social skills which determine the motivation and ability of individuals to gain access to, understand and use information in ways which promote and maintain good health'. The definition goes on to explain 'health literacy means more than being able to read pamphlets and successfully make appointments. By improving people's access to health information and their capacity to use it effectively, health literacy is critical to empowerment' (Nutbeam, 2000, 264).

Strategy for engaging vulnerable families in research   **179**

Given the apparent benefits experienced by parents who were able to access the information resources, we began to consider how we might better support and empower parents for whom standard information resources were not sufficient. This seemed important in order to ensure that existing health inequalities are not reinforced. This led to our idea for a main study to develop/co-create an HL intervention for socially disadvantaged parents to develop HL as an 'asset' (Nutbeam, 2008) via which individuals may feel empowered to confidently manage common childhood illness and exercise greater control over a range of factors that contribute to their families' health and wellbeing. This would involve qualitative work with parents to inform the development of a needs-led intervention. In order to ensure that the study design was feasible and capable of recruiting the needed participants, we embarked on formative research using a multimethods approach.

Formative research questions and approach

The overall aim of the formative research was *to develop an appropriate design for a subsequent main study to co-create an HL intervention to empower socially disadvantaged parents/carers of children aged zero to four years to manage common childhood illness and confidently navigate health services.*

We were guided by two main research questions:

1. Which parent/child groups across Hampshire possess characteristics associated with low HL?
2. How should we access/engage with these vulnerable groups in research about their HL support needs?

To answer these questions, we undertook an iterative programme of work using a range of methods, each of which contributed insights that allowed us to determine an appropriate design for the main study. The methods encompassed

- a scoping literature review;
- desk research to identify, profile and map socio-economically deprived communities in Hampshire; and
- qualitative PPI work with parent and practitioner stakeholders.

Literature review

As the first stage in the formative research, we conducted a scoping literature review. To contribute understanding to our two main research questions, we were interested to find out more about the following issues:

- i. The nature and definitions of HL
- ii. The effects of low HL and who is most at risk
- iii. Interventions that have been shown to improve HL

180 Amanda Lees and Kit Tapson

We used broad search terms encompassing our topics of interest, including 'HL', 'effects of low HL on health', 'HL and socio-economic disadvantage'; 'HL interventions'; 'research approaches for vulnerable groups'; and so on. We employed a purposive and inclusive approach to literature reviewing using search engines and databases, including Google Scholar, Google, Web of Science and Academic Search Complete. Following up citations within relevant articles also proved fruitful. Eighty-three papers were reviewed with notes and summaries made of contents in the bibliographic software Mendeley.

Literature review findings

The main findings from the literature review are discussed next.

Low HL and health inequality

Groups that have been identified as being at heightened risk of low HL include minority ethnic groups; those born outside the UK, without English as a first language; highest level of qualification below that expected by age 16 years; not in work, in low-grade work, with a low income, non-homeowner; and living in areas of socio-economic deprivation (Rowlands et al., 2015, 383). Low health literacy is linked with social inequality, meaning HL can be considered a social determinant of health. A US-focused systematic review by Sanders et al. (2009) looking at links between literacy and child health produced a model depicting the way that low HL acts as a social determinant of child health (which is likely to carry forward into adulthood). The authors suggest that family factors of income, education, language, culture and social support, as well as social factors of geography, educational resources, public health support and environmental health, work together to determine the collective HL of the child, parents and other caregivers, which then affects health behaviours and interaction with the health system (the ease of which is determined by its accessibility, written information and providers).

Low HL is linked with a range of adverse health outcomes. According to the Patient Information Forum (2013), patients with low HL

- suffer poorer health status,
- experience higher rates of hospitalisation/emergency admissions,
- are less likely to adhere to treatments and self-care plans,
- experience more medication/treatment errors,
- make less use of preventative services and more use of unscheduled ones,
- have poorer knowledge about disease management and living healthily,
- have lower ability to communicate with health professionals and participate in decision-making,
- are less able to make appropriate health decisions, and
- sustain higher health costs.

Low parental HL is detrimental to dependents' health. Children with long-term health conditions who have caregivers with low literacy use more health services (Public Health England, 2015a), and a US-focused systematic review by Sanders et al. (2009) concluded that low HL in caregivers is associated with poor preventative behaviours and poor child health outcomes. Low HL can make parents feel uncertain about managing their children's health problems and can lead to high use of health-care services for common childhood illnesses (Sanders, Thompson and Wilkinson, 2007).

In view of this, there have been calls for interventions to improve HL as a means to combat inequalities, improve outcomes and reduce health-care costs. For example, the Patient Information Forum (PIF) state:

> Low health literacy is…closely associated with significant health inequalities between different groups in the UK; and one key objective for health literacy interventions is to help reduce such inequalities in health and access to health-care services by targeting consumer health information and education at low literacy, hard-to-reach and disadvantaged groups.
>
> (PIF, 2013, 42)

They also identify the potential returns associated with such interventions:

> In the UK, patients with low health literacy have poorer health status and incur higher health costs than other patients. Improving engagement among patients with low health literacy would not only deliver much greater savings than for any other group, it would also help reduce health inequalities.
>
> (PIF, 2013, 13)

Interventions to address HL

HL is 'a two-sided issue, reflecting both the individual's ability to understand and use information to make decisions about their health and care, and a "systems issue" – reflecting the complexity of health information and the health care system' (Public Health England, 2015a). As such, interventions designed to address HL have been focused on health systems, as well as at the individual/community level. In some instances, interventions have addressed both elements.

Systems-focused interventions: Much of this work has emanated from the States and the Institute of Medicine's (2004) report 'Health Literacy a Prescription to End Confusion'. This work views low HL as a risk factor linked to poor health outcomes, which needs to be mitigated via systems change (Nutbeam, 2008). An example of this approach is that of De Walt et al.'s (2010) 'universal precautions' approach, which is focused on improving the accessibility of health services for all. Such 'precautions' are designed to improve spoken, written, support and 'empowerment' systems. De Walt et al. provide a toolkit of suggested interventions that health services can implement according to their organisational needs and priorities. Such tools include advice on using the 'teach-back' method, communicating with patients, following patients up, considerations for telephone conversations and so on. The authors report positive results associated with the various tools – for example, an easy-to-read brochure resulted in an increase in uptake of colon cancer screening, and symptoms of depression improved in a group of patients referred to a literacy group, in comparison with the control group.

In 2014, National Health Service (NHS) Scotland published 'Making It Easy, a Health Literacy Plan for Scotland'. As part of this, NHS Tayside established a Health Literacy Demonstrator site, which is implementing a range of tools to improve the health literacy of health services, including training staff, implementing the teach-back method, HL walkthrough of a hospital clinic and following up DNAs ('did not attends'). Whilst initial web-based feedback from the Demonstrator site is encouraging, formal evaluation of these interventions is not yet available.

Following on from work in Scotland, a demonstrator site has also been established in England. At the East Midlands Demonstrator Site (Public Health England, 2016–2017), systems-level interventions have focused on training staff (health, care and wider workforce) to enhance awareness of issues of low health literacy and the exploration of the feasibility of developing of an undergraduate HL module to embed awareness into professional development. The Public Health England (2016–2017) evaluation of the site states that recipients of staff training reported increased understanding of health literacy and how low HL can impact patients; enhanced understanding of how HL is relevant to their role; increased confidence in speaking to colleagues, patients, etc., about HL and improved confidence/skills to implement the learnt approaches/techniques into their practice. Whilst these early findings are encouraging, as yet there is no indication of associated impacts for patients.

Another approach introduced with a view to facilitating patient involvement with health-care systems is the introduction of decision aids, designed to supplement patient/professional consultations. Decision aids provide patients with information about different options and courses of action available to them and guide them through a decision-making process about which best suits their needs. These have been shown to improve patients' knowledge about health care, involvement in decision-making and appropriate uptake of services (O'Connor, 2003, reported in Coulter and Ellins (2007)). There is some evidence from the US that these groups are particularly beneficial to disadvantaged groups and have the potential to improve HL.

Stigma associated with low literacy levels may mean that universal approaches are sensitive and effective (Easton Entwistle and Williams, 2013). However, such approaches may fail to reach those currently not engaging with health services.

Educational interventions to improve HL: There are also a number of specific examples in the literature of educational interventions designed for people with low HL. A number of these interventions have been run within the auspices of health-care services, delivered by health-care professionals. An example of a professionally led intervention for lower literacy groups is Rothman et al.'s (2004) primary care–based diabetes management programme for people with low literacy (cited by Public Health England, 2015a). This study involved eight hours of teaching geared to low

Strategy for engaging vulnerable families in research **183**

literacy groups, supported by pharmacist adjustment of medication dose and resulted in 42% of the intervention group achieving their haemoglobin levels compared to 15% of the control group. Another example of HL intervention delivered by health professionals is the Stanford Nutrition Programme (cited by Public Health England, 2015a), which involved six sessions of education on lower-fat nutrition for adults with limited literacy. This approach relied on activities rather than written materials and included goal setting and problem-solving. This resulted in a significant report of the reduction in fat and saturated fat intake.

Other educational interventions have been community based, in partnership with the voluntary sector and social enterprise. These have had a broader educational focus, designed to enhance wider life skills, as well as specific health-related knowledge. These approaches operate from within a paradigm of developing HL as an 'asset' (Nutbeam, 2008) via which individuals may exercise greater control over a range of factors that contribute to health and wellbeing.

The Skilled for Health programme (2003–2009) used health-focused material as a hook to engage adult learners from disadvantaged communities to improve their literacy, language and numeracy skills. Skilled for Health classes took place in 157, mainly community, settings, for 3,500 participants. The class material included a 'health and wellbeing' module, which included advice on how to stay healthy and well and a 'services and health-care' module, with guidance on self-care and how to make the most efficient use of services. The evaluation found that the classes successfully engaged individuals and communities who do not traditionally engage in adult learning or other forms of public health promotion material (Public Health England, 2015a). Another important initiative has been NHS England's/Tinder Foundation's work to deliver digital skills training to facilitate the use of online health information and advice. This project was developed in response to the 'digital divide' whereby socially disadvantaged groups are hampered from accessing relevant information due to limited digital skills. The evaluation showed that 93% of participants had increased understanding of how NHS Choices could help them manage their health, nearly three-quarters were more confident in using online tools and nearly a fifth reported using fewer offline services as a result of increased use of online services (Public Health England, 2015a).

In a US study aimed specifically at parents, Herman and Jackson (2010) describe HL training for low-income parents on how to deal with common childhood illness delivered in the States by 55 Head Start agencies (Head Start and Early Head Start are government-funded programmes to support disadvantaged families). The intervention was delivered by Head Start agency staff who received 'train the trainer' input to prepare them for this role. The intervention provided a comprehensive, easy-to-read booklet for low-income parents with low literacy on a range of childhood conditions, along with training on how to use it (a two-hour training session delivered at an appropriate literacy level and offered in a range of languages), plus an in-home, follow-up session monthly for the following six months. Parents who completed the programme 'graduated' at the end of the intervention and follow-up. In the first stage pilot study, families that received both the book and the training, compared with the families who received only the book, showed

184 Amanda Lees and Kit Tapson

a 48% decrease in A&E visits and 38% primary care visits over a six-month period (Herman and Mayer, 2004; Herman and Jackson, 2010). In the follow-on full study, amongst parents receiving book and training, average A&E and primary care visits decreased 58% and 41%, respectively. The authors also signal the cost savings that could be anticipated through a wider roll-out of this approach. Missed working days by the primary caregiver and missed school days also decreased. The impressive results reported in this study signal the usefulness of 'a carefully tailored intervention with intensive reinforcements and follow-up in order to address the underlying motivation for behaviour regarding use and clinic visits and to maintain this change over time' (Herman and Jackson, 2010, 896).

Peer support roles: Lay-led community education approaches have also been found to be effective in addressing low HL. In Tower Hamlets and Hackney, Social Action for Health trained and supported over 70 local people to become their own-language 'health guides' for their own communities. Health guides share information about local services to facilitate access and share feedback received with local agencies to assist service improvement. Since its launch in 2004, the project has trained health guides from many communities including Bengali, Congolese, Nigerian, African Caribbean and Turkish/Kurdish. In an evaluation of 13 mental health guides, participants appreciated learning from a local community member/service user; and were motivated to change and to access further sources of information about their health. They also benefitted from peer sharing and support.

In a similar initiative, NHS Ashton, Leigh and Wigan employed health champions as a means to improve community health. Health champions are people who encourage and support other individuals and communities to engage in health promotion activities. Health champions can act as consultants to local authorities and community partnerships to help them develop activities to improve the health of local people. Qualitative evaluation of the work in Ashton, Leigh and Wigan showed that the health champions successfully engaged with members of the local community with low HL skills, to encourage healthy behaviours (Public Health England, 2015a).

Harris et al. (2015) conducted a substantial realist review to investigate the mechanisms by which community-based peer support could promote HL and reduce health inequalities. They found that peer supporters are most effective when allowed to exercise their experiential knowledge and autonomy to deliver culturally tailored support and involved in the co-design of programmes. This could be hampered by health researchers and professionals taking an authoritarian approach to programme design and implementation. Projects forming part of their review included peer support programmes for breastfeeding mothers, healthy living for older people, healthy eating and smoking cessation.

How the literature review shaped our approach

In summary, the literature shows the link between low HL and health inequality and provided helpful pointers to the groups most at risk of low HL (minority ethnic

Strategy for engaging vulnerable families in research **185**

groups; those born outside the UK, without English as a first language; highest level of qualification below that expected by age 16 years; not in work, in low-grade work, with a low income, non-homeowner; and living in areas of socio-economic deprivation; Rowlands et al., 2015, 383). This learning shaped subsequent stages of our formative research – especially the desk research/mapping exercise described next.

The literature indicates the usefulness for vulnerable groups of peer support, community-based and co-constructed interventions. This also resonated with the experience we had during the Healthier Together evaluation described earlier where recruitment in the known community settings of children's centres, facilitated by trusted children's centre workers proved a successful strategy. The identified themes were also relevant for the initial stage of PPI to be conducted as part of the formative research and signalled the likely usefulness of engaging parents/carers from harder-to-reach groups in known community settings and avoiding an 'authoritarian' approach.

Qualitative PPI work with practitioners and parents

In this formative research, we were seeking the input of parents and people from organisations that work with parents into the design of our subsequent main study. We also asked people (practitioners and parents) whether they would be willing to be involved in the subsequent main study research as part of an advisory panel. It is perhaps worth mentioning that it is not necessary to seek ethical approval to carry out PPI activities.

Practitioner PPI

Firstly, we (KT and AL) engaged with several groups of practitioners who represented organisations working with socio-economically disadvantaged parents/carers. This encompassed meetings with the following:

- Hampshire public health leads
- One community organisation supporting vulnerable families in New Forest
- South East Hampshire–based health visiting team
- A locality manager and a health visitor team leader
- A public health engagement officer

These meetings were run as focus groups/interviews and consisted of the research team laying out plans and findings to date and seeking the opinions of the group (or individual) in general and in relation to specific questions. This process of contacting professionals happened concurrently to the desk research/Lower Super Output Areas (LSOA) mapping. As such, it began at quite a broad level and then funnelled down once we had a clearer idea of the 'patches' of particular interest to us.

186 Amanda Lees and Kit Tapson

Key findings that arose from this element of the PPI were as follows:

- There was a general consensus about the importance of this area of research/work and that low HL was a recognised issue for practitioners who would value more skills/resources to empower parents.
- There was a recognition that existing information and resources were not suited to parents with low HL who often rely on social media and/or their children for support.
- A recognition of the differing profiles of vulnerable groups, especially in terms of ethnicity, led to discussion about *group-specific* engagement techniques. Some communities are more cohesive by nature of their shared faith/ethnicity and could be accessed via community leaders who are likely to be important gate-keepers for research.
- Other groups are not necessarily cohesive. This may be more likely amongst white British economically deprived groups where social isolation can be a problem. For these parents, access via existing outreach services could be a useful strategy. Trust can be a big barrier for socially isolated parents, so the importance of brokering contact by those already known to parents was stressed.
- Some useful link organisations and contacts to perform this brokering role were identified.

This led us to some initial research design ideas whereby parents could be 'recruited' either via existing community groups with which they were involved and/or by researchers 'piggy backing' on visits carried out by professionals with whom parents already have contact – e.g. health visitors. We felt that parents could be interviewed in-home or engaged in focus groups in known community locations, bearing in mind the provisos identified earlier.

Parent PPI

As we were beginning to come to some outline ideas about a design for our main study in terms of ways of sampling and collecting data, we now needed to gain the input of parents themselves into these ideas to really be sure that they were suitable and to identify factors that may encourage or deter from participation in research.

We held two PPI focus groups for parents to seek their views on the proposed research design. These groups were convened in two settings serving our target sampling area. The first of these was within a children's centre (whose attendees were all white British mums) and the second, brokered for us by the public health engagement worker, was held as part of an Afghan Women's Breakfast Club. Whilst we would have liked to have held more parent PPI events, the good numbers of attendees at both groups did ensure that several voices were represented. At both groups, KT attended to explain our reason for wanting to carry out the study and how it might be conducted and to ask for feedback and suggestions. KT took simple 'prompt' material along to the groups to assist with explanations. Time was taken

Strategy for engaging vulnerable families in research **187**

to explain the various possibilities related to the research design and to seek participants' views on this.

Responses to the proposed research design are shown in Table 8.1.

TABLE 8.1 Findings from PPI groups

Group	Findings/suggestions
My Time Group for Vulnerable Parents, Children's Centre	• A key finding from this group was that parents did not wish to be interviewed on a one-to-one basis and would prefer to answer questions in a group. They felt this would remove the spotlight from individuals and suggested that their anxiety levels would be eased if they could have some sort of distracting activity whilst answering questions. The researcher observed that at the session she was attending the parents were filling in diet sheets for their children. It was judged to be a helpful activity as parents did not feel pressurised to respond to her questions in a set way. • As a venue, parents suggested an existing meeting point, as this is something they have already factored into their week and they are all there together. For example, baby clinics, family points, drop-in sessions, My Time Group, Sure Start, part of health visitor's review. An alternative suggestion was that groups of parents could all go to one parent's house, although this was not so popular. Nurseries/preschools not seen as suitable because pickup/drop-off times can be pressurised and stressful. • Childcare and snacks would be desirable.
Afghan Women's Breakfast Club	• Parents were enthusiastic about the research, and some volunteered to be members of the parents steering group. • Parents stressed that crèche facilities would be necessary. • We sought advice in advance on whether interpretation would be necessary for the Women's Breakfast Club but were advised that most of the women who attended spoke good English and were able to act as interpreters for the couple of attendees who did not.

Desk research to identify, profile and 'map' socio-economically deprived communities in Hampshire

Following findings from the literature review, we undertook this work to identify, profile and 'map' the most deprived areas in Hampshire using the Index of Multiple Deprivation (IMD). The IMD is used to measure relative deprivation for small areas

188 Amanda Lees and Kit Tapson

in England (LSOA). LSOAs are fixed statistical geographies of about 1,500 people designed by the Office for National Statistics. Every LSOA in England is given a score for each of the domains and a combined score for the overall index. This score is used to rank all the LSOAs in England from the most deprived (1) to the least deprived (10), identifying how deprived areas are relative to others. An LSOA ranked 1 is amongst the 10% most deprived LSOAs – i.e. the most deprived decile. An LSOA ranked 10 is in the least deprived decile/amongst the 10% least deprived LSOAs. Accessing these groupings via the IMD provides a very reliable indicator for areas of deprivation. The domains that contribute to deprivation scores (1–10) are shown in Table 8.2:

TABLE 8.2 The seven domains of the IMD

Income	The proportion of the population in a LSOA that live in income deprivation. The definition of low income used includes both people who are out-of-work and those who are in work but have low earnings (and who satisfy the respective means tests).
Employment	The proportion of the working-age population in an area that is involuntarily excluded from the labour market. This includes people who would like to work but are unable to do so due to unemployment, sickness or disability or caring responsibilities.
Health, deprivation and disability	This includes measures of premature death, comparative illness and disability ratio, acute morbidity, rate of emergency admission to hospital and measures of mood and anxiety disorders.
Education, skills and training deprivation	This sub-domain measures the lack of attainment and skills in the local population relating to children and young people (key stage 2 and 4 attainment, secondary school absences, post education 16 and entry to higher education) AND lack of attainment and skills in the local population relating to adults (the proportion of working-age adults with no or low qualifications; the proportion of working-age adults who cannot speak English or cannot speak English well).
Barriers to housing and services	The barriers to housing sub-domain measures issues relating to access to housing, such as affordability, overcrowding and homelessness.
Crime	The crime domain measures the risk of personal and material victimisation and is made up of several indicators based on the recorded numbers of violent crimes, burglaries, thefts and criminal damage.
Living environment	This includes measures of air quality and road traffic accidents and measures of the quality of housing.

It can be seen that measures relating to education, skills and training deprivation, and health deprivation and disability are likely to bear a direct relationship with low HL, with other measures having a potentially more indirect bearing. For the purposes of our study, we decided to focus on parents/carers living in an area falling within the 10% most deprived in England – i.e. with a rank of 1 on the IMD. It was our assertion that respondents living within areas of highest multiple deprivations are likely to exhibit one or more characteristic of low HL and by definition fall within at least one group identified by Rowlands et al. (2015) as being at heightened risk of low HL – i.e. minority ethnic groups. Those born outside the UK, without English as a first language; highest level of qualification below that expected by age 16 years; not in work, in low-grade work, with a low income, and non-homeowner; and living in areas of socio-economic deprivation (Rowlands et al., 2015, 383).

As a first step, we identified a list of all 46 LSOA 1s in Hampshire and Isle of Wight and downloaded maps of each LSOA to identify the exact geographic location, for example, Figure 8.1.

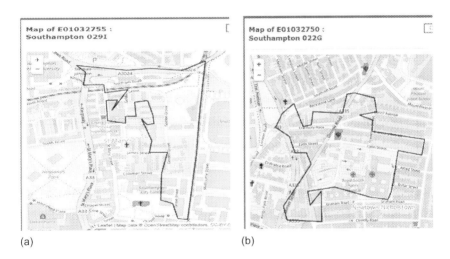

FIGURE 8.1 Example of LSOA maps

We were also keen to get a sense of the demographic profile of inhabitants of these LSOAs, especially regarding ethnicity, as being in an ethnic minority group has been highlighted as one of the risk factors for low HL. We were able to do this by running a query on the NOMIS website of the demographic profile of residents within individual LSOAs. In Hampshire, the large majority of LSOA 1 areas are predominantly white British. Out of the 46 LSOA 1s, there were only three in which 'white British' accounts for less than half of the population. These three areas fell within central Southampton.

The ethnic breakdown for these three LSOAs available from NOMIS is shown in Table 8.3:

190 Amanda Lees and Kit Tapson

TABLE 8.3 The ethnic breakdown for three LSOAs

Ethnic Group	LSOA E01017154: Southampton 022B	LSOA E01032750: Southampton 022G	LSOA E01032755: Southampton 029I
White: English/Welsh/ Scottish/Northern Irish/ British	40.9	40.7	37.9
White: Irish	0.6	0.7	0.9
White: Gypsy or Irish Traveller	0.6	0.3	0.0
White: Other White	10.3	25.9	11.1
Mixed/multiple ethnic groups	5.2	3.7	5.3
Mixed/multiple ethnic groups: White and Black Caribbean	1.4	1.4	1.1
Mixed/multiple ethnic groups: White and Black African	1.1	0.4	1.5
Mixed/multiple ethnic groups: White and Asian	1.7	1.1	1.7
Mixed/multiple ethnic groups: Other mixed	1.0	0.8	1.0
Total White	52.3	67.5	49.9
Asian/Asian British: Indian	6.4	5.7	5.4
Asian/Asian British: Pakistani	5.2	4.1	3.6
Asian/Asian British: Bangladeshi	1.8	1.7	3.0
Asian/Asian British: Chinese	0.7	2.9	0.6
Asian/Asian British: Other Asian	12.6	4.4	15.0
Total Asian/Asian British	26.7	18.8	27.7
Black/African/Caribbean/ Black British: African	9.7	4.1	10.8
Black/African/Caribbean/ Black British: Caribbean	1.9	1.3	1.1
Black/African/Caribbean/ Black British: Other Black	1.2	0.7	2.8
Black/African/Caribbean/ Black British	12.9	6.2	14.7
Other ethnic group: Arab	0.7	2.5	0.6
Other ethnic group: Any other ethnic group	2.1	1.4	1.8
Other ethnic group	2.8	3.9	2.5

Because we were keen to consider issues around ethnicity and English as a second language as part of our work, we decided that these areas of central Southampton would be important sampling areas. To ensure representativeness, we decided that we should also sample from predominantly white British areas of the city and subsequently sought advice from Southampton Public Health's engagement worker to help us to refine our choice (see later section) and to determine how we might recruit parents within these areas.

We then carried out a further mapping exercise in which we cross-referenced the LSOA maps with more detailed street views using Google Maps. This allowed us to get a better sense of the geographic location of the LSOAs and to identify obvious community centres/venues that may be existing meeting places/possible points of access. For an example, see Figure 8.2.

Google Maps search shows one temple and infant/junior schools in this LSOA.
Other relevant agencies/centres identified in other LSOAs included children's centres, churches, parish offices, etc. This exercise also identified LSOAs that were not in proximity to any obvious community centres/services, e.g. LSOAs close to the sea/parkland.

FIGURE 8.2 Example mapping exercise

How the desk research shaped our approach

The desk research shaped our research approach by identifying suggested sampling areas that could represent a mix of ethnicities/geographic locations. By cross-referencing the LSOAs with the use of Google Maps, we were able to identify possible access points in terms of community centres/services, etc. We still needed to 'drill down' further in terms of firming up which possible organisations/services may act as useful gatekeepers for the research and facilitate recruitment and retention. We also needed to know how we might best work with these organisations for these purposes. To find answers to these questions, we needed to employ a more qualitative approach and to seek the opinions of relevant organisations and parent groups. We describe this stage of the formative work as 'qualitative PPI'.

How the PPI work shaped our approach

Findings from our PPI work, particularly with parents, changed our proposed approach for the subsequent main study. Unlike our original plans, parents did not favour the use of in-home or individual interviews but preferred to meet with peers in known locations that form part of their everyday routine. This, therefore, became the proposed data collection approach for the main study. PPI work also highlighted special considerations, including the preference for the provision of food and child-care. We were also pleased to find that parents were interested in the research and (some) agreed to engage as parent advisors for the subsequent study.

Concluding reflections

The formative multimethods approach has enabled us to put together a well-considered research design for a main study that we believe to be capable of recruiting and retaining its target population. This study commenced in January 2021.

Through a combination of scoping literature review, desk research and mapping and PPI work with practitioners and parents, we developed a strategy for sampling in specific areas, known both to represent a mix of ethnicities and to be likely areas of high health service use/low HL. In particular, the PPI work with parents allowed us to develop our data collection strategy – we prioritised the strategy of engaging parents in groups of their peers within already known informal settings (rather than through in-home interviews as was one initial thought or conducting interviews in settings such as preschools or nurseries). We also learnt about the importance of providing childcare and the value placed on providing food. Because of the flexible nature of multimethods design, we were able to use the findings from one method to shape the approach taken by another – this was the case where findings from the analysis of the IMD and NOMIS shaped our decision to conduct PPI within particular areas of Southampton. Whilst we fully integrated our findings at the end of the work, in fact, there was also some interplay during the process of data collection.

This was an enjoyable and informative endeavour which provided much useful information and that has subsequently informed not only the design for the main study but also other avenues for research and development. We also developed a network of useful contacts through our PPI work with parents and practitioners. Learning to use the IMD and NOMIS extended our skill set and was an interesting challenge. As highlighted at the start of the chapter, it is important not to underestimate the amount of time and energy that went into this formative work.

As Bonevski et al. (2014, p. 23) point out,

> Developing relationships with communities and community groups, including their involvement in the development of procedures and study resources, and extensive formative research and pilot testing, require a considerable amount of time.

Given the extensive effort required to successfully engage with hard-to-reach groups, Bonevski et al. (2014) also highlight the potential for the establishment of research collaborations committed to high-quality research with socially disadvantaged groups. They identify potential benefits of this to include shared funding and resourcing, access to multidisciplinary expertise, developing a research culture in this field and, crucially, developing and expanding links with community groups to enhance the conduct of and recruitment to future research studies. We would also hope that such an initiative would have reciprocal benefits not just for the research community but also for the communities involved. In our region, we are currently involved in taking the first steps towards networking with other researchers also working in this field and hope that this could develop in the way that Bonevski and colleagues have described. It is also encouraging to see the opening up of funding streams dedicated specifically to the development of PPI networks via funders such as the School of Primary Care Research.

Perhaps another issue to highlight is that like the secondary data collection, the face-to-face data collection activities we conducted did not require ethics approval, as they were classified as PPI. So whilst they used similar techniques to interviews and focus groups, we did not need to seek consent from our stakeholders to record (in written form, not audio) and report their views. This did feel like a slight tension in writing the chapter, but we have tried to anonymise people's views as far as possible, even if we are not 'ethically' obliged to. We hope, however, that seeking to improve the research process such that it is sensitive and inclusive is an ethical activity in itself.

There are a couple of things we would have done differently on reflection. As alluded to at the start of the chapter, at the time of carrying out the various elements of this formative work, we did not really conceive of it as a piece of research in its own right, rather as an iterative sequence of approaches employed to gather the required information to determine the best design for our proposed main study. This limited the way that we have written up and disseminated our findings. Whereas a 'normal' piece of research would entail a formalised process of analysing/writing up and disseminating, we tended to record just what we perceived as the key findings – i.e. that were useful for the purpose of shaping the funding bid for the main study. We have thus probably rather 'under sold' the work that we have done and the findings we have gleaned.

Neither did we fully disseminate our findings back to those involved in PPI work, which on reflection, we feel we should have done, especially in view of the need to form relationships based on trust and continued engagement when working with 'harder-to-reach groups'. Putting together this chapter has been an interesting exercise in reconceptualising the work. It has made us wonder if there are other avenues for sharing the findings of the various elements of this project, perhaps with health and care practitioners and/or other researchers undertaking similar endeavours. It would be good to maximise learning and outputs from this multimethods project, especially in view of the resource and time it took.

Methodologically, such sharing could also 'fly the flag' for seeing the value in such multimethods formative approaches – we expect there may be a lot of this type of work that has gone on, as other researchers have done preparatory work for big bids – the learning from which may well not have been truly realised. It is interesting to think about what happens to 'all that knowledge'.

In conclusion, the multimethods research process we have described in this chapter stood outside our previous experience of research design, and as such, we tended to undervalue it and view it as a means to applying for funding for the subsequent main study. On reflection, we see that this multimethods approach has been a valuable programme of research in its own right, based on pragmatism and selecting the relevant tools to answer our questions. It has resulted in creative, paradigm-crossing work, which we believe has equipped us with a feasible design for our proposed main study, through which we will seek the views of parents and carers living in socially disadvantaged areas about the types of HL intervention they feel would help them to become more confident in looking after their young children's health and navigating services. It has also led us to appreciate the usefulness of the multimethods approach to health and wellbeing research.

Questions for discussion and further reflection

Why do the authors describe their approach as multimethods rather than mixed methods, and what are the related philosophical assumptions?

How has the data been integrated to this piece of work?

How does PPI differ from primary qualitative data collection?

What differences do you see between this formative approach and other studies described in this reader?

References

Aldridge, J. (2014). Working with vulnerable groups in social research: dilemmas by default and design. *Qualitative Research*, 14 (1), 112–130.

Baird, B., Charles, A., Honeyman, M., Maguire, D. and Das, P. (2016). *Understanding pressures in general practice.* Available at: https://www.kingsfund.org.uk/sites/default/files/field/field_publication_file/Understanding-GP-pressures-Kings-Fund-May-2016.pdf.

Bonevski, B., Randell, M., Paul, C., Chapman, K., Twyman, L., Bryant, J., Brozek, I. and Hughes, C. (2014). Reaching the hard-to-reach: a systematic review of strategies for improving health and medical research with socially disadvantaged groups. *BMC Medical Research Methodology*, 14, 42.

DeWalt, D., Callahan, L. F., Hawk, V. H., Broucksou, K., Hink, A., Rudd, R. E. et al. (2010). *Health literacy universal precautions toolkit* [online]. Available at: https://www.ahrq.gov/health-literacy/quality-resources/tools/literacy-toolkit/index.html

Graham, J., Grewal, I. and Lewis, J. (2007) *Ethics in social research: The views of research participants.* Available at: https://assets.publishing.service.gov.uk/government/uploads/system/uploads/attachment_data/file/497222/ethics_participants_tech_tcm6-5784.pdf. (Accessed 26 September 2018).

Harris, J., Springett, J., Croot, L. et al. (2015). Can community-based peer support promote health literacy nd reduce inequalities? A realist review. *Public Health Research*, 3 (3), 1–192.

Herman, A. and Jackson, P. (2010). Empowering low-income parents with skills to reduce excess pediatric emergency room and clinic visits through a tailored low literacy training intervention. *Journal of Health Communication*, 15 (8), 895–910.

Herman, A. D. and Mayer, G. G. (2004). Reducing the use of emergency medical resources among Head Start families: a pilot study. *Journal of Community Health*, 29 (3), 197–208.

Hesse-Biber, S.N. (2016) Introduction: navigating a turbulent research landscape. In S.N. Hesse-Biber and R. Burke Johnson (eds.), *The Oxford handbook of multimethod and mixed methods research inquiry*. Oxford: Oxford University Press.

Holden, B., Egan, M., Snijders, V. and Service, S. (2017). *Why do parents bring children with minor illness to emergency and urgent care departments? Literature review and report of fieldwork in North West London*. Available at: https://www.bi.team/publications/why-do-parents-bring-children-with-minor-illness-to-emergency-and-urgent-care-departments/.

Hunter, A., and Brewer, J. D. (2006) Designing multimethod research. In S. N. Hesse-Biber and R. Burke Johnson (eds.), *The Oxford handbook of multimethod and mixed methods research inquiry*. Oxford: Oxford University Press.

Johnson, R. B., Onwuegbuzie, A. J. and Turner, L. A. (2007) Toward a definition of mixed methods research. *Journal of Mixed Methods Research*, 1 (2), 112–133.

Kossarova, L., Cheung, R., Hargreaves, D. and Keeble, E. (2017). *Admissions of inequality: emergency hospital use for children and young people*. London: Nuffield Trust.

Lees, A., Tapson, C. and Patel, S. (2018). A qualitative evaluation of parents' experiences of health literacy information about common childhood conditions. *Self Care*, 9 (1), 1–15.

Marmot, M., Allen, J., Boyce, T., Goldblatt, P. and Morrison, J. (2020). *Health equity in England: the Marmot review 10 years on*. London: Institute of Equity.

Morse, J. M. (2017). *Essentials of qualitatively driven mixed-methods designs*. Abingdon: Routledge.

NHS Digital. (2009). *Trends in consultation rates in general practice – 1995–2009*. Available at: https://digital.nhs.uk/data-and-information/publications/statistical/trends-in-consultation-rates-in-general-practice/trends-in-consultation-rates-in-general-practice-1995-2009. (Accessed 3 June 2019).

NHS Digital. (2018). *Hospital accident and emergency activity 2017–18*. Available at: https://digital.nhs.uk/data-and-information/publications/statistical/hospital-accident--emergency-activity/2017-18. (Accessed 3 June 2019).

Nutbeam, D. (2000). Health literacy as a public health goal: a challenge for contemporary health education and communication strategies into the 21st century. *Health Promotion International*, 15 (3), 259–267.

Nutbeam, D. (2008). The evolving concept of health literacy. *Social Science and Medicine*, 67 (12), 2072–2078.

Patient Information Forum (PIF). (2013). *Making the case for information*. Available at: https://www.pifonline.org.uk/wp-content/uploads/2013/05/PiF-full-report-FINAL-new.pdf.

Public Health England/UCL. (2015a). *Local action on health inequalities improving health literacy to reduce health inequalities practice resource*. Available at: https://assets.publishing.service.gov.uk/government/uploads/system/uploads/attachment_data/file/460709/4a_Health_Literacy-Full.pdf.

Rowe, B., Cook, C., Wootton, R. and Brown, T. (2017). *A&E: studying parental decision making around non-urgent attendance among under 5s*. Available at: https://www.revealingreality.co.uk/wp-content/uploads/2017/03/Revealing_Reality_DH_non-urgent_attendance.pdf.

Rowlands, G., Protheroe, J., Winkley, J., Richardson, M., Seed, P.T. and Rudd, R. (2015). A mismatch between population health literacy and the complexity of health information: an observational study. *British Journal of General Practice*, 65 (635), 379–386.

Sanders, L. M., Federico, S., Klass, P. et al. (2009). Literacy and child health: a systematic review. *Archives of Pediatrics & Adolescent Medicine*, 163 (2), 131–140.

Sanders, L. M., Thompson, V. T. and Wilkinson, J.D. (2007). Caregiver health literacy and the use of child health services. *Paediatrics*, 119 (1), e86–e92.

Sutton, L. B., Erlen, J. A., Glad, J. M. and Siminoff, L. A. (2003). Recruiting vulnerable populations for research. *Journal of Professional Nursing*, 19 (2), 106–112.

Public Health England/UCL. (2015b). *Local action on health inequalities improving health literacy to reduce health inequalities practice resource*. Available at: https://assets.publishing.service.gov.uk/government/uploads/system/uploads/attachment_data/file/460709/4a_Health_Literacy-Full.pdf.

WHO (2009). *Track 2: health literacy and health behaviour*. Available at: http://www.who.int/healthpromotion/conferences/7gchp/track2/en/.

Woods, M. N., Harris, K. J., Mayo, M. S., Catley, D., Scheibmeir, M. and Ahluwalia, J. S. (2002). Participation of African Americans in a smoking cessation trial: a quantitative and qualitative study. *JAMA*, 94 (7), 609–618.

9

MIXED METHODS IN COMMUNITY-BASED HEALTH AND WELLBEING PRACTICES

Geoffrey Meads

The novel context is twofold: the expansion of faith based social enterprises in community health services and their inclusion of more informal sector resources, including both individual volunteers and social networks. For this contemporary context, four methodological approaches are presented for identifying and formulating policy through trend analysis, future scenarios and models and case exemplars. Essential stages in the process of secondary data research applications are detailed, from preparatory scoping reviews to the innovative use of both theoretical frameworks and perspectives from beyond standard health research.

The chapter seeks to demonstrate that the use of mixed methods is especially important now as a means of contributing sound data sources to the modern health policy-making mixture. They can enable research findings to have an extended reach as powerful stimulants for service and organisational development.

Introduction

The focus of this chapter is secondary data: its capture, its range and role and its analysis. The use of mixed research methods applies to both how this data has been derived and how it is then examined. The context for the chapter is contemporary and often rapid change in the organisational developments of health and wellbeing, including the move towards the delivery of health and wellbeing services by social enterprises and charitable agencies. The purpose of the chapter is to encourage and enable researchers – and especially those addressing future change agendas in these subject areas – at both the early and later stages of their research careers, to first recognise and then utilise effectively the data sources that can be available to them. These are expanding rapidly in volume and range. As a result, so too are the opportunity and scope for application and impact.

DOI: 10.4324/9780429263484-10

For illustrative material, this chapter draws on the author's recent experience of organisational research in primary and community health-care settings. In the UK and the local service evaluations, scoping reviews and evidence syntheses referred to in the pages that follow, many of the organisational developments in the health and wellbeing sector have been faith related in origin or orientation. They are part of the growing international trend towards mixed economies of individual and community health providers, which require less reliance on either simply public taxation or private investments for the delivery of comprehensive health and social care.

Such developments to the health and wellbeing sector are intrinsically complex and dynamic. They cannot be understood through single research methods, whether quantitative or qualitative. They may only be appreciated retrospectively. Particularly for the purposes of policy formulation and evaluation, multiple sources of evidence are needed to identify what is possible, potentially productive and even popular.

The approach adopted in this chapter is not that of simply regarding research findings as pure reflections of the data captured through disciplined investigation, with the validity of findings corresponding directly to the accuracy of the mirrored image. This classic scientific stance is, of course, paramount in the positivist tradition and current practice of clinical and cluster trials and meta-analyses. However, it is not necessarily either essential or even appropriate if successful application to policy, and thence to the organisational changes which policies promote, are the principal aim of a research project or programme. For these data capture and analysis are processes which can be legitimately designed to create the stimulus of new ideas and awareness of potential innovations which can be adapted, if not adopted. Such processes extend, but do not contradict, the scientific approach that underpins conventional systematic research designs. The pursuit of what is now often termed 'transferable learning' is especially important in times such as the present transformational period in health and health care when decisions have to be taken quickly at a pace for which conventional trials–based research reporting cycles are simply no match.

Within this dynamic context, an approach to acquiring research data as a trigger mechanism rather than as a mirror means more than just being opportunistic. Such an approach is not merely journalistic reporting dressed up as academic research by, for instance, trying to enhance perceptions of a report's status and the justification for ensuing action. It is also not just about partial truths, while nevertheless accepting that it is designed to help piece together future plans and proposals and can often be distilled into a gap analysis. What research is about when 'trigger' data is gathered principally for change agent purposes is termed 'development', accepting and recognising that development in health services and systems is an intrinsically political process. It is essentially research driven by expediency.

As such research data functions for its clients alongside values, relationships and resources. In both individual health services and overall health systems, policy outcomes arrive out of developments which are a mixture of all of these. Appreciating this does not diminish the role of research or its value but rather lays on the researcher an enhanced responsibility to produce empirically sound findings which should have applications in practice. Secondary data is well suited to the task. It is non-personalised. It is usually readily and expeditiously accessible, and it can often

Community-based health and wellbeing practices **199**

be in available public documents, including, increasingly, research data repositories of public universities and research institutes. This data may well be associated with primary research projects and publications of established credibility and accepted as a welcome next step as a result. And, of course, sometimes it may even offer answers to questions which were at best either supplementary or subliminal in the original primary research programme but turned out, over time, to be of more significance than the previous and original research propositions.

Design

In moving on now from the chapter's scene-setting section, it is now essential to clarify what is meant here by secondary data. As we look to provide empirical support for future developments, we need to define its particular attributes in relation to contemporary mixed-methods research. In this chapter, the data referred to is first that obtained in formal research-based projects which has significance beyond the remit of a particular project's commissioned aims and objectives. This occurs, usually when it is aligned by association or aggregation with such data from other research projects or documents. The data can be from past or ongoing qualitative and/or quantitative research programmes and projects. The sources are often such as appendices and supplements referenced in public documents and databases, issued from such agencies as the UK Department of Health and Social Care, Home Office or interior ministries and the UK Office of National Statistics. Secondly, the secondary data can be derived from 'grey' sources, such as conference proceedings, dissertations and theses, databases, websites, media entries and expert commentaries.

In this chapter, the particular local illustrations offered are largely derived from mixed-methods studies which revolved around interviews, focus groups, Delphi-style panels and different levels of participant observation, with statistical returns confined to such as simple Likert survey scores and service profile mapping exercises. Elsewhere, of course, in the same subject areas of primary and community care, the balance will be different with sophisticated statistical analyses of obvious utility (e.g. Zahner and Corrado, 2004) given the range of formative factors operating in today's increasingly hybrid systems.

Of the various qualitative research sources available for secondary data studies, structured observational data often offers the richest return. This is because of its breadth, detail and scope for comparison between different organisational settings with common features and characteristics. As a consequence, it can lay claim to possessing (and asserting) consistent variables. Such an assertion allows, for example, a researcher to identify, interpret and make meaningful as a cluster or grouping, different critical incidents or similar narratives and discourses. And, moreover, the researcher is able to do so without naming locations while still remaining true to the actual events. The use of secondary data can also mean that the need for local research ethics committee approvals is not required for data capture processes and permissions, although this should be checked on a case-by-case basis.

Individual secondary data research project designs depend on their agreed and authorised remits. As in primary research, a carefully articulated purpose should still determine the methodology. For example, if guidance on best practice is the objective in a central policy communication, then an 'ideal type' model, bringing together exemplary interventions across widely dispersed sites, may be employed in the collection of relevant data samples from an eclectic portfolio of past research. An 'ideal type' is a theoretical construct. It is an example of how theory, along with performance requirements and policy imperatives, can legitimately supply the alternative frameworks for collecting, collating and classifying secondary data. In turn, this data may itself be the source for suggesting rigorous revisions to theory, of even new theory. Fundamentally, as this example of the 'ideal type' suggests, we are operating in the territory of concept-oriented research, often using findings from previous ethnographic work (including observations, interviews and so on). Such research is founded on the premise for effective policy promulgation that an idea can be particularly powerful when it chimes with multiple experiences across a diverse range of settings. As earlier commentators on the subject of 'idealist orientations' in this mode of research through mixed-methods data capture and integrated analysis have noted, its pursuit of improvements can mean that the findings may well only report an emerging social phenomenon 'more or less faithfully' (Sandelowski and Barosso, 2007; Heyvaert, Hannes and Onghena, 2017).

Accordingly, the principal research products of secondary data studies for prospective applications are those with malleable and negotiable boundaries as follows:

- trend or network analyses
- agency models
- case exemplars
- future scenarios

These research approaches are described and illustrated in detail in the following sections, and they are not, of course, an exclusive list. They are also not completely discrete: for instance, both gap and risk analyses are closely identified with studies designed to stimulate future scenario planning and options appraisals. However, the four end-point products listed earlier do together clearly highlight the worth of secondary data for decision-making in health and wellbeing. Policymakers will often look to have all of the four 'empirical' sources of evidence lined up in support when they look to justify and promote a decision, especially, of course, if it is controversial.

Take, for instance, the thorny issue of community rehabilitation. To know how much to invest in alternatives to mainstream medical services is notoriously difficult. There is a relative shortage of evidence on the efficacy of interventions from 'positivist' primary research through clinical trial designs and follow-on meta-analyses. Such decisions depend on at least a workable partial understanding of changing trends in the preferred employment status of the relevant therapy practitioners, awareness of novel incentives and options for commercial and charitable agency delivery, evidence of cost efficiencies from good practice examples which possess adequate quality safeguards in selected local settings, and viable routes for the expanded or diminished resource allocations required. This example is just one of

Community-based health and wellbeing practices **201**

so many. For decision-makers in health and wellbeing, often entering new territories of organisational change and development, and desperate at times for the crutch of empirically sustainable arguments, 'perfect' positivist and provisional investigative results can often feel like the elusive enemy of 'good enough' research. Too often their findings are termed by their researchers as 'preliminary'.

From this perspective, sound, well-designed secondary data analyses meet the policymakers' needs and, quite literally, fit the bill for making expeditious and defensible decisions. To understand in more detail how the design of secondary data studies can be tailored for situations where expediency is an overriding consideration, it is helpful here to review specific studies where this has happened. The next section of this chapter describes the mixed elements of the secondary data enquiry process and then four local pieces of research involving methods of secondary data capture and analysis. These are drawn from the recently published work of the research team hosted by the Faculty of Health and Wellbeing at the University of Winchester in the UK.

Mixed methodologies

All secondary data investigation begins with a scoping exercise to locate what evidence is available and in what formats. The latter may well extend from conventional research databases, such as Medline and Scopus, to YouTube videos and the minutes of meetings. The search is a structured one, derived for its keyword terms from the commissioning remit: for example, the tenets of a central policy, a set of institutional principles, performance metrex or even a past programme theory. The second stage is to filter the findings eradicating duplications and removing those items which do not meet the study's contextual parameters for transferable learning. For example, these may be such as the exclusion of autocratic states, the inclusion of only peer-based decision mechanisms or particular profiles of professional human resource profiles. The third stage is that of codification across different types of study to obtain consistency of grouped subject matter and to give an initial weighting to the findings. While coding begins with the terms of the research remit, it should involve relevant inputs from the prospective research recipients. The last then continue their engagement in the final stage of interpretation in which repetition of incidence, demonstrable impact on practice and transferability are the key determinants.

As the following accounts of local research highlight, these four stages can easily overlap as opportunism takes over. Each stage can be perceived and recognised as a principle, but all are susceptible to the forces of pragmatism which prevail in both health policy and the emerging world of wellbeing.

Trend analysis

Sometimes significant change can be taking place right in front of our eyes, but because it is almost too close, as an everyday occurrence, we do not really notice it. We lack the objectivity to see its significance. Somehow our mindsets get stuck,

202 Geoffrey Meads

and we are unable to discern the emerging patterns of behaviour and common processes which constitute trends or emerging networks. This block certainly applies to the rapid expansion of wellbeing provider outlets and their impact on the front line of health services. The article that is referred to here, as an illustration of a trend analysis, actually arose from a discussion between researchers at the University of Winchester in which such an assertion of dramatic contemporary change was treated with some scepticism. To support the claim that the translation of the concept of wellbeing into practice was then 'revolutionising' the 'High Street' through a proliferation of health- and wellbeing-related businesses required empirical backing. The evidence before our eyes was just not enough.

The empirical backing was supplied by re-visiting, in this case, two sets of observations and interviews undertaken across the public and independent service sectors in the cities of Melbourne and Winchester. Both are award winning as 'liveable' cities. Both could legitimately be regarded as a purposive sample or exemplar of wellbeing values and initiatives. Winchester hosts the university at which this chapter is being written. Melbourne hosts Monash University where in 2014/2015, the chapter author was seeking to pull together some of the lessons to be discerned from a series of previous primary research projects, through the use there of a series of expert witness interviews and workshops on organisational developments in primary health care. And Melbourne is the capital of the State of Victoria: a global pioneer of 'bridging social capital' measures for enhanced community wellbeing, through the use of its cross-sectoral and empirically based 'Framework for Health Equity' to underpin and monitor health service interventions (Mason et al., 2015).

The secondary data capture was remarkably simple. First, the interviews and observations offered the opportunity to identify and profile new wellbeing service outlets through collating and coding their citations in interviews and research diary entries and, in many cases, noting the location of the interviews themselves. This exploratory work provided a basis for the construction of an initial inventory of wellbeing agencies. This could then be expanded through a locality mapping exercise.

The second stage of mapping utilised current and past Google Maps and websites to count, over a set three-year period, changes in the overall numbers by randomly selected suburbs and to record, on the basis of physical proximity, apparent combinations or clusters of wellbeing outlets. The finding was that wellbeing agencies had expanded in range so rapidly that, by 2017, they consistently occupied between a quarter and a third of frontline shop premises: second only in number to cafes, restaurants and other hospitality venues. A threefold increase was noted in three years. The titles of proprietors and their marketing material suggested much of this growth was linked to ventures undertaken by new immigrants. (For instance, in one Melbourne suburb, no fewer than 14 types of 'holistic' body massage were available.)

A third stage study of civic documents then confirmed that during the three-year period, local authorities in Melbourne had offered financial incentives in relation to low rentals for commercial premises, including deferred payments and reduced rental fees, while at Victoria State, major discounts were being provided for

Community-based health and wellbeing practices **203**

block bookings on one-year vocational training programmes in further education colleges. Life coaches, nutritionists, counsellors and personal trainers were identified in the documentation as typical new practitioner products of such courses across Victoria State sites in Australia.

The academic research product of triangulating the three secondary data sources – interview and observation notes from previous primary research, historic and current website entries and formal documents – was a short scoping review article. This employed a standard World Health Organization (WHO) policy framework for multi-disciplinary primary health care (WHO, 1978) to first collate the different data sources and then to define a future research agenda. The ensuing published article highlighted some of the empirical shortfalls apparent in relation to the efficacy of new wellbeing initiatives (Meads, 2016). The future research questions posed in the article were classified according to the long-established WHO principles of equity, participation and cross-sectoral collaboration (WHO, 1978). They pointed to the need to understand better the issues arising from commercial and social enterprises co-existing in the High Street, the implications for general medical practice and health system regulators and future governance requirements. The article included short comparative case studies drawn from the secondary data sources and a research topic guide.

While the article, on the face of it, drew on quite straightforward and even relatively superficial sources to analyse trends, its aggregated data did still offer quite a profound insight into the potential dilemmas that might arise if and when economic drivers usurp health gain as the main purpose of new wellbeing initiatives. This prospect may apply to both their service provider practitioners and their business entrepreneurs, with privatisation to commercial status a recurring outcome for charitable endeavours which initially adopted a social enterprise status. Accordingly, a concluding question in the article summed up the concern by asking, 'What are the risks and benefits for health care investments arising from increased levels of private and co-payments for frontline wellbeing services?'

Agency models

As boundaries between publicly and privately funded public health and health-care interventions have become more blurred, so interest has increased in organisational developments which seek to combine the energies, services and skills previously understood to be prevalent in different alternative sectors. In the UK, as elsewhere, and especially in primary care settings, all kinds of hybrid ventures have come to the fore in what is clearly a time of organisational experimentation and uncharted waters for both local health systems and national policymakers. Confederations, coalitions, collaboratives, private-public partnerships and, above all, new networks abound, and to avoid simply adopting a trial-and-error approach, basic reference points are often sought from research sources so that articulated criteria for change can at least have some legitimacy in empirical terms. In consequence, they can be expressed in explicit and contestable language.

204 Geoffrey Meads

This is the background for the production of models which can help define the agency that can be appropriate for the delivery of health-care future interventions. Such models are of utility when they categorise, classify or frame agency to incorporate inputs from practitioners previously outside the boundaries of institutional providers, such as mainstream university or district hospitals. Of course, most of these come under the umbrella term of 'wellbeing' and have been either commercially or charitably financed and supported. As a result, new alliances, exchanges and combinations across sectoral boundaries produce real tensions and dilemmas, especially in relation to issues of probity and accountability.

These issues come together in the subject area for health management and policy research of governance: an umbrella term which encompasses the processes and procedures of agency accountability. The study chosen to illustrate the value of secondary data studies on this subject is one which recognises that achieving effective and enduring governance arrangements in hybrid health and wellbeing systems, at this stage of their evolution, is a real challenge. It can be one which is fraught with pitfalls. Practical setbacks and continuous structural change seem almost inevitable. Accordingly, the 'ideal type' of agency model comes into its own because it so neatly brings together actual examples of good (or even best) practice coherently into a single comprehensive framework while still explicitly acknowledging that, in overall terms, the model cannot and does not exist. Or at least as a whole it does not yet exist and will not in the foreseeable future. This agency model may be 'merely' conceptual, but it can also be practically invaluable in complex political contexts of multiple 'countervailing' forces (Light, 1997).

An 'ideal type' for community governance in modern primary health-care organisations was derived from three researchers re-visiting their primary research in separately published and peer-reviewed studies on local engagement developments in primary health care across three WHO global regions, undertaken over the same ten-year period prior to 2016 (Meads, Russell and Lees, 2016b). The data capture was again threefold but in five phases. Accordingly, the first two stages involved structured literature reviews to first define an initial theoretical model for an ideal type of public participation and then, at the second stage, to refine this in response to policy mandates identified in relevant WHO documentation. At the second stage, individual components of the model with their linkages and clusters were visible structurally in an overall framework. This was then followed, in the third and final stage, by a detailed review of interview records from 34 national case study sites which had the common characteristic of devolved resource management roles for lead primary care professionals (usually general medical practitioners). This review was completed with a further refinement of the model's component features. The modifications made now came through identifying significant repeated contributions to service delivery in the case study data. Repetition is the key here in the analysis, across two or more settings to formulate learning which is not bound by context. No local or personal identification is necessary or, in ethical terms, desirable excepting for beacon sites.

Community-based health and wellbeing practices **205**

In addition, for each organisational dimension or category, illustrative practices were specified and collated in tabular form within a single inventory and overall classification. The result was a distinctive contribution to the growing literature on the new collaborative (and community) governance models which, across sectors, are recognised as essential if stakeholder-based corporate accountabilities are to be performed effectively in practice.

Case exemplars

By definition, exemplars highlight excellence of practice, 'wicked issues' (of novel complexity and difficulty), outliers, future directions of travel and exceptional ideas. They invite emulation, re-creation and adaptation. They can make the impossible, or previously un-thought of, seem possible and feasible; so long as they are accurately described, take account of particular contexts and have clear criteria for such as success and failure or benefits and shortfalls. In their potential for early adoption as implementable developments, case exemplars go well beyond the illustrative examples of an agency model described earlier. The reports that contain exemplar accounts are, in consequence, often the most read forms of research publication, particularly in relation to primary care development topics (Turner, Meads and Garfield-Birkbeck, 2013).

As a general rule, the more specific detail there is in a case exemplar, the better it is for application purposes. And for exemplars to be appropriately specific and detailed as sources of applied learning, they invariably must be located within frameworks which are simple and meaningful for health professionals and managers. This is not to patronise but simply to recognise the political and patient pressures under which the latter operate. Accordingly, the researcher needs to design or draw upon frameworks and linguistic forms which are succinct, accessible in their wording and/or use of acronyms and credible on an everyday basis. No more than six headings are ever required, and the rule of less is more applies. Accordingly, secondary data should be used sparingly, not to tell the whole picture but rather to whet the appetite and to enable those whose task is implementation to feel the end product is theirs and theirs alone: credited as 'all their own work'.

This approach to encouraging legitimate plagiarism can lead to what seems like quite crude methodical research. Our recent study of the extended informal relationships which provide support for older people employed just a simple framework of four sub-titles for recording exemplars in 'physical, mental, social and spiritual networks' (Meads and Lees, 2019). Obviously, such networks as absolute and discrete entities do not exist. Of course, all four overlap, and their often faintly drawn boundaries blur. But in this instance, gathering together under these headings, data from across a series of previously published and approved wellbeing studies (e.g. Ralph, 2015; Meads, Lees and Tapson, 2016a; Jones, 2017) to augment the case material available in the notes of our own previously cited UK and Australian studies allowed the 'leadership hubs' and their knowledge bases to be identified. Table 9.1 provides a summary of these using actual job and subject titles.

206 Geoffrey Meads

TABLE 9.1 Relational wellbeing networks for older people: leadership exemplars

Wellbeing network	Activity	Leadership hub	Knowledge base
Physical	Sports and exercise (e.g. in seniors' academies and Strava links)	Life coaches	Physiology
Mental	Arts and creative crafts (e.g. in meditations, mindfulness and colour charts)	Counsellors	Psychology
Social	Meetings and mobility (e.g. via Good Neighbours schemes and book clubs)	Community organisers/agents	Social work
Spiritual	Reflection and fellowship (e.g. yoga classes and house groups)	Pastoral gurus	Religions

Few new topics are more instantly attractive to implementers than that of leadership, especially if, as in this case, the specific exemplars are associated with low or minimal costs. To shape secondary data for the purposes of achieving such an appeal depends on utilising frameworks which can have traction in the world of action and decision-making. Accordingly, in the secondary data study of relational networks, the functional frameworks used were those developed in handbooks and now drawn together in central community development practice guidance (GOV. UK 2017). Some of these frameworks are derived themselves from pioneering secondary data studies (e.g. Grundy and Holt, 2001), and they increasingly align with the objectives (and performance indicators) promulgated by national governments and voluntary sector councils for seniors' wellbeing (Grube et al., 2019, Zaidi et al., 2021). Table 9.2 gives an indication of the kind of outputs which can be achieved through adopting such a pragmatic perspective. In this example, the very specific nature of the case material allows a clear comparison of networks at what implementers tend to see as the two (opposite) ends of the spectrum in respect of physical and spiritual wellbeing. By just using broad headings of 'Aims', 'Scale' and Activities', however, the applied learning is not of competing or contradictory practices but of the potential for complementary and mutually supportive 'Connections' with the profound prospect of a dual 'Ethos' that can become more culturally embedded.

Putting together data 'highlights' for the purpose of detailing case exemplars as a means of applied early learning is not merely a random or *ad hoc* methodological process for the researcher. What is presented to the reader and what the researcher sees are quite different. The crude simplicity of the end product is deceptive. While the effectiveness of the case exemplar may depend on its ready accessibility its production depends, rightly, on the academic rigour of the production process. An inverse law applies here. In the relational network example drawn upon here in this chapter, it was the sifting of the burgeoning research literature on networks through an incremental cascade approach which identified the underpinning actor networks

Community-based health and wellbeing practices **207**

TABLE 9.2 Exemplar senior/older people's networks: characteristics and cultures

Network	Aims	Scale	Activities	Connections	Ethos
Physical	Enhanced sports performance, exercise routine with targets, egalitarian approach across generations and gender	Daily schedules, kettlebells, warmups and regular workouts, standard pool and sea usage, green gyms	Cycling routes, jogging and power walking, flexibility sessions, Pilates, small court ball games	Personal trainers, exercise physiologists, muscular skeletal practitioners, physios, first aiders and occupational therapy, gym suites	Individual and self-managed actualisation
Spiritual	'Missional' fellowship and reciprocal support, life–cycle awareness, redemptive self–exploration, palliative and restorative	Seasonal observances, religious occasions, ongoing witness, truth seeking study and narrative sharing	Scriptural texts, shrine attendances and divinely sourced worship, contemplative sanctuary, soulfulness sessions and retreats	Key writers and inspirational speakers, churches and study group hosts, churches and cults, yoga classes	Meta-physical and supernatural/ superordinate

theory, and it associated the notion of 'social materials' as the most relevant and applicable to the secondary fieldwork data being used in the project (Hassard and Law, 1999; Latour, 2005). Decisions on which 'living materials' to then include in the published article and report were then taken by the researchers only after consultation with, in this instance, a virtual advisory group. This was largely made up of those who had offered contributions as advisors to the original primary research studies. For academic development purposes, as opposed to practical application, such continuity is important when the ultimate aim is the creation of a genuine new body of knowledge.

Future scenarios

Future scenarios are the most fun outcome for those engaged in secondary data research. They are actually fun at every stage: to formulate, to communicate, to test and to revise and update. Intellectually, they give licence to the researcher to be creative and experiment and to not worry too much about their reception. If it is not quite 'anything goes', it is not so far off, and the thresholds for validity and credibility are more flexible than for almost any other mode of research investigation and enquiry. The golden rules are simply to ensure the scenarios proposed do offer authentically alternative routes to the same end point, with out-of-sight horizons which are well beyond the timescales for effectively resolving present operational challenges, tasks and issues – however, daunting these may currently seem – and agreed upon macro-level milestones for formative development along the way. And, of course, future scenarios must be rooted empirically in professionally gathered research data.

The rapid growth of new wellbeing interventions and their agencies offers a glorious opportunity for designing and defining future scenarios. Nobody can really know, in specific detail at least, where we are heading. Lots of legitimate options are on offer. In this context, conscientious interpretation by the researcher is justified. This is especially true if the outcomes have a more profound impact than scenarios which merely masquerade as likely developments but which fail to mask expressions of personal opinions and/or a priori assumptions. Writing future scenarios properly and well means not just pointing to worst- and best-case outcomes or converting past data into a source of advocacy for positive responses to a favoured unmet need or personal interest. Future scenarios are not about championing a particular cause by the back door, but rather they should be designed to help readers rise above the mire of daily workloads and consider the fundamentals that must be addressed effectively in and for future development. At the level of whole health systems especially, they are critically important.

This is apparent when the future of the increasingly multi-professional and cross-sectoral primary health-care sector is considered. New wellbeing interventions are a changing world in which, only recently, medical and nursing professions held sway through their clinical monopolies and control of community health centres. So the end point of more service outlets, more interfaces between them and more complex health and wellbeing systems as a result is generally accepted. So too, inevitably, is the challenge they face at all levels of achieving functional integration. In terms of future scenarios, this is beyond the horizon: a long way off and out-of-sight. All that is clear from the standpoint of present operational activity is that key relationships will need to be examined and enhanced if increased diversity is not to be damaging or even destructive.

Which are these relationships? Which are those critical to integration, and which formative relationships require attention along the way? Secondary data lends itself to retrospective gap analyses. Our recent re-visiting of research in local areas where new social enterprises are operating provided a valuable means of identifying not only emergent new relationships across health and social care agencies but also the strengths and shortfalls in these which can assist and hinder future integration processes. In this particular study, a validated relationship audit tool (Ashcroft and Meads, 2006) was applied to the data. Two empirically established components of integration, continuity and directness (Schluter and Lees, 1993), were applied to measure and assess (Meads, 2018).

Accordingly and in summary, data from periods of participant observation were investigated so that the frequency of face-to-face contacts with openness of dialogue and exchange could be counted and understood. The findings pointed to three relationships as fundamental to future health system formulations: (1) between

Community-based health and wellbeing practices **209**

senior decision-makers authorised in newly participative health and social care accountability structures, (2) across and within separate new wellbeing service specialty practices themselves and their dispersed outlets and (3) actually for health researchers and their clinically focused faculties with the ever-expanding wellbeing service sector. The future scenarios are of these three relationship sets intertwining in different (and alternative) ways, with behavioural patterns that will assuredly create the health and wellbeing systems of tomorrow.

Table 9.3 provides a list of further relational dimensions beyond just directness and continuity, with a brief explanation of each.

Drawing on such relational variables as those previously listed allows the researcher to highlight high and low scores currently in relationships across agency boundaries, which may be key factors for the long-term future. For example, their very novelty means that many colour- or diet-based therapists have little shared experience with nursing or medical professionals, while public service trustees can be similarly detached or even alienated from the commercial stakeholders of spa- and sauna-linked business ventures. In this context, the staging posts defined by researchers in future scenarios they articulate may well revolve around the search for joint objectives, common educational curricula and overall unity of purpose.

In summary

The four local case examples described in this chapter point to the richness and range of secondary data research and its potential worth in situations of high uncertainty. A single research methodology in each instance could not have produced sufficient up-to-date levels of data or 'power' for a persuasive argument. The learning from such studies for future researchers is especially important in terms of getting to grips with emerging contemporary issues that might de-stabilise increasingly complex health and wellbeing systems. For many of these issues, there are few precedents, and systematic literature reviews would reveal only a dearth of research. This clearly applies, for instance, to the advent of many new wellbeing service enterprises for which public health regulatory powers seem likely to be less influential than those for market competitiveness. Much the same can be said in respect of issues around probity.

Accordingly, while each of the case examples is self-evidently opportunistic in its choice of both subjects and data capture techniques, all are shaped by motives of applied learning for the common good. This is critical and fundamental. Secondary data research should never be about second-guessing or parading the false wisdom of hindsight. While formed by the events of what has happened in the past, secondary data studies are essentially formulated to meet the needs of the future. This is a guiding principle.

In summary, then, by collating the common elements of the local case studies described earlier, and their several counterparts, we can identify three requirements for the successful exposition of this guiding principle. For secondary data projects as contemporary mixed-methods health and wellbeing research, these are the

TABLE 9.3 Relational variables: examples of integration

Commonality	Breadth	Reciprocity	Continuity	Directness	Parity	Values
Common terms and language	Understanding roles and responsibilities	Exchange of knowledge and goods	Regular contact over time	Openness of communication	Equivalence of status and contributions	Codes of behaviour
Shared aims	Complementary skills and resources	Goodwill on both sides	Planned meeting points	Face-to-face contact	Mutual respect	Practice ethics
Cultural compliance	Sensitivity to personal and professional agendas	Informal and formal cooperation	Meaningful encounters	Integrity of process	Balance of power and influence	Joint regulation

Community-based health and wellbeing practices **211**

imperatives of investigation, in particular, for future organisational researchers in the fields of health policy and management.

First, it is essential to check and compare the relevant social policy as formally expressed in official documents with that which is informally espoused in behaviour. This imperative is particularly evident in the use of civic and church documents in the trend analysis and exemplar case illustrations described earlier. Secondary data analyses, because of their time frames, offer a unique opportunity to evaluate difference and often dissonance between asserted and actual outcomes in policy implementation. Accordingly, for evaluative purposes, drawing on the distinction between expressed and espoused statements is essential.

Secondly, the re-visiting and review of secondary data derived from observational and/or broader ethnographic work must be soundly structured by appropriate, relevant and defensible theory or performance criteria and categories. If the latter data are to be used, as in the case of the community development handbook cited earlier (Skinner and Wilson, 2002), then the common perception of the terms employed should be that they are non-partisan and politically neutral. Simply relying on a grounded theory approach is insufficient. This lays the researcher open to the charge of being excessively interpretative: of pedalling a personal opinion or promoting a political position. Studies which involve the secondary use of data are absolutely not about having a second chance or an axe to grind.

Thirdly, and finally, there is the methodological imperative of applying a cross-boundary perspective. Insight in secondary data studies comes from employing a new research viewpoint. While ensuring participants in the primary research are anonymised and protected, it does not come from simply repeating the original data capture and analytical process. The new perspective comes from addressing the data from the stance of another subject or sector. In the local studies described earlier, for example, the management dimensions of collaborative governance were identified with the aid of sociological tenets in respect of 'countervailing forces', while both theological and psychological scales of wellbeing helped in the classification of alternative network hubs for older people. The student of secondary data is a 'boundroid' researcher, preferably by dint of personal temperament as much as by professional disposition. It helps a great deal if the starting point is a non-institutional mindset and an openness to the value of applied learning from elsewhere.

These three directions for secondary data research methods are fundamental to the evaluation of and for health policy, inter-professional and multi-disciplinary practices and new social enterprise. Together, they safeguard research as empirically based, independent and creative. These are three qualities on which the viability of tomorrow's increasingly hybrid health and wellbeing systems may well depend if they are to achieve functional degrees of integration.

The bigger picture

The local case studies highlighted in this chapter are, of course, part of a larger picture in which multiple big datasets and their computer-based access mechanisms

212 Geoffrey Meads

are increasingly being established and made available. This growth is big business. It is increasingly supported by novel templates for research protocols and literature reviews – such, for example, as SQUIRE (British Medical Journal, 2015) and eMERGe (Cunningham et al., 2018) – that are well suited to the discipline of secondary data research. NVivo is the most popular of the many computer-based tools for identifying themes in interviews, focus groups and expert panels, with others such as Atlas.ti able to delineate patterns and ideas in particular discourses, exchanges and narratives through its structured storage facility for common data coding exercises. The tools and techniques for secondary data research are now such that an eclectic approach to their selection and mix can be adopted easily, and indeed appropriately. The local case studies in this chapter point to how different combinations of data capture are feasible and effective. As those who have studied how to study to produce credible social research, mixed research methods are an essential prerequisite (Bryman, 2012). In short, form fits function.

This emphasis on eclecticism in research methodology selection tallies directly with the range and variety in subject matter of increasingly hybrid health systems. Health and wellbeing services that depend on public, private and, increasingly, independent voluntary sector investments and interventions can only be understood if data capture processes respond to their very different business requirements for service delivery. What rates as 'patient confidentiality' in one setting ranks as 'commercial-in-confidence' in another. The need to match data capture to this extension in sites and settings does help pave the way for legitimately combining previously distinct and separated secondary data sources while still using the principle of such as realist synthesis or triangulation to ensure the appropriate collating and interpretation of the gathered and aggregated data (Pawson et al., 2010).

The need to include a wider range of cross-sectoral data sources becomes especially apparent in the context of integration. Today, this is the foremost value in clinical and social care, driving both UK and continental policies in the pursuit of more efficient resource utilisation and holistic public health. Since the WHO's revision of its seminal 'now more than ever' primary health-care philosophy a little over a decade ago (WHO Annual Assembly, 2007), integration, founded upon the much greater involvement of non-statutory agencies, has been the value around which its 'pillars' of participation, partnership and equity (MacDonald, 1992) coalesce for their contemporary expression. And research in those leading universities for the promulgation of primary health-care development has recognised this change through their own eclectic approaches to disciplinary linkages designed to create mutually reinforcing bodies of knowledge. Exemplars now proliferate: Medicine and Manufacturing at Warwick in England, Politics with Community (and Communist) Health Development at Bologna in Italy, Marketing with Pharmacology and Genetics in the Life Sciences movements of Minneapolis and Boston in North America and, above all, Business Economics with multi-professional Health Education initiatives in the universities such as Ghent, Maastricht, Upsalla, Linjoping, Tampere and, especially, Utrecht, across the Low Countries and the States of Scandinavia. At each of these venues, the pursuit of knowledge has meant traditional boundaries between academic disciplines have been cast aside in parallel with the merging of public and private agencies across the health and wellbeing sectors. Mixed-methods secondary data studies belong to the growing movement for evidence syntheses which underpin this knowledge production. The researchers of tomorrow will be well advised to view this as a 'new normal'.

Together, all the different elements in the agenda for integration lead to a bigger picture for health researchers. As indicated earlier, this certainly means more mixed methods and broader remits. It also means more imaginative approaches to research implementation and dissemination. Findings should not simply rely on internal validity for their currency. Compliance with a host institution's commissioned brief is no longer enough. Transferability of outcomes and application of outputs across sectors are increasingly critical review criteria. For example, for health technology and public health feasibility studies commissioned at the National Institute for Health Research in England, follow-up research depends on not only demonstrating a satisfactory and acceptable research process but also a likely positive impact in the 'third sector' – through such public-private partnership change agents as the Academic Health Science Networks and various National Health Service (NHS)/ local authority leadership collaborations for knowledge exchange and transfer. The bigger picture does contain traditional institutions, such as the NHS in the UK, but movements, networks, cooperatives and coalitions are just as prevalent and becoming ever-more prominent as we move towards the integration programmes of tomorrow.

In this more complex world, one-dimensional primary research based on a limited range of variables, often in constrained environments, is less attractive and perceived by policymakers as less relevant. Attempts at control for experimental purposes are more likely to be aborted. Secondary data sources will abound, and their employment in research appears certain to become ever-more mainstream.

Conclusions

It is time to recap and review. Putting aside the padding of peripheral points, what are the key lessons for the next generation of researchers? First and foremost is the underpinning assertion of the increased value of secondary data studies in contemporary health and wellbeing research. In essence, this is because contemporary health systems do now deliberately incorporate wellbeing interventions and have become more complex and cross-sectoral as a result. The shift to secondary data research reflects and corresponds to this development: multiple sources for multiple services. And moreover, many of the latter in the private and voluntary sectors are only accessible to the health researcher through secondary data in the form of such as marketing documents, websites and media reviews. The clinical research regimes of primary medical research can either be a cultural anathema or a practical and political barrier to this sector's participation. In this context, with realist and big data research methods now increasingly available to frame investigations, secondary data research comes to the fore.

214 Geoffrey Meads

Secondly, secondary data is shaped by identified future needs for effective implementation. Policy relevant, properly structured and cross-boundary provides expedient and sufficiently empirical findings for early and rapid adoption into practice through new models and concepts, indicative exemplars and trends and projected assessments of risks and benefits. Multi-disciplinary, with different datasets and sources carefully cross-referenced, secondary data research is becoming a main vehicle for transferable learning. For reviewers, it may well score higher on application than quality, but this for now, and more especially for tomorrow, appears to be an acceptable trade-off.

Lastly, secondary data health research is intrinsically eclectic in its mixture of sources and tools. This is true, in particular, of its methodology, as our local illustrations from the University of Winchester in this chapter have sought to demonstrate. But it is also true of its research team membership and its target clients and sponsors. Secondary data study depends on viable and committed stakeholders from a range of organisations that make up the new mixed economy of health and wellbeing. These may include church ministers, social enterprise owners and foodbank volunteers. These may well be new to the academic world. In this, as in many aspects of secondary data research, there is new ground to be broken and fresh knowledge to be gained. At the beginning of this chapter, it was noted that many of the ground-breaking social enterprises are faith oriented or based, with revelation an important element in their motivation. Not all secondary data researchers are spiritually inspired in this way, of course. Nevertheless, it is reasonable to suggest that for this type of secondary data study, it will be imagination, along with reason, that will lead the way.

Questions for discussion and further reflection

Why does Geoffrey suggest that the use of secondary data can be particularly useful to consider novel developments in practice and policy?

Which types of secondary data are discussed? How do these relate to those identified in Chapter 5?

This chapter described a number of ways to analyse secondary data for policy purposes (e.g. trend/network analysis, case exemplars). Can you see an application for any of these in your own work?

In what ways does this chapter challenge your conceptualisation of mixed-methods research?

References

Ashcroft, J. and Meads, G. (2006). *The case for collaboration in health and social care*. Oxford: Blackwells.

Bryman, A. (2012). *Social research methods*. Oxford: Oxford University Press.

Cunningham, M., France, E. F., Ring, N. et al. (2018). *Developing meta-ethnography reporting guidance for research and practice*. Southampton, UK: National Institute for Health Research.

Community-based health and wellbeing practices **215**

GOV.UK. (2017). *Community development handbook.* London: Central Digital and Data Office.

Grube, M., Mohler, R., Fuchs, J. et al. (2019) Indicator-based public health monitoring in old age in OECD countries: a scoping review. *BMC Public Health* 19, 1068. https://10.1186/s12889-019-7287-y.

Grundy, E. and Holt, G. (2001). The socio-economic status of older adults: how should we measure it in studies of inequalities? *Journal of Epidemiology and Community Health* 55(12), 895–904.

Hassard, J. and Law, J. (1999). *Actor network theory and after.* Oxford: Blackwell.

Heyvaert, M., Hannes, K. and Onghena, P. (2017). *Using mixed methods. Research synthesis for literature reviews.* Thousand Oaks, CA: SAGE Publications.

Jones, S. (2017). *Top tips for spreading new care models across the health and care system.* London: NHS Confederation.

Latour, B. (2005). *Reassembling the social: an introduction to actor-network theory.* Oxford: Clarendon.

Light, D.W. (1997). The rhetorics and realities of community health care: the limits of countervailing powers to meet the health needs of the twenty-first century. *Journal of Health Politics, Policy and Law*, 22, 105–145.

MacDonald, J.J. (1992). *Primary health care. Medicine in its place.* London: Routledge.

Mason, C., Barraket, J., Friel, S. et al. (2015). Social innovation for the promotion of health equity. *Health Promotion International*, 30 (2), 116–125.

Meads, G., Russell, G. and Lees, A. (2016b). Community governance in primary health care: towards and ideal type. *The International Journal of Health Planning and Management*, 32 (4), 554–574.

Meads, G. (2016). Wellbeing agencies in the High Street: the rebirth of primary health care? *The Open Public Health Journal*, 9, 3–12.

Meads, G., Lees, A. and Tapson, C. (2016a). Creational narratives for new housing communities: evidence synthesis. *Housing, Care and Support*, 19 (3/4), 1–9.

Meads, G. (2018). New wellbeing interventions in primary health care: reviewing the relational agenda. *Biomedical Journal of Scientific and Technical Research*, 9 (4), 1–3.

Meads, G. and Lees, A. (2019). Health and wellbeing networks for older people: a scoping review for future research. *Journal of Quality in Health Care and Economics*, 2 (4), 1–11.

Pawson, R., Greenhalgh, T., Harvey, G. et al. (2010). Realist review. A new method of systematic review designed for complex policy interventions. *Journal of Health Services Research and Policy*, 10 (1), 21–34.

Ralph, N. (2015). *Good neighbour support scheme impact briefing.* Portsmouth: Winchester Social Enterprises.

Sandelowski, M. and Barosso, J. (2007). *Handbook for synthesizing qualitative research.* New York: Springer.

Schluter, M. and Lees, D. (1993). *The 'R' factor.* London: Hodder & Stoughton.

Turner, S., Meads, G. and Garfield-Birkbeck, S. (2013). International health management research: a two way street for the UK. *International Journal of Advances in Management Science*, 2 (3), 87–91.

WHO. (1978). *Primary health care. The Alma Ata Declaration. Annual report.* Geneva: WHO.

WHO Annual Assembly. (2007). *Primary health care: now more than ever. Annual report.* Geneva: WHO.

Zahner, S.J. and Corrado, S.M. (2004). Local health department partnerships with faith-based organizations. *Journal of Public Health Management and Practice*, 10 (3), 258–263.

Zaidi, A., Green, M., Iparraguirce, J. et al. (2021). *Index of wellbeing in later life.* London: Age UK.

CONCLUSION

Developing mixed-methods research practice in wellbeing and health

In this concluding section, we aim to draw together the learning from the preceding chapters and to distil the important messages they contain about the practice of mixed-methods research in wellbeing and health. The included chapters have covered a wide range of wellbeing and health-related issues and tackled them with a variety of approaches. In the introduction, we drew on a broad definition of wellbeing to highlight the diversity of topics that may be of interest to researchers. These included the natural environment, personal wellbeing, our relationships, health, what we do, where we live, personal finance, the economy, education and skills and governance (see What Works Centre for Wellbeing, 2020). Our chapters have dealt with many of these subjects; for example, the natural environment is an important feature of Chapter 6 (Brear), where participants live is an important focus in Chapters 7 (Gray, Manning and Oftadeh-Mogadam) and 8 (Lees and Tapson), education and skills of Chapters 2 (Locke, Bell and Scallan) and 5 (Harrison, Medisauskaite and Rees) and governance of Chapter 9 (Meads). We recognise, too, that there are many more areas for exploration, and we hope that you will find lessons from these situated studies to be transferrable to the range of contexts within which you may be researching. We hope that whether you are a student, researcher or practitioner working in the area of health, social care or wellbeing, the included studies have helped you to appreciate the value of mixed-methods approaches in these and similar fields. It has been our ambition in producing this reader to make a difference in the way in which research in wellbeing and health is carried out. With this in mind, towards the end of this overview, we have highlighted a series of 'thinking points' derived from the content of the chapters that we would encourage you to consider as you design and execute mixed-methods designs in your own areas of interest.

DOI: 10.4324/9780429263484-11

Ahead of this, we return to the questions that we posed ourselves, as editors, in the introduction to this collection of studies. These were as follows:

- How can we define mixed-methods research in the context of wellbeing and health research?
- What happens to 'philosophical position' when we mix approaches from two different paradigms?
- Why employ mixed methods in wellbeing and health research?
- What are the challenges and benefits of mixed-methods research designs?

These questions have stayed with us as we have read and digested the contributions, and we have drawn our own conclusions to their answers, which we share with you next.

How can we define mixed-methods research in the context of wellbeing and health research?

As stated earlier, although all relating to the subject matter of wellbeing and health, the aims and questions of the included studies are broad and, of course, only represent a small subsection of possible research topics in this arena. We argue, therefore, that in such a multifaceted landscape, what is needed is a definition of mixed methods that is capable of encompassing a whole range of mixing and a whole range of methods. We suggest that any definition should be inclusive, not overly complicated and sit comfortably with researchers from a range of backgrounds. Our authors have variously used the terms mixed methods, qualitatively driven mixed methods, multimethods, multi-modal and so on, and they have mixed quantitative and qualitative approaches, secondary with primary data, combined different forms of secondary data and employed techniques that would not ordinarily be included in research methods teaching. We applaud this all! We feel that researchers should use the definition of mixed methods that best suits their own study and context (and there are many of these available in the academic literature), but if we had to choose a definition that draws together all the strands in this reader, it would be *'research that employs more than one technique, approach or method with a view to answering its questions in the fullest and most reliable way possible'*. We feel that the broadness and inclusivity of this definition is important in that it is capable of encompassing a range of mixed-methods designs and approaches and makes room for researchers to tackle wellbeing and health research questions free from any methodological constraints.

What happens to 'philosophical position' when we mix approaches from two different paradigms?

The authors in this book have taken different views on the research paradigm. As we highlighted in the introduction, some authors have taken qualitatively driven approaches – e.g. Chapters 1 (Flower), 2 (Locke, Bell and Scallan), 6 (Brear) and 7

218 Conclusion

(Gray, Manning and Oftadeh-Mogadam) – which can be associated with a constructivist underpinning philosophical position. Chapter 3 (Mitchelmore) describes a quantitatively driven approach (underpinned by positivism, with a qualitative element that would most likely fall into the critical realist position) and authors of Chapters 5 (Harrison, Medisauskaite and Rees), 8 (Lees and Tapson) and 9 (Meads) situate their stance as pragmatic, driven by the questions to be answered rather than one dominant paradigm. In putting together this collection, we have become convinced of the utility and neatness of taking a pragmatic approach to mixed methods in wellbeing and health research, that so often deals with very practical problems. In this way, there is no need to become tangled up (as PhD students often may!) in complicated debates about how best to reconcile competing paradigms; instead, such issues can be put aside, and research designs derived by deciding on the methods that could best be employed to answer the research questions. Nevertheless, there are certainly examples in this reader of studies where the study's main thrust is clearly qualitative or quantitative, and in these cases, we have found the terminology of 'qualitatively (or quantitatively) driven' to be very helpful (Morse, 2016; Morse and Cheek, 2015).

Why employ mixed methods in wellbeing and health research?

A number of common threads have presented themselves throughout the chapters as reasons for, and benefits of, undertaking mixed-method designs. These are provided in bullet point form below:

- Mixed methods enable a voice to be given to those who may otherwise not participate in research and who have often been marginalised (Chapter 1, Flower; Chapter 2, Locke, Bell and Scallan; Chapter 7, Gray, Manning and Oftadeh-Moghadam; Chapter 8, Lees and Tapson). This approach is, therefore, described as being inclusive in that it seeks to hear/explore the real lived experiences of a range of participants.
- The use of mixed methods enables deep, rich and more robust understandings of a phenomenon and the most complete understanding possible through a commitment to employing a range of techniques (that may often fall outside of the 'traditional researcher tool box'). In this way, it recognises and embraces the complexity of human experience that may otherwise be difficult to access and recognises the importance of a range of diverse perspectives (Chapter 2, Locke, Bell and Scallan; Chapter 7 Gray, Manning and Oftadeh-Moghadam).
- Adopting mixed methods in their broadest sense is a way of personalising research and offering different methods to suit different participants (Chapter 2, Locke, Bell and Scallan).
- This choice of design adapts well to research which adopts a holistic view of wellbeing and health and takes place within traditional practice settings, as well as within the broader community.
- Research that adopts a mix of methods appeals to a range of sponsors/ commissioners of research because it can generate policy- and change-relevant

Conclusion **219**

insights (Chapter 4, Steven and Wilson). This also results in benefits for the wider community (i.e. wider than scientific and academic) by reporting policy implications through good communication (Chapter 5, Harrison, Medisauskaite and Rees). An example that stands out from the book is the need for soap in the WaSH project (Chapter 6, Brear). As such, mixed-methods research has significant practical value and provides applied learning for the common good.

- Finally, mixed-methods research is of benefit in that it disrupts taken-for-granted narratives about a topic, making the familiar surprising and so can lead to novel findings that are enlightening. This approach of looking for the unexpected is a key feature or characteristic of practitioner research (which is considered and covered in several chapters in this reader, including Chapter 1, Flower; Chapter 2, Locke, Bell and Scallan; and Chapter 7, Gray, Manning and Oftadeh-Moghadam).

What are the challenges and benefits of mixed-methods research designs?

The complexity of the real world is reflected in the challenges that researchers encountered in undertaking mixed-methods research in wellbeing and health. It can be that in undertaking mixed methods, the researcher is entering new territory as their particular combination of mixed methods has not been tried before or not with a particular topic or population. Therefore, there may not be any existing protocols to follow. This can result in a number of challenges that were discussed in the chapters:

- Several authors highlighted that undertaking their research designs required them to come to grips with new research techniques/skills and approaches. It is important that mixed-methods researchers are willing to learn, to try new things and to allow time in the research process to achieve this.
- Linked to the fact that undertaking mixed-methods designs may become something of a voyage of discovery, the need to be reflexive in the practice of mixed methods is highlighted (Chapter 4, Stevens and Wilson). This allows us to determine what has worked well and what could be done better, as well as the examination of our beliefs, judgements and practices during the research process and how these may have influenced us as researchers. Reflexivity involves questioning one's own take-for-granted assumptions. We should not, for example, assume which methods are suitable or that would-be participants are too busy to engage in research. There is a need for transparency. Reflexive issues should be drawn out and addressed by being collaborative and in frequent and ongoing conversations with others during the research process (Chapter 1, Flower).
- With a mix of methods, there is a need to ensure that research processes, including data collection and analysis, align (Chapter 5, Harrison, Mediasauskaite and

220 Conclusion

Rees). The engagement with a dataset needs to be thorough, and a readiness on the part of the researcher is required to go between data and interpretation iteratively (Chapter 7, Gray, Manning and Oftadeh-Moghadam).

- The chances are that there will be a lot of data generated from the mix of research methods (Chapter 7, Gray, Manning and Oftadeh-Moghadam). Our book contributors issue a caution against doing too much in one study and ensuring that there are good data management processes and training in place.

- Whilst several authors have highlighted their desire to give voice to respondents who are not easy to access in research, some also acknowledge that there is further to go in this regard. Flower (Chapter 1), for example, highlighted the desire to develop research designs that are more inclusive for children without language. To achieve this, mixed-methods researchers may need to draw on the experience and expertise of those working in disciplines accustomed to participatory and innovatory approaches to collecting data. This further highlights the potential for cross-disciplinary, as well as mixed-methods, approaches.

- The relational work of research in general is something to consider and may perhaps be particularly pertinent for mixed-methods approaches which aim to engage more fully with research phenomena at various levels. With participants, the researcher's role is to facilitate inclusion by being kind, giving voice, allowing unloading and avoiding unspoken assumptions that may limit inclusivity, even from the best motivations. There is also a need to build strong relationships with sponsors/funders of research, organisations, policymakers and gatekeepers (Chapter 3, Mitchelmore).

- Finally, the challenge is raised in this reader as to how the quality of mixed-methods research can be assessed (Chapter 7, Gray, Manning and Oftadeh-Moghadam). We would like to flag this as an issue for further future consideration and about which more work is needed in terms of the research community sharing their good practice.

'Thinking points' to assist research design

Inspired by the previous points and the themes that have arisen across the book's chapters, we would like to finish by offering some 'thinking points' for researchers to consider as they plan and carry out mixed-methods research on wellbeing and health topics. In some places, we have linked these back to our chapters, to provide some examples and assist and motivate students, researchers and practitioners going forward to develop their own research practice.

Research topic and context

This thinking point relates to the need to fit research strategy to research context. We highlight the need to think ahead about which contextual issues will necessarily influence the approach taken and also flag the importance of surfacing any taken-for-granted assumptions that you may hold, which could limit what you aim

Conclusion **221**

to achieve. A good example of a study that has worked hard to design research that fits within the constraints of a clinical organisation is Flower's study in Chapter 1. Example questions to consider are:

- What are contextual challenges related to my proposed topic/context in well-being and health?
- How can these be addressed?
- What are any unspoken assumptions that may be placing limits on data I believe could be collected?

Study design and preparation

This thinking point recognises that mixed-methods research, especially with vulnerable groups, often requires considerable preparation and formative research. Such activities can include carrying out patient and public involvement (PPI), seeking relationships with key stakeholders and collaborators who can inform your research approach and often developing your own skill set. On this subject, see Lees and Tapson's approach in Chapter 8. Issues to bear in mind include the following:

- What skills do I need to develop/advice do I need to take?
- Have I considered insights from PPI?
- Have I given thought to building relations and developing collaborations?
- What role will I adopt as a researcher?

Methodological approach

Whilst not always uppermost in the mind of practitioner-researchers, methodological thinking is very important for students, especially at the postgraduate level. As we suggested earlier, pragmatism appears to us to be a very helpful approach to answering practical and policy-relevant questions, but there are, of course, studies that are truly driven by one specific philosophical approach. Here are some prompts to guide you through this sometimes-tricky issue.

- What is my own research philosophy with regard to this mixed-methods study?
- For example, is the information required more important than theoretical considerations – pragmatism (see, for example, Chapter 5 written by Harrison, Medisauskaite and Rees)?
- Is my research most strongly aligned to constructivist principles, with some larger-scale/numerical information required – qualitatively driven (see, for example, Brear's Chapter 6)?
- Is my research driven by positivist assumptions but with a need for deeper areas of knowledge – quantitatively driven (see, for example, Mitchelmore's study in Chapter 3)?

222 Conclusion

Methods

Linked to the previous thinking point, this relates specifically to the choice of methods within mixed-methods designs. We encourage you to think about 'ways of finding out', which may not always be traditional research methods at all. It is also important to consider whether your subject matter lends itself best to primary or secondary research (or both) and to consider creatively the sources that may be available to you. See for example Meads chapter in this regard (Chapter 9)

- What are the limits and benefits of single-methods approaches in wellbeing and health research?
- Is a mixed-method design more appropriate, and which methods are relevant?
- What are the limits on the possibility to collect primary data in this context? Is secondary data needed?
- What do I need to do to access the information I need (even if these are not 'traditional' approaches)?

Integration and ordering

For some of the research studies included in this reader, certain elements of data collection have informed subsequent stages. In other studies, results are not synthesised until the end. Therefore, think about the ordering of your various activities in advance, and ask,

- Will certain elements of data collection inform the others, which to do first and when to bring the findings together?

Ethics

Ethics are important in any research. Additionally, we would reiterate here the potential of mixed-methods approaches to access the voices of those who are harder to reach in research terms and, therefore, their potential to address issues of social transformation and justice. This in turn may necessitate even more careful thinking about ethics and the sensitive application of research designs. Refer to Chapters 6 (Brear) and 7 (Gray, Manning and Oftadeh-Moghadam) on this subject of research aiming for social justice and transformation. Useful prompts for your own research are as follows:

- What are the ethical implications of my approach, especially with regards to the involvement of vulnerable groups?
- Is this research aiming to address issues of social transformation and justice?

Reflection and reflexivity

We have been very impressed by the reflective stance taken by a number of our contributors. For some authors, it appears that the opportunity to write a chapter on their research has provided an opportunity for reflection and for resultant new learning to emerge. Bearing this in mind, we urge researchers to build reflexivity into their research designs and to share this thinking and learning wherever possible.

- Can I build opportunities for reflection (with peers, participants, stakeholders, etc.) into my research process?
- How can I incorporate reflection into the interpretation of my results?
- What would I do differently next time? How can I share learning about my research process, along with learning about findings?
- (If relevant) Can I build in opportunity to reflect across a body of work? Are there common threads that I can see across a number of studies I have been involved in (as, for example, Locke, Bell and Scallan and Steven and Wilson have done in Chapters 2 and 4)?

Final thoughts

We hope that you have enjoyed reading this book and that you have learned from the contributing authors, as we as editors have done. As we conclude this book, the UK is once more in the state of national lockdown in response to the coronavirus pandemic, and we are living in a time which has repeatedly been referred to as 'unprecedented'. Perhaps if the last 12 months have shown us anything, it is that we cannot say for certain what the contextual challenges and issues will be most pressing for researchers in the future, although we already see issues relating to mental health, health inequalities and socio-economic disadvantage looming large. Whatever the issues and contextual challenges arising, we hope that you have been inspired to apply creative, flexible and inclusive mixed-methods approaches in order to produce robust findings that are relevant to both the practice and policy of well-being and health in the twenty-first century.

References

Morse, J. M. (2016). *Essentials of qualitatively-driven mixed-method designs*. New York: Routledge.

Morse, J. M. and Cheek, J. (2015). Introducing qualitatively-driven mixed-method designs. *Qualitative Health Research*, 25, 731–733.

What Works Centre for Wellbeing (2020). *About wellbeing*. What Works Centre for Wellbeing. Available at: https://whatworkswellbeing.org/about-wellbeing/. (Accessed November 2020).

INDEX

Page numbers in **Bold** refer to table; Page numbers in *Italic* refer to figure; page numbers followed by 'n' refer to footnotes number; Page numbers in underline refer to box

Abrams, B. 21
Abshire, M., et al. 72
Academic Health Science Networks 213
Academic Search Complete 180
Adshead, F. 92
Afghan Women's Breakfast Club 186, **187**
agencies: accountability 204; boundaries 209; commercial and charitable 200; Head Start and Early Head Start 183; health and social care 208; HESA <u>118</u>; in LSOAs <u>191</u>; models 7, 200, 203–205; non-statutory 212; social enterprise and faith 7; of wellbeing 202, 208
agency: child's potential for 11; individual *94*
Aigen, K. 11, 13
Aked, J., et al. 11
Aldridge, J. 175
Alexandrov, A.V. 63
Allgood, N. 12
Allida, S., et al. 68
Amorrortu, R. P., et al. 65
analysis, types of: abductive 135; composite 160; conversation/discourse 18, 73, 159; descriptive 84; documentary 59; gap 198; integrated 135, 146–147, 151, 200; interpretative phenomenological (IPA) 16, 19, 23; interpretive 147; meta- 34, 55, 198; predictive 122; primary and secondary 114, 137, 147; qualitative 113; qualitative data 42, 97, 119; qualitatively

driven 151; quantitative 119; secondary 83, 84, **85**, 87, 104; statistical 35, 68, 70, 128; thematic 42, 91, <u>118</u>, 147; trend 197, 201–203, 211, 214; *see also* reflexivity; video microanalysis
Andersen, M. B., et al. 102
anonymity 96, 99–100, 137, 168, 211; *see also* confidentiality
Ansdell, G. 11
Ansdell, G., et al. (2010) 13, 17
Ansdell, G., et al. (2016) 13, 15, 20, 27
appraisal: annual peer 44; Mixed Methods Appraisal Tool (MMAT) 169; revalidation 44, 57
Asghar, Z., et al. 40
Ashcroft, J., et al. 208
assessment: of cardiovascular health 56; CDS 10–11; performance related 44; research quality 169; risks and benefits 214; *see also* data types
assumptions: challenging negative 42; about participants 97–98; philosophical 194; a priori 208; researchers 96–100, 103–104, 111, 157, 220–221; study design 88, 90, 92; survey terminology 136
Atkinson, P. 33
Atkinson, S. 158

Baird, B., et al. 177
Balint group **38**, 39
Balme, E., et al. 32, 34

Barnes, B. R. 166
Barras, C., et al. 119
Bartlett, R., et al. 56, 61, 69
Bartram, J., et al. (2010) 133, 136, 143
Bartram, J., et al. (2014) **134**, 135–137
Batty, E. 102–103
Bell, J. 32
Bell, J., et al. 32
Berge, E., et al. 55, 62, 72
Bergstrøm-Nielsen, C. 25
Berrow, D., et al. 43
Biomedical Admissions Test (BMAT) 117–118, 121
Blanco, M. A., et al. 82
Blazeby, J. M., et al. 62
Bochner, A. P. 32
Bohman, B., et al. 36
Bond, V., et al. 136
Bonevski, B., et al. 174–175, 192–193
Booth, A. 36, 38
Bostock, S., et al. 66
Bowe, M., et al. 156–157
Brannen, J. 160
Braun, V., et al. 38
Brear, M. R., et al. (2018) 137, 138n4, 147, 152
Brear, M. R., et al. (2020) 139
Bressers, G., et al. 35
Briel, M., et al. 63
British Association for Music Therapy 10
British Educational Research Association (BERA) Conference (2017) 1
British Medical Association (BMA) 42; funding 92; mentoring research 101–102; study design 93
British Medical Journal 32, 34, 212
British Psychological Society Code of Ethics and Conduct (2018) 168
Brookfield, H., et al. 157, 162
Brown, B. 33
Brown, S. D., et al. 157, 162
Bryman, A. 2, 111, 212
Bryman, A., et al. 169
Bucci, S., et al. 61, 64
Buddeberg–Fischer, B., et al. 81–82
Buetow, S. 88–89
Bunniss, S., et al. 32
Burke Johnson, R., et al. 156–157
Business in the Community (BITC) Workwell model 92–94, 93

Campbell, D., et al. 34
Campbell, D. T., et al. 156
Cardoso, G., et al. 68

Carroll, C., et al. 27
Carter, S. M., et al. 14
Castillo, J. L. A. 72
Chamberlain, K., et al. 4, 157
Charmaz, K. 16
Chelsea and Westminster Hospital (NHS Trust 2017a/b) 10, 12
Cheong, C. W. S., et al. 81
Cheong, K. X. 81–82
Chiang, J. Y. K. 12
Child Development Service (CDS) 5, 28; 'context' for music therapy 10–12, 16; medical model 11–12
Choudry, A., et al. 119
Clarke, R. 33
clinical equipoise 62–63, 67
clinical practice: dyslexia 40, 43; inappropriate 43; performance issues 6, 33, 43, 89; strategies 41
Clinical Practice Research Datalink (CPRD) 113
clinical researchers' key traits 69–72, 74
clinical trials: participation issues 62–66; protocol development 60; qualitative techniques before/during trials 67–69, 72–73; randomised control trials (RCT) 6, 34, 47, 55; recruitment and retention 55–56, 60; trial documentation 65–66; trust 65; unanticipated events 72; *see also* clinical equipoise; reflective practice
clinical video material *see* video
Cohen, S., et al. 23
Collins, K. M., et al. 167
community: centres 185, 191, 208; community based research 5, 135; co-researchers 135, 137–139; development 133; (dis)engagement of young people 162; governance 204; health and health care services 150, 152; organisers/agents **206**; participatory approach 135, 137; peer support 184; rehabilitation 200–201; research communities 58, 137, 169, 220; supportive culture 94; *see also* health and wellbeing; research design
complexity: of datasets 128, 167–170, 218; mentoring 83, 90; mixing data types and methods 125; music therapy 9, 12, 14, 20, 24, 26; participant–researcher relationships 101–104; the real world 219; WaSH 133, 136–137; *see also* mixed methods; multi-modal methods
confidentiality 42, 98–99, 212; *see also* anonymity
Connor, M., et al. 80, 83, 99

226 Index

consent: informed 46, 61, 63, <u>118</u>, <u>120</u>, 125–126, <u>126</u>; parents 17; written 38
Contzen, N., et al. (2015a) 133, 136
Contzen, N., et al. (2015b) 136
Cowan, J. 43
Cox, J., et al. 34, 43
Crawford, A., et al. 162
Creswell, J. (2018) 90, 92–93
Creswell, J. W. (2003) 157–158
Creswell, J. W. (2011) 169
Creswell, J. W., et al. 98
Crisp, G., et al. 80
Cross, M., et al. 81–82
Crotty, M. J. 87
Cruz–Correa, M. 82
Cunningham, M., et al. 212
Curry, L., et al. 110

data collection: complementary 37, 161; face to face 193; interviews 90; multi-modal 168; rigour 35; qualitative data 47, 55, 97, 101, <u>124</u>, 128, 144, 147; quantitative data 55–56, 147; techniques 39, 40–41, 44–49, 175; 'think-aloud' 163, 165; workshops 164; *see also* focus groups; surveys; triangulation
Data Safe Haven <u>118</u>, <u>120</u>
dataset(s) 166, 214; administrative 126; analysis of 93, 137; archives 113; big 122, 125, 128–130, 211; BITC Workwell model 93; coding 146; CPRD 113; focused 146–147; linking 125; LRMP <u>120</u>, <u>122</u>; secondary 126–129; UK Medical Education Database (UKMED) 113; UK population health 113; WaSH <u>128</u>, 135, 137, **138**, 147, 151
data sources 4, 7, 45, 88, 114, **138**, 197; challenges 130; cross-sectoral 212; multi-sourcing 113; secondary 203, 212–213; *see also* datasets
data types: assessment **112**; categorisation 111; mixing 111–114, <u>119</u>, 121–125, 129; paper-based 141; primary qualitative (& PPI) 194; primary and secondary 112–113, **114**, 118–120; qualitative 32–33, 55, 110, 124, 137, 144; quantitative 55–56, 136; the 'real' data 137; structured observational 199; *see also* secondary data; secondary data research
Davies, S. 57
De Backer, J., et al. 24
Dekker, S. 34, 45
Dellinger, A. B., et al. 166
DeNora, T. , 16

Denscombe, M. 158
Denzin, N. (1978) 2, 111
Denzin, N. K. (2011) 156
Department of Education database 113
De Walt, D., et al. 181
Dickson–Swift, V., et al. 102–103
disadvantaged (socially): areas 174, 194; communities 183; families 183; groups 174–175, 181–183, 185; parents and carers 176, 179, 185
Dixon, J., et al. 157
doctors: engagement with work 36; fear of being 'outed' 47; 'harmful' stress 35, 36–40; poor performance 35–36, 43–47; reluctance 81, 99; under-researched 36, 41; wellbeing 79–80; *see also* dyslexia; mentoring
Dodge, R., et al. 54
Donovan, J., et al. 67
Dowell, J., et al. 129
Doyle, L., et al. 160
Driessen, E., et al. 80
Drolet, B. C., et al. 82–83
Duff, C. 158
Dures, E., et al. 156
Dutta, R., et al. 82
dyslexia 34–35, 40–43, 45–47; 'workarounds' 35, 40–41

Eccles, D. W., et al. 159
Edwards, J. (2011) 12
Efstathiou, J. A., et al. 81
Eide, P., et al. 101
Eisen, S., et al. 82
Elliott, D., et al. 55, 64
Elmer, R. 32
Elton, C. 34
eMER.GEe 212
'enactment': hygiene 152; music therapy 9, 15–16
engagement: community 164; continual and reflexive 166; with data 135, 166, 220; formative 175; health services 174–175; interventions 165; local neighbourhoods 102; mentoring 83–84, **86**, 92, 97; with researchers 163; with research participants 163–164; with research questions 163; for socially disadvantaged 174; with stakeholders 175; with work 36; *see also* health literacy (HL); public health engagement officer
EPPI–Reviewer 4 software 37
Epstein, R. M., et al. 32, 34, 36
Equality Act (2010) 41

Eraut, M. (2000) 92
Eraut, M. (2004) 92
Eswatini: community of co-researchers 135, 137, **138**, 139, 141, 146, 149; community participation study 135–155; health workers 150, 152; *see also* WaSH
ethics: approval 60, 65, 118, 168, 185; approval not required 193, 199; consent 62, 126; ethical considerations 14–15, 131; ethical sensitivity 10, 38, 48; fear of exposure 42; in mixed methods research 79, 84, 87, 152–153, 168–169, 222; obligations 101–103; principles 56; trial recruitment 61; viewing video 26; *see also* reflexivity
ethnographies 19
evaluation: of health literacy 182–184; of health policy 209–211; mentee evaluation sheets 90–91; of mentoring for psychiatrists 84, 87–89; qualitative 178; of qualitative process 72–73; *see also* doctors; realistic evaluation (RE)
evidence-based medicine 34
evidence-based practice 55

Fàbregues, S., et al. 111
Farkas, A. H., et al. (2019a) 81
Farkas, A. H., et al. (2019b) 81
Farmer, E. A., et al. 34, 45
Farrugia, P., et al. 60
feedback 1, 159, 161, 184, 186; participant and researcher 168; stakeholder 89; web-based 182
Feldman, M. D., et al. (2009) 82
Feldman, W. B., et al. (2016) 61–62
Fetters, M. D., et al. 135, 137
Fielding, S., et al. 70
Finlay, L. 14
Fish, D., et al. 32
Fleming, B., et al. 84
Flower, C. (2008) 11–12
Flower, C. (2019) 16, 24
focus groups 1, 6–7, 16, 37–40, 48, 82, 99, 112, 137–139, 144, 146–147, 150, 158, 166, 185–187, 193, 199
formative research 7, 174–177, 185, 221; 'multi' rather than mixed methods 192–194; questions and approach 179–180; *see also* patient and public involvement (PPI)
Fortney, L., et al. 37
Francis, R. 34
freedom of information: Act (2000) 45; requests 40, 42, 44
Frei, E., et al. 81–82

Friedson, E. 44
funding: 'big funders' 175; funders 87, 96, 103; requirements 84
Futch, V. A., et al. 158

Garr, R. O., et al. 81
Gauthier, A., et al. 69
Gawande, A. 33
General Medical Council (GMC) 34, 43
geographic information system (GIS) analysis 159, 161, 166
Geraci, S. A., et al. 81
Gerada, C. (2016) 32
Gerada, C. (2017) 32
Gibbs, G. 57
Gibbs' reflective cycle 58
Gibson, S., et al. 40
Gilbert, K. R. 102
Gilboa, A., et al. 17
'giving voice' *see* voice; you ng people
Glass, G. 114
Goffman, E., cited in Riddick, B. (2001) 41
Golby, M., et al. 32, 39
Gong, Z. X., et al. 81
Goodwin, D., et al. 98
Google: Earth 141, 143; Maps 4, 191, 202; Scholar 36, 180
Graduate Medical School Admissions Test (GAMSAT) 117
Graham, J., et al. 175
Grant, M. J., et al. 38
graphic score 24–27
Gray, D., et al. 157–158
Greene, J. C. 82, 157
Greenhalgh, T., et al. 32
Greig, A. D., et al. 162
Griffin, D., et al. 62
Gunning, R. 66
Gunning's–Fog Index 66

Hackney *see* Tower Hamlets
Hadidi, N., et al. 63
Hammersley, M., et al. 35
Hampshire *see* Healthier Together network
Hanson, W. E., et al. 156, 161
Harden, J., et al. 164–165
Harrington, S. 80
Harris, J., et al. 184
Harrison, J., et al. 34
Haslam, C., et al. 158
Haslbeck, F. B. 18, 23
Head Start *see* agencies
health and wellbeing 2, 54–55, 90, *94*, 99, 114, *116*, 120, 153, 158, 160, 169, 200,

208, 212–214; children 9–10; community 202; contexts 7; environmental 133; hybrid 204, 211; inadequacy of a single research method 198; multi–methods approach 194; physical, psychosocial and social 92; 'on a social scale' 115; systems 209; 'unimpaired flourishing' 11; *see also* mentoring; psychological research

health capability analysis 147

Health Care and Professions Council 10

health champions 184

health, definition 54

Healthier Together network 177–178, 185

health literacy (HL) 179–191; engagement 181; and ethnicity 190–191; group specific techniques 186; 'harder to reach' groups 193; local engagement development 204; *see also* low health literacy (LHL); patient and public involvement (PPI)

health service 5; health centres 208; providers 198; settings 185–186, 191; workers 150, 152

Heath, C., et al. (2007) 17

Heath, C., et al. (2010) 17

Heeneman, S., et al. 81

Henry, S. G., et al. (2011) 16, 18

Henry, S. G., et al. (2012) 18–19

Henson, K. E., et al. 69

Herfath, H. H., et al. 61

Herman, A, D., et al. (2004) 184

Herman, A., et al. (2010) 183–184

Hesse-Biber, S. N. 177

Heyvaert, M., et al. (2013) 169

Heyvaert, M., et al. (2017) 200

Hickey, G. L., et al. 60

Higher Education Statistics Agency (HESA) 118

Holck, U. 17–18, 21–22

Holden, B., et al. 177

Home Office 199

Hong, Q. N., et al. 169

Hospital Trusts 41

Hox, J., et al. 112–113

Huggett, K. N., et al. 81

Hunter, A., et al. 177

Hunt, J. 115

Hutton, G., et al. 133, **134**, 135

Illing, J. 32

inclusivity 37, 47, 49, 104, 180, 218; in definition of mixed methods 217, 223; in research design 115, 220; in research process 115, 193; the under-researched 36

Index of Multiple Deprivation (IMD) 187–189, 192; seven domains **188**

Institute of Medicines 181

Interpretative Phenomenological Analysis (IPA) 23

interventions: community-based 183, 185; development 174–175; digital sleep 7, 159–161, 163; educational 36–41, **38**, 183; efficacy 59, 136, 200; enhancing trial running 72–74; health and health-care 203–204; information based 177; interventional research studies 54–55; systems focused 181–182; wellbeing 208, 213; *see also* low health literacy; voice; WaSH

interview(s): in depth 67; face to face 144; longitudinal 97, 101; medical 117; multiple-mini 117; narrative 120; qualitative 102; qualitative follow-up 161, 163, 167; qualitative think-aloud 159; semi-structured 41, 45; semi-structured qualitative 87–88, 91, 101, 118, 122; sequential 100; UKMACS 124; *see also* video elicitation interview

Irwin, L. G., et al. 163

Irwin, S. 84, 87

Jacobsen, S. L., et al. (2014) 12, 27

Jacobsen, S. L., et al. (2017) 13

James, A., et al. 162

Jayatilleke, N., et al. 57

Jetten, J., et al. 158

Johnson, R. B., et al. (2007) 110, 176–177

Johnson, R., et al. (2004) 156–157

Johnson, W. B. 80

Jones, H., et al. 62

Jones, S. (2017) 205

Jones, S. R., et al. (2003) 60

Journal of The Royal Society of Medicine **85**, 86

Kalen, S., et al. (2012) 81

Kalen, S., Ponzer, S. and Silen, C. (2012) 82–83

Kasenda, B., et al. 55, 61

Kashiwagi, D. T., et al. 81–82

Kay, A. 32–33

Kearney, A., et al. 72

Kelley, P., et al. 162

Khoushhal, Z., et al. 119

King's Fund (2019) 115

Kinman, G., et al. 34

Kirk, S. 164

Kirsch, J. D., et al. 82

Knoblauch, H. 17

Koch, T. 88
Kolb's reflective cycle 57
Kossarova, L., et al. 177
Kow, C. S., et al. 81
Kram, K. 80
Krueger, R. A., et al. 16
Kurré, J., et al. 81
Kvale, S. 88

Lake, J., et al. 32
Lasagna's law 55
Launer, J. 44
Law, J. 15
Lee, F. Q, H ., et al. 81
Lees, A., et al. (2017) 27
Lees, A., et al. (2018) 174, 178
Lee-Treweek, G., et al. 102
Liao, L., et al. 81
Light, D. W. 204
Likert scales 87; survey scores 199
Lincoln, Y. S. 157
List of Registered Medical Practitioners
    (LRMP) 119–220, 122
literature review(s) 1, 7, 37, 39, 44–45, 48,
    84, **85**, 93, 118, 179–185, 187, 192, 204,
    209; influence on approach 184–185;
    templates 212
Locke, R. 42
Locke, R., et al. (2013) 43
Locke, R., et al. (2015) 40
Locke, R., et al. (2017) 40, 42
Locke, R., et al. (2020) 36
Locock, L., et al. 55, 62, 65–66
Loder, E., et al. 32
London NHS Trust 10
Longitudinal Educational Outcomes 113
Lonner, W. J. 161
Loosveld, L, M., et al. 81
Lower Super Output Area (LSOA): ethnic
    breakdown 190; mapping 185
low health literacy (LHL): A&E attendance
    177; effects of 179–180; health inequality
    180–181; interventions 7, 175–176, 179,
    181–184, 194; in the literature 184–185;
    parental 181; parent/child groups 179;
    parents and carers 176; social deprivation
    178; stigma 182
LRMP see datasets
LSOA see map(s)
Luff, P., et al. 17
Lyons, B., et al. 32

Maben, J., et al. 34
Macdonald, J. J. 212
Macdonald, R. A. R., et al. 11

Malterud, K., et al. (2005) 32
Malterud, K., et al. (2009) 32
Manning, R. & Gray, D., (forthcoming)
    157–158, 162
Mann, M. P. 81
Mann, R., et al. 82
mapping 6–7, 87, 163, 165, 192;
    collaborative spatial (CSM) 158,
    160; data 166, 168; exercise 185, 191,
    199, 202; LSOA 185; methods 162;
    participatory 138n2, 138n3, 140–141,
    143; photography 141
map(s): community 145, 146, 159; data
    145; focus groups 166; group based 167;
    and identity 158–159; of local area 158;
    LSOA 188, 189; social constructionist
    accounts 166; social memories 162;
    spatial 159; water sources 141; young
    people's 159, 168; see also Google
Marmot, M. 115
Marmot, M., et al. 174, 175
Marsh, L. 68
Mason, C., et al. 202
Mason, J. 60
Mays, M., et al. 37
McCann, C. M., et al. 34
McKendree, J., et al. 40
McKinley, N., et al. 34
McManus, S. 116–117
McMichael, C. 134, 136–137, 152–153
McNamara, N., et al. 158
Meads, G. (2016) 203
Meads, G. (2018) 208
Meads, G., et al. (2016a) 205
Meads, G., et al. (2016b) 204
Meads, G., et al. (2019) 205
medical ethics 117
medical model see CDS
Medical Schools Council 116
Medline 201
Melbourne 202
Melia, K. 35
Mendeley 180
mental health and wellbeing 34, 54–55;
    doctors 39, 43; parents 13
mentee: benefits 82, 87; composite vignette
    (context, process, outcome) **95**
mentor: role 80, 103; training 84, 92; see also
    mentoring
mentoring: benefits 82, 84–87, 91, 103–104;
    definition 80; evaluation 79, 84, 87,
    90–91, 93; four studies 83–96; in medicine
    and medical research 79, 80–82; national
    mentoring groups 102; outcomes 94;
    stigma 81, 99; types of 80; unanticipated

230 Index

research area 96, 103; and wellbeing 82–83, 91; *see also* doctors; qualitative research methods

meta-analytic design 81

methodological approach 221; 'pluralism' 157; *see also* paradigm(s); philosophy(ies)

microanalysis *see* video elicitation interviews; video microanalysis

MICS and mentoring 79, 83, 92

Miles, S. 32

Mintzberg, H. 44

Misselbrook, D. 11

Mitchell, F. 84

mixed and multi-m odal methods 6; challenges 167–170; comparison 176–177

mixed methods 1; assumptions 96–98; benefits 4–5, 10, 35–36, 38–39, 47, 49, 96, 100, 157, 160–165, 169–170, 197; challenges 33, 40, 44–45, 47–49, 103–104, 165–170, 219–220; core and supplementary combination 176–177; definition 3, 6, 33, 82, 110–111, 129, 157–158, 176, 217; a distinct methodology? 110; enhancement 2, 59–60, 111; incompatibility between methods 156–157; purpose 2, 123, 217–219; qualitatively driven 5, 135, 137, 158, 217; rationale 2, 123, 160; research design 3, 16, 114–120, 130; understanding complexity (WaSH) 13, 67, 136–137, 160–162; value of 36, 47–49; *see also* mixed and multi-modal methods; qualitative research; quantitative research

Moberley, T. 34

Modified Grounded Theory 16

Monash University (Melbourne) 202

Monster Study (1939) 65

Montgomery, K. 33–34

Moorcraft, S.Y., et al. 61–62, 65–66

Moran-Ellis, J. 166

Morris, D., et al. 41

Morris, M. C., et al. 62

Morrow, V. 158, 162–163

Morrow, V., et al. 163

Morse, J. M. 3, 35, 147, 218

Morse, J. M., et al. (2015) 3, 135, 137, 218

Morse, J. M., et al. (2017) 176

Muller, A. E., et al. 14

multi-modal methods: complexity of human experience 4, 157; innovative and sustained engagement 7, 157, 163; making the familiar surprising 162; multiple voices 164

music therapy: description 10; ethical considerations 14–15; 'gentle empiricism' 13, 15; graphic score example *25*; integrated themes **19**; trio/duo 12; and wellbeing 9–11; *see also* clinical video; video microanalysis

My Time Group **187**

National Health Service (NHS): Choices 183; Digital 113; government policy 115; Long Term Plan (2019a) 115; People Plan (2019b) 115; Scotland 182; Tayside 182; Tinder Foundation 183

National Institute for Health Research 213; Applied Research Collaboration 174; Clinical Research Network survey 61; UKMACS 117

network(s): actor 206; emerging/ new 202–203; erosion of traditional support 177; literature on 206; mentoring 90; older people's **207**; physical, mental, social, spiritual 205; PPI 175, 193; relational **206**

Neumayer, E. 135–136

Newcastle, University of **85, 86**

Newlands, F., et al. 40–42

Ng, K.Y. B., et al. (2020a) 81

Ng, Y, X., et al. (2020b) 81–82

NOMIS 189, 192

Nowell, L., et al. 81

Nutbeam, D. (2000) 178

Nutbeam, D. (2008) 178–179, 181, 183

NVivo 38, 212

O'Brien, B. C., et al. 34

O'Cathain, A. 156

Office for National Statistics (ONS) 188, 199

Ofri, D. 32

Olckers, L., et al. 56

Oldfield, A., et al. 12

Oliver, M. 41

O'Neill, N., et al. 13

Ong, J., et al. 81

Onwuegbuzie, A. J., et al. 135, 137

OpenAthens 36

O'Reilly, K., et al. 136

Ortega, G., et al. 81–82

Overeem, K., et al. 82–83

Oxley, J. 80

Oxley, J., et al. (2003) 81–84, **85**

Oxley, J., et al. (2008) 82

pandemic 3–4; coronavirus 223; Covid–19 175

Index **231**

paradigm(s): incompatibility of quantitative and qualitative approaches 156; mixing 217–218; positivist/realist vs constructivist/interpretivist 4, 81; qualitative 33, 35, 49, 158–159; 'third paradigm' 4, 156, 170; underpinning 100, 131

Paradis, E., et al. 35

participants: and researcher 101–104; sustained engagement 163–165; working with clinical groups 63, 67–69; *see also* consent; ethics

Pasiali, V. 17

patient and public involvement (PPI): contacts 175, 192; ethics 193; findings from PPI groups **187**; 'harder to reach groups' 175; influence of IMD and NOMIS 192; insights 221; networks 175, 193; parents 186–187, 192; practitioners 185–186, 192; primary qualitative data collection 194; representative 175; *see also* data collection; health literacy; research design

Patient Information Forum (2013) 180

Pavlicevic, M. O. 11

Pavlicevic, M. O., et al. 23

Pawson, R. 90–92

Pawson, R., et al. (1997) 90–92

Pawson, R., et al. (2010) 212

Pereira, S., et al. 55

Peters, D. 34

Pethrick, H., et al. 81

Pfund, C., et al. 82

philosophy(ies): assumptions 100, 194; definition 112; logic model 90; 'position' 1, 217–218; principles 177; underpinning 1, 80, **85–86**, 89, 131; *see also* multi-methods; paradigm(s)

photography 4; art and drawing 157; WaSH 6, 137, **138**, 141, 148

Picillo, M., et al. 61

Platt, D., et al. 37

Polese, J. C., et al. 61

Polley, C., et al. 80

Pompili, M., et al. 69

Ponterotto, J. G., et al. 160–161, 164

Popay, J., et al. 158

PPI *see* patient and public involvement

practitioner PPI 185–186

practitioner research 5, 42, 175–176

pragmatism 4, 21, 83, 157, 177, 194, 201, 221

Prendergast, H. M., et al. 82

Price, T., et al. 47

primary data: assessment **112**; definition 112; types 112–113

primary health care 202; community governance 204; cross-sectoral 208; exemplars 212; multi-disciplinary 203

Probst, B. 14

Procter, S. 14–15

Professional Support Unit (PSU) 41

Prüss-Ustün, A., et al. 133

psychological research: aspects of health and wellbeing 158; mixed and multi-methods 156; reliant on quantitative research designs 156; *see also* qualitative and quantitative methods

public health engagement officer 185–186

qualitative and quantitative methods: differences 59; incompatibility 156–157; integrated 3, 6–7, 33, 35, 101, 145–147, 151–153, 159–160; mutually enhancing 137; strengths and limitations (WaSH) 135–136; *see also* data collection; mixed methods

'qualitative PPI' *see* patient and public involvement

qualitative research 32; enhancing trials 56, 59–60, 67, 72–73; limited use in mentoring 81–82; in mixed methods design 3; providing depth and insight 158; qualitatively driven 3–4, 49, 147, 151, 154, 217; strengths and limitations 135–136; *see also* mixed methods

quantitative research 81; in curricula 34–35; in medical practice 34; medicine's traditional reliance on 81–82; providing breadth 161; supplementary function 135, 158; unsuitable for mentoring 83; *see also* data collection

questionnaires 2, 82, **85**, **86**, 87, *88*, 90–91, 103, 118, 120–121, 124; anonymity 99–100; design 122; online 97, 127; sampling 111; top down 97; UKMACS 126, 127

Rabkin, J. G., et al. 68

Ralph, N. 205

Ramani, S., et al. 88

Ramer, S. L. 36

randomised control trial (RCT) *see* clinical trials

realistic evaluation (RE) **86**, 90–92, *93*, 94

Reavey, P. 4, 157

recruitment 6, 40–41, 47–48, 60–61, 175, 185, 191, 193; improving 66, 73; Lasagna's law 55; poor 55–56; stages 61; strategies 59; *see also* clinical trials; ethics; retention

232 Index

reflection(s) 5, 26–27, 49, 56, 129–130
reflective practice 56–59, 96–98; cycles;
Gibbs' *58*; Kolb's *57*
reflexivity 14, 88–89, 166, 219, 223; *see also* ethics
research design 5, 14, 27, 47, 154, 175–177, 192; design model 90; participatory 137–139; and PPI 186–192; qualitative 32–33; responses to **187**; 'Thinking points' 187, 220–223
researcher(s): design and development 119, 125; important traits **70**; integrated 124; multiple 124; primary medical and data 214; qualitatively driven 221; qualitative and quantitative 135–137; quantitatively driven 4, 218; quantitative and qualitative researchers 58, 73; strong research instruments, alignment 125; *see also* questionnaires; survey(s)
research methods 10, 17, 97, 100, 124, 139, 161, 198, 209; teaching 217; traditional 222; *see also* mixed methods; survey(s)
resilience 34; community *94*; GPs 39
retention 6, 34, 61, 65, 73, 191; factors affecting 119, 123; improving 66, 72–73; *see* clinical trials; recruitment
Revalidation Support Team (Department of Health) 46
rigour: methodological and analytical 36, 38, 42, 47–48; reflexivity 88–89; triangulation 35
Riley, R., et al. 34
Rodda, J., et al. 68
Rogers, C. G., et al. 66
Rolvsjord, R. 11, 16
Rossetto, K. R. 101–102
Rowe, B., et al. 177
Rowlands, G., et al. 180, 185, 189
Rowles, G. D. 162

Sambunjak, D., et al. (2006) 80–81
Sambunjak, D., et al. (2010) 81
Sandelowski, M., et al. 200
Sanders, L. M., et al. (2007) 181
Sanders, L. M., et al. (2009) 180–181
Sawyer, R. K. 20
Sayan, M., et al. 81
Scallan, S. 42
Scallan, S., et al. 44
Schluter, M., et al. 208
Schön, D. A. 35, 42, 48
Scopus 201
secondary data: accessing 127–130; analysis 7; meaning 6, 112, 199; scoping exercise

201; sources 113; types 113; *see also* data collection; datasets; data types
secondary data research: future needs 209; future scenarios 207; policy oriented research 7; project designs 199; protocols and literature reviews 212; research products 200–209; shift to 213; stakeholders 214; three directions for 209–211; tools and techniques 212; vehicle for transferable learning 214
Selewski, D. T., et al. 61
Sharkey, A., et al. 164
Shaw, A., et al. (2009) 69
Shaw, S. C., et al. (2016) 41
Shaw, S. C., et al. (2017) 40–41
Shaw, S. C., et al. (2018) 40
Shaw, S. C. K. (2018) 42
Shaw, S. C. K. & Anderson, J. L. (2017) 41
Sheri, K., et al. 81–82
Shrewsbury, D. 34, 40–41
Sikic Micanovic, L., et al. 103
Sills, S., et al. 101
Silver, J., et al. 157, 162
Silverman, D. 88
Sinclair, S. 33
Skilled for Health Programme 183
Skjevik, E. P., et al. 81
sleep and health 162
SleepWise 159–160; *see also* interventions
Sligo, J. L., et al. 84
Smith, J. A. (2011) 19
Smith, J. A., et al. (2009) 16–17, 19
Smith, L. T. 152
Smith, T. C., et al. 61
Sng, J. H., et al. 81
Social Action for Health *see* Tower hamlets
Sorel, S. 18
'sounding boards' 88–89
South Africa 5
Southampton 189, **190**, 191–192
Sparkes, A. C 156
SQUIRE 212
Stacey, M. R. 34
Stamm, M., et al. 81–82
Standing Committee on Postgraduate Medical and Dental Education (1998) 80
Stanford Nutrition Programme 183
Steele, M. M., et al. 82
Steiner, J. F., et al. 82
Steinert, J. L., et al. 135–136
Stenhouse, L. 42
Steven, A. (2008) 82, 84, **85**, 87, 89
Steven, A. (2015) 84, **86**, 90–91
Steven, A., et al. (2008) 82–84, **85**, 87, 100
Steven, A., et al. (2016) 116

Steven, K., et al. 92, 96
Stige, B., et al. (2009) 14, 26
Stige, B., et al. (2010) 11
Stige, B., et al. (2012) 27
stigma: 'disabling' 158; harmful 39; open defecation 137; among students 55; vulnerability 36; work-related 36–37; *see also* doctors; low literacy stress
Strange, J. 13, 18
Streeton, R., et al. 127
Stroke Association (2012) 71
stroke research 56, 61, 63, 68–69, 70–71
Stryker, J. E., et al. 66
Suls, J., et al. 159
Sun, Z., et al. 55
Sure Start **187**
survey(s) 6, 40, 81, *93*, 97, 99, 118–120, 122–123, 127, 137, 138; cross-sectional 81–82; demographic and health (DHS) 135, 139, 142; online 41, 99, 101; *see also* assumptions; WaSH
Sussman, A. L., et al. 55, 60
Sustainable Development Goals (SDG) 133, 135, 137, 153
Sutton, L. B., et al. 174
Suvini, F., et al. 24
Swann, A., et al. 82

Tashakkori, A., et al. (1998, 2003) 156–157
Tashakkori, A., et al. (2007) 167
Thayabaranathan, T., et al. 55, 61, 64
'think-aloud' technique 159, 163, 165
'third paradigm' *see* paradigm
Thistlewaite, J., et al. 43
Thomas, C. 73
Thompson, G. 13
Thompson, G., et al. 13
Tower Hamlets and Hackney, Social Action for Health 184
Treweek, S., et al. 55
triangulation 35, 114, 120, 121, 123–124, 160, 176, 203, 212; data linkage 125; definition 2, 111; in mixing methods 130; validation 176
Trondalen, G. 23
Trondalen, G., et al. (2012) 11
Trondalen, G., et al. (2016) 16, 21
Tselebis, A., et al. 68
Turner, S., et al. 205
Tuskegee Study 65

UK 1998 Standing Committee on Postgraduate Medical and Dental Education 80
UK Department of Health 46, 84

UK Department of Health and Social Care 199
UK Medical Applicant Cohort Study (UKMACS) 6, 117–119; ethics and consent 126; widening coverage 127
Understanding Career Choices in Psychiatry (UCCiP) 6, 119–120, 122; sampling 127
UNICEF 135, 152
Universities and Colleges Admissions Service (UCAS) 118
University Clinical Aptitude Test (UCAT) 117, 118, 121
Uprichard, E., et al. 136

Varpio, L., et al. 32
video: clinical video material 10, 17, 26; ethical implications 26; and interviews 17–20, 27; microanalysis 20–21, 27; *see also* video elicitation interviews (VEI); video microanalysis
video elicitation interviews (VEI) 5, 16–17, 18–20
video microanalysis 5, 16–17, 24
Vlachova, Z., et al. 18
voice (in research): disenfranchised 174; doctors 32, 36–37, 39–40, 46, 47–49; 'giving voice' 3, 5, 8, 15, 21, 27, 218, 220, 222; parents 186; *see also* young people
vulnerability: families 174–196; historically unsuitable for investigation 35; and medical professionals 33–34; *see also* doctors; dyslexia

Walters, S. J., et al. 61
Walworth, D. D. 12
WaSH: access issues 133; community participatory approach 135; data sources **138**; definition 133–134; enhancing resources 133; hygiene 143–144, 150–151; influences on health, infrastructure and related practices **134**; integrating data 151–153; meta-inference(s) 135, 137; participatory mapping and photography 141; qualitative studies 136; sanitation 141–143, 149–150; WaSH variables **140**, **142**, **144**; water 139–141, 147–149; *see also* datasets; mixed methods
Watson, P. M. 61
Web of Science 180
Welch, J. L., et al. 82
wellbeing of: benefits/risks to patient care 34; of caring professionals 34–35; of child, parent, therapist 11; emerging

234 Index

contexts 7; health on a social scale 115–117; meaning of 2, 54; mental health disorders 55; of mentors not considered 96; networks **206**, **207**; participant and researcher 104; political and socio-economic factors 54; research 8; ten dimensions of 2–3; unanticipated findings 6, 79–80, 103; unsuited to traditional mixed methods approach 33; *see also* doctors; mentoring
West, M., et al. 34
What Works Centre for Wellbeing 2, 216
White, J. 41
Wilding, P. M. 57
Williams, K. E., et al. 13
Wilson, G., et al. 82–83, **86**, 92
Winchester, City of 1, 202
Winchester, University of 32, 214; ethics policy 46; Faculty of Health and Wellbeing 2, 201
Wisdom, J., et al. 110
Wood, J., et al. 12
Woods, M. N., et al. 174
Woolf, K., et al. 32, **114**
'workarounds' *see* dyslexia

World Health Organisation (WHO) 44, 54, 142, 149, 151, 178, 203; Annual Assembly 212; definition of health 11; primary health care philosophy 212
Wosch, T., et al. 21

Yanchar, S. C., et al. 157
Yardley, L. & Bishop, F. L. 160
Yardley, L., et al. 159, 165
Yelland, L. N., et al. 62
Yin, R. K. 17
Yoon, L., et al. 81
young people: challenges for other researchers 165–169; complex experiences 160; connected identity 162; disrupting reality 161–162; engagement with 163; 'favourite' places 159; 'giving voice to' 7; 'insideness' 162; understanding of identity 158; visually and verbally discovered identity 166; *see also* music therapy
YouTube videos 201

Zaharoff, B., et al. 61
Zahner, S. J., et al. 199

Printed in the United States
by Baker & Taylor Publisher Services